Praise for *The Cultural Foundations of Nations*

"Once again, Smith proves himself to be the doyen of nationalism studies. In The Cultural Foundations of Nations, written with his customary erudition and clarity, he reveals the variety of forms that nationalism has taken over the ages. This exploration of the 'dating' and 'shaping' of nations is a powerful demonstration of historical sociology at its very best."

John Stone, Boston University

"Anthony Smith remains the most original scholar working in the field of nationalism. In this important book, he throws new light on premodern traditions of the nation and offers a new chronology for the emergence of nationalism."

John Hutchinson, London School of Economics

"An important development has occurred with the publication of The Cultural Foundations of Nations: Smith has significantly furthered and deepened our understanding of nations and nationalism through an historical analysis of three patterns of social relations – hierarchy, covenant and republic – that rightly recognizes the relative independence of culture. His analysis is carried out with impressively wide-ranging and historical nuance – a powerful analysis that properly not only tolerates but also invites numerous ambiguities and complications as any serious investigation into nations should. With the publication of this book, all scholars of nations and nationalism, once again but more so as never before, owe a debt of gratitude to Anthony Smith."

Steven Grosby, Clemson University, author of Nationalism: A Very Short Introduction

"An intellectual tour de force: bold, carefully argued and provocative. Smith identifies different historical forms of nation and distinctive public cultures emerging from Antiquity up to the Global Age. He explores the legacy of hierarchy, covenant and republic upon modern nations and offers a compelling analysis of nationalisms as forms of a secular religion of the people which have evolved alongside or in opposition to traditional religions."

Montserrat Guibernau, Queen Mary College, University of London

In memory of my Grandmother

The Cultural Foundations of Nations

Hierarchy, Covenant, and Republic

Anthony D. Smith

Blackwell Publishing

BLACKWELL PUBLISHING
350 Main Street, Malden, MA 02148-5020, USA
9600 Garsington Road, Oxford OX4 2DQ, UK
550 Swanston Street, Carlton, Victoria 3053, Australia

First published 2008 by Blackwell Publishing Ltd

1 2008

Library of Congress Cataloging-in-Publication Data
Smith, Anthony D.
The cultural foundations of nations: hierarchy, covenant and republic / Anthony D. Smith.
p. cm.
Includes bibliographical references and index.
ISBN 978-1-4051-7798-6 (pbk.: alk. paper) — ISBN 978-1-4051-7799-3 (hardcover: alk. paper)
1. State, The. 2. Nationalism. I. Title.

JC311.S5355 2008
320.1—dc22

2007026882

A catalogue record for this title is available from the British Library.

Set in 10.5/13pt Galliard
by Graphicraft Limited, Hong Kong
Printed and bound in Singapore
by C.O.S. Printers Pte Ltd

The publisher's policy is to use permanent paper from mills that operate a sustainable forestry policy, and which has been manufactured from pulp processed using acid-free and elementary chlorine-free practices. Furthermore, the publisher ensures that the text paper and cover board used have met acceptable environmental accreditation standards.

For further information on
Blackwell Publishing, visit our website at
www.blackwellpublishing.com

Tradition, when it is accepted, is as vivid and vital to those who accept it as any other part of their action or belief. It is the past in the present but it is as much part of the present as any very recent innovation.

Edward Shils

The second [sc. species of religion], limited to a single country only, gives that country its special patrons and tutelary deities. Its dogmas, its rites and its external cult are prescribed by law; outside of the single nation which follows it, it regards everything as infidel, foreign and barbarous; it extends the rights and duties of man no farther than its altars.

Jean-Jacques Rousseau

God wished to have the nations as separate individualities, like human beings, in order that they might be his instruments to influence the whole of mankind and to establish the necessary harmony of the world.

Kazimierz Brodzinski

Contents

Illustrations

Preface

This book arose out of a paper I presented to the fourteenth annual conference of the Association for the Study of Ethnicity and Nationalism at the London School of Economics in April 2004. The theme of the conference, "When is the Nation?," became the subject of the book by that name, edited by Dr. Atsuko Ichijo and Dr. Gordana Uzelac, who had also organized the highly successful conference. I owe a great debt of gratitude to them, both for honoring me on my retirement in such a signal manner, and for their initial stimulus and constant support.

However, I soon found that what had started as a contribution to the debate about dating the nation evolved into a larger exploration of the different "characters" of nations. In one sense, of course, nations are unique, if only because their members tend to believe them to be so. In another sense, we can also isolate recurrent features of the historical forms of communities and identities designated as "nations" and "national identities" – as opposed to other types of community and identity. However, between these poles of particularity and universality, it is also possible to discover recurring patterns which are most clearly exemplified in certain types of the distinctive public cultures of nations. I came to see that these were strongly influenced by long-standing cultural traditions stemming from the ancient world, and that, in changed forms, they have continued to make their influence felt, even in a highly secular and interdependent world.

Clearly, this is a vast theme, and I have found it necessary to severely restrict its scope, if only because of my lack of competence in so many historical fields. I have therefore concentrated on areas with which I am most familiar – the ancient world and early modern and modern

Europe – leaving the exploration of equally important periods and culture areas, like those of the Far East, to others. In this respect, the essays in *Asian Forms of the Nation*, edited by Stein Tønnesson and Hans Antlöv, mark an important engagement with some of the issues of this book; while those in the collection edited by Len Scales and Oliver Zimmer, entitled *Power and the Nation in European History*, do much the same for the medieval period.

In the course of preparing this book, I found I had to revise my ideas on two key issues. The first concerned the "ethnic origins" of nations. While continuing to regard ethnicity and ethnic ties as central to the formation of nations, a broader view of the cultural foundations of nations highlighted the importance of other political and religious kinds of community and identity; this is reflected in the prominence given to both "hierarchy" and "republic" as cultural traditions emanating from the ancient Near East and the classical world. The second issue concerned the dating of the ideology of national*ism*. Again, while I hold to the view that as a doctrine, nationalism emerged in the eighteenth century, I came to see that several of its elements emerged considerably earlier, and more specifically that as a political programme, a certain kind of popular and vernacular nationalism could be found in some seventeenth-century states like England, Scotland, and the Netherlands – and perhaps elsewhere, too. This in turn meant revising the modernist chronology of national*ism*, as well as of nations.

Such a view is underlined by the centrality of the idea of solemn compact or covenant, a form of commitment stronger and more lasting than a simple contract. Oath-swearing and public compacts have been central to the idea and history of the popular nation, and that was why so many of the educated classes harked back to models of covenant and compact in classical antiquity and the Old Testament. Hence the choice by the Regents of Amsterdam of the subject of the Batavian myth of Dutch origins for the Amsterdam Town Hall, and the resulting painting by Rembrandt of *The Conspiracy of Claudius Civilis* against the Romans in 70 AD – though Rembrandt's light-filled and realistic version failed to please and was soon taken down and cut up, so that today only a fragment remains in the Stockholm National Museum and a drawing of the whole conception in Munich. For all that, Rembrandt's magnificent fragment conveys the hushed sense of an ancient solemn compact on the part of the participants to resist alien rule and free their country, just as the contemporary Dutch had done some years earlier.

The bulk of this book is devoted to a historical sociology of nations and nationalism, but inevitably that has raised the vexed issues of definition and theoretical paradigm. It is, indeed, hardly possible to write a book about nationalism which does not raise these issues in one form or another. Accordingly, I have tried to deal with them in the introduction and first two chapters, setting out my own version of what has come to be known as an "ethnosymbolic" perspective. Such a perspective I see as a useful supplement and corrective to the dominant modernist orthodoxy, but in no sense a theory; and I have therefore limited discussion to chapter 2. Since, too, the aim of the book is to give a sociohistorical account of the formation and shaping of different kinds of nations, I have kept critique, beyond the initial disagreement with the modernist reading of the nation, to a minimum, particularly in the Notes.

My debts to scholars are deep and numerous. But I particularly want to single out Walker Connor for his continuing stimulus and robust argument, as well as for his great kindness. To John Hutchinson I want to express my gratitude for many lively discussions and for his constant support. I am also indebted to my former research students, and those of ASEN, as well as my friends on the editorial team of *Nations and Nationalism*, for their interest, above all, to Seeta Persaud for her unfailing help. I am especially grateful to my wife, Diana, for her constant support in often difficult times, and to Joshua for the sheer delight he affords us.

Responsibility for the views expressed herein, and for any errors and omissions, is mine alone.

Anthony D. Smith
London

About the Book

When is the nation? The question of the periodization of nations and nationalism has preoccupied scholars recently, since it was raised by Walker Connor in 1990. His conclusion, that present-day nations were unlikely to have originated earlier than the late nineteenth century, goes beyond the conventional modernist view that sees nations and nationalism emerging with the French and American Revolutions. It takes to its logical conclusion the assumption of many scholars that nations and nationalisms are mass political phenomena with unified mass cultures, and as a result, it is only with the advent of modernity, however defined, that we can begin to speak of nations and nationalism. It is just these assumptions that this book sets out to challenge, and with them, the whole edifice of modernist thinking.

In *The Ethnic Origins of Nations*, I set out the case for regarding modern nations as, in large part, formed on the basis of pre-existing ethnic ties and sentiments. While such a view holds for a great number of cases, there are enough examples where ethnicity played a secondary, or posterior, role in forging modern nations. Ethnic ties were of undoubted importance in various periods, for example, in the ancient Near East and early modern Europe, but other political forms of community and collective identity like the city-state, tribal confederation, and even empire have contributed to the formation of nations.

Perhaps more important, they have also set their mark on the subsequent varied character of nations and nationalisms. This provides a clue to the initial problem of periodization. Rather than a single date or period of formation, different historical forms of the analytic category of nation emerge in successive periods, each of them displaying different kinds of distinctive public cultures. The latter in turn are strongly influenced by one or other of the three main cultural traditions of antiquity: hierarchy, covenant, and civic-republic. Through the example of Rome and its successor empires and city-republics, as well as through Jewish and Christian beliefs and practices, these cultural traditions retained their hold over the European educated classes from England to Russia and from Sweden to Spain.

As a result, questions about the chronology of nations are *ipso facto* also issues of the cultural foundations of nations, of the "shaping" as well as the "dating" of the nation. But this also raises issues of definition and theoretical perspective. Accordingly, the book begins with discussions of the theoretical background, definitions of concepts, and underlying social and symbolic processes and cultural resources of the formation and persistence of nations. The bulk of the book is devoted to a historical sociology of nations and nationalism, in the ancient world, the European Middle Ages, the early modern, and the modern eras, and is rounded off with a discussion of the alternative destinies facing modern nations as a result of their often multi-stranded character.

Plan of the Book

Introduction. This sets out the initial problems of "dating the nation" in the wake of Walker Connor's arguments, and the main theoretical paradigms – modernist, perennialist, and primordialist – which have dominated the field of nationalism studies and which can throw light on the question of periodization.

Chapter 1. Here I analyze the problems of a modernist conception of the nation, and show how it is properly restricted to dealing with only one part of the field, that of the "modern nation." A broader conception of the nation is required, one which distinguishes the nation as a general category of analysis from the descriptive enumeration of historical forms of the nation. By defining the nation in ideal typical terms, it becomes possible to relate a variety of historical forms of the nation in different periods, so avoiding the arbitrary restrictions of the modernist perspective and enriching our understanding of nations as cultural resources and felt communities.

Chapter 2. Before proceeding to a historical sociology of nations, we need to explore the main factors in their formation and persistence.

Nations are best viewed in relation to the antecedent types of collective cultural and political identities like city-states, empires, tribal confederations, and, above all, ethnic and ethnoreligious communities. But it is only with the development of key social and symbolic processes like self-definition, symbolic cultivation, territorialization, dissemination of public culture, and standardization of laws and customs that communities can approximate to the ideal type of the nation; and only with certain cultural resources like myths of election, memories of golden ages, and ideals of mission and sacrifice that communities are likely to persist over time.

Chapter 3. A historical sociology of nations must begin with the ancient Near East. Despite the dearth of examples of nations, the ancient world was characterized by the widespread presence of ethnic categories and communities. Ethnicity was intertwined with other forms of collective cultural and political identity, such as ancient empires, city-states, and tribal confederations. However, only in a few cases – ancient Egypt, Judah, and later Armenia – can we really discern the makings of nations. Even in ancient Greece, for all its strong ethnic sentiments both at the pan-Hellenic and *polis* levels, the territorial and legal dimensions of nationhood were lacking.

Chapter 4. But the ancient world also bequeathed to its European successors something even more important: the three vital legacies and cultural traditions of hierarchy, covenant, and republic, derived respectively from ancient Mesopotamia and Egypt, ancient Judea, and ancient Greece. Mediated through both republican and imperial Rome, as well as the Bible and Christianity, these cultural traditions were continually revived in Europe as Christendom's monarchs sought to legitimate their rule and strengthen their states, notably in Muscovy, France, England, and Spain. By the late Middle Ages, we witness the emergence of "hierarchical" nations in which rulers and elites of western states evinced strong national sentiment and identity.

Chapter 5. By the sixteenth century, there was considerable evidence of widespread elite national sentiments in several European states from Russia and Poland to England, France, and Denmark. But the "breakthrough" to popular nations and to the earliest nationalisms occurred in the wake of the Reformation. By returning to the Old Testament and the Covenant of Israel, radical Reformers, notably the Calvinists, broadened the idea of election to include churches and whole communities – and nations. In Scotland, England, and Holland, but also in the Swiss cities and the American colonies, growing identification of the national community with the potential elect among the Puritans mobilized much larger numbers of people and gave them a dynamic vision of communal salvation through political unity, autonomy, and identity of fate. The resulting "covenantal" nations and nationalisms became the seedbeds and models for later secular versions.

Chapter 6. Rather than marking a rupture with all that had gone before, the secular "republican" nation was forged under the influence and inspiration of covenantal nations. Similarly, for all its radical secularism, civic-republican nationalism was often modeled on the rituals, liturgies, and practices of traditional religions. As a "secular religion of the people," nationalism was able to combine a purely human and terrestrial citizen compact with public worship of the nation. During the French revolutionary *fêtes*, this combination of the secular and the religious, of the revived patriotism of the ancient city-states and of the sacred compacts of myths of election and Covenant, was able to mobilize great armies and inspire widespread enthusiasm. The triumph of republican nationalism both within Europe and the West, and outside, is in no small part due to its "sacred" and popular dimensions.

Chapter 7. However, far from sweeping away previous historical forms of the nation, secular republican nationalism finds itself continually challenged by persisting cultural elements of earlier forms of the nation. This is exemplified in the modern history of Greece, where the republican Hellenic project was challenged by, and then combined with, a "Byzantine" national ideal which itself was composed in equal measure of hierarchical (imperial) memories and Greek Orthodox covenantal beliefs. Not only do we find survivals of hierarchical elements, for example in Britain's monarchy, but also republics like the United States, Israel, and France remain imbued with myths and beliefs that derive from earlier covenantal nations and nationalisms, thereby presenting each generation of the community with alternative ethnohistories and national destinies. Though these different cultural traditions may engender ideological conflict within national communities, their rivalry and synthesis can also strengthen national consciousness and maintain the fabric of the nation.

Conclusion. The book concludes with a summary of my account of the historical sociology of nations, and briefly spells out some of the longer-term implications for nations and nationalism in the contemporary world.

Introduction
The Theoretical Debate

The purpose of this book is twofold: to trace the cultural foundations of nations in different periods of history by means of an analysis of their social and symbolic processes and cultural resources, and to throw some light on the vexed questions of the definition and dating of "the nation." The two questions are closely linked, for both relate to the more fundamental issue of whether we can speak of a single concept of the nation, and if so, how it relates to the various forms of nations in different periods of history.

These forms of national community, I shall argue, are dependent on certain cultural traditions stemming from antiquity which have shaped their members' ethos and sense of national identity. But, before we can explore these traditions, we need to focus on questions of definition and periodization. These, in turn, are embedded in different theoretical approaches. In this introduction, therefore, I shall first briefly outline the main approaches in the field and their answers to the problem of "dating the nation." This will afford an entry into the basic issues of the definition of the category of "nation" and the social formation of the historical forms of nations, which will in turn allow us to embark on a historical sociology of the formation and persistence of national communities in different historical periods.

A good starting place is the short article published by Walker Connor in 1990, entitled "When is a Nation?" Here he argued that scholars have always focused on the question of "what is a nation?," but had neglected the equally important and interesting question of "when is a nation?" Even if the first was logically prior, of itself a definition of the concept of the nation could not settle the problem of dating specific nations. That required in addition historical data, as well as a model or theory of nation formation. And Connor supplied both a definition, and model of how modern nations, at least, were formed. (1)

For Walker Connor, nations are really self-aware ethnic groups. They constitute the largest group formed on the basis of a conviction on the part of their members that they are ancestrally related. That they may not be ancestrally related, that they may well stem from a variety of ethnic stocks, as is often the case, is irrelevant. It is not factual history, but felt history that counts in the making of nations. That is why modern nationalists liken the nation to a large family, and that is why their appeals to "blood" always strike a chord with the members of the nation. How does the nation form from its ethnic base? For Connor, this may be a long-drawn-out process, for nations emerge in stages. But modernization, because it brings many groups into close and regular contact, acts as a powerful catalyst; and ideas of popular sovereignty and the equation of alien rule with illegitimate rule have since the French Revolution excited successive ethnic groups to aspire to become independent nations. However, we cannot really speak of nations coming into being until the majority of their members know not just who they are not, but who they are; and, more important, feel that they belong to the nation and participate in its life. In a democracy, that means that we cannot speak of a nation until the majority have been enfranchised – something that did not begin to occur until the end of the nineteenth or early twentieth century. Ethnic groups may be a "fixture of history," found in every period, but existing nations are modern and really quite recent. (2)

Modernism

Connor's dating of the advent of nations is consonant with that of the majority of scholars today, who for this reason may be called "modernists." For modernists, both nations and nationalisms are recent and novel, and both are products of "modernization." They differ, of course, as to the exact reasons why nations are recent and novel, some seeking the causes in industrial capitalism, others in the rise of the centralized, professional state, and others still in the nature of modern mass communications and secular education. But my concern here is not with their reasons but with their periodization and the underlying categorical assumptions behind their dating. (3)

In the modernist perspective, nations not only do not, they cannot exist before the advent of modernity, however the latter is defined. In practice, this means that we cannot talk of nations or nationalism before the late eighteenth century, at the very earliest. According to Ernest Gellner, nations could not emerge before the onset of modernity. In what he calls "agro-literate" societies, tiny elites ruled over the vast mass of food-producers, and the literate culture of these elites was entirely different from the many "low," oral, and vernacular cultures of the peasant masses. The elites had no desire or interest to spread their culture, and even the clergy who did have such an interest lacked the means to do so. Only the mobility required by industrial societies creates the need for specialized literate "high cultures" which Gellner equates with nations. (4)

For other modernists like John Breuilly and Eric Hobsbawm, the premodern masses had purely local and religious loyalties. At best, we may call some of their communities "proto-national." But, as Hobsbawm is at pains to show, there was no necessary connection between these regional, linguistic, or religious communities and modern territorial nations. Only in those few cases where there was some continuity with a medieval state or church may we be permitted to entertain the possibility of a link with modern national identity in earlier times. But, in general, it is only with the rise of the modern state, urbanization, and economic growth that the mass of the population can be mobilized and feel an allegiance to wider, national communities. (5)

In fact, if we would seek the immediate causes for the timing of the rise of nations, we need look no further than the nationalist intelligentsia. It is nationalists who, according to Gellner, create nations rather than the other way round; just as it was the Enlightenment, according to Elie Kedourie, that shaped the secular culture of nations and spawned imitative and reactive intelligentsias across first Europe and then the globe. This marks the watershed of nationalism. For the Enlightenment outside its homelands created a generation of alienated and frustrated youth – "marginal men" – who felt their chances of worthy employment and status commensurate with their secular education were thwarted by aristocratic or colonial rejection. Their ensuing discontent sought in nationalism a millennial political solution. The result was appeals by successive waves of nationalist intellectuals to "their" co-cultural masses to forge the political nation in which the intellectuals would have an assured leadership role. It was only after the French Revolution that such appeals could begin to stir the masses, beginning with the Romantics in Germany – which again would place the formation of nations in the nineteenth century. (6)

A similar dating, and shaping, is implied by Benedict Anderson's analysis of the role of "print-capitalism" in the origins of nations and nationalism. For Anderson, the union of printing and capitalism in the production of books may start in the late fifteenth century. But it was not till the eighteenth century, with the mass production of newspapers ("one-day best-sellers"), that large numbers of peoples were brought into the political arena and could begin to "imagine" the nation as a finite, sovereign, and cross-class solidarity. And in this they were greatly assisted by a revolution in our conceptions of time: from an earlier messianic, cosmological understanding of time before the onset of modernity, we have now come to see it as moving in linear fashion – through "empty, homogeneous time" – measured by clock and calendar. (7)

"Neo-Perennialism"

Of course, this confident modernism is not universally shared. Just as the modernists had challenged the earlier prewar orthodoxy which tended to see nations, if not nationalism, as perennial and recurrent in every historical epoch and continent, so a rising tide of "neo-perennialist" historians, especially in Britain, issued a powerful counterblast to modernist assumptions.

Their general case has been put most forcibly by the late Adrian Hastings. He argued that nations were to be found emerging from ubiquitous but fluid oral ethnicities as the result of the introduction of a written vernacular, because a literature fixes the field of a vernacular language and defines its reading public, or nation. In fact, Hastings contends, nations and nationalisms were endemic to the Christian world. This was the result of two features of Christianity. The first was that Christianity, as opposed to other religions, sanctioned the use of vernacular languages and translations. The second was that Christianity adopted the Old Testament with its narrative of a monolithic model of nationhood in ancient Israel, one that fused land, people, language, and religion. (8)

For Hastings, as for Patrick Wormald, John Gillingham, and even Susan Reynolds, there is sufficient evidence, especially in the case of England, to undermine the contention that nations as well as nationalism are the product of "modernity." While they may disagree as to the exact dating of the origin of an English nation, they all agree that a late eighteenth- or nineteenth-century dating is far too late, that there existed long before in England, but also in Scotland and Ireland, and perhaps in Wales, a firm sense of national identity, and that in the English case, that sense of identity was well defined already in late Norman and medieval England from at least the thirteenth and fourteenth centuries onwards, if not already in the late Anglo-Saxon period. For these medievalists, the sources are quite clear: the term *natio* was widely used in the Middle Ages, not just for Church Councils and student bodies in universities, but also in legal and ecclesiastical documents, royal decrees and travelogues, as well as in general correspondence. True, these are all the work of tiny elites. The great mass of the people, the illiterate and isolated peasantry, left no written records. But, then, how many records did peasants leave in the nineteenth century, the heyday of burgeoning nations, according to most modernists? (9)

This brings us back to Walker Connor's central claim that nations and nationalism are "mass phenomena," and that because the peasant masses in premodern epochs were illiterate and "mute," we cannot speak of nations existing in periods before they entered the political arena of the nation, which, in the case of existing nations – Connor allows for the possibility of nations in earlier periods of history, given sufficient evidence – was not until the end of the nineteenth century. There are several rejoinders to Connor's argument. To begin with, absence of evidence is not the same as evidence of absence, and an argument from documentary silence is often two-edged. For the neo-perennialists, this silence could be construed as much one of peasants accepting, or taking for granted, their ethnic or national attachments as of their lack of any sentiment of national belonging. Moreover, to claim, as Connor does, that "very often the elites' conceptions of the nation did not even extend to the masses," goes beyond our evidence and suggests that we have more insight into the beliefs of the premodern masses than did their elite contemporaries. At this distance in time, we simply cannot be sure whether the peasant masses in the Middle Ages or earlier did or did not share the conceptions of the elites. Such general arguments do not allow us to infer that the vast mass of the peasantry could not or did not possess some kind of ethnic or even national sentiments at certain times. (10)

Alternatively, the relevance of peasant mass sentiment to the determination of the existence of a nation can be questioned. One could equally claim that, given their absence from history and politics in most epochs, whether and what the peasants felt and thought about the nation is largely irrelevant. Cultures and polities are forged by minorities, usually by elites of one kind or other. All that matters is that quite a large number of people outside the ruling class should come to feel that they belong to a given nation, for it to be said to exist. On the other hand, we can also point to the fact that we do indeed know something about the wider beliefs of (some of the) peasantry at various times, for example, their tendency to rise in defense of religion, as in the Vendée in 1793, or their appeal to the memories of Wilhelm Tell in the Swiss Peasants' War of 1653. So, if the peasants are not always "mute," we should be careful not to dismiss *a priori* the possibility that some of them may have felt some attachment to a translocal *ethnie* or nation – as, for example, was evidently the case with the ancient Israelite tribes at various times, or among growing numbers of Swiss valley-dwellers, even if they retained their cantonal loyalties. (11)

Yet again, one might challenge the notion of nations and nationalism as "mass phenomena" by recalling that most nationalisms, however they couched their appeal, were distinctly minority affairs well into the twentieth century. For example, the nationalists on the barricades in the Spring of Nations in 1848 could, for the most part, be numbered in the hundreds; and much of the political violence in, say, the Balkans in the early twentieth century was committed by small dedicated cadres of fervent nationalists. As for nations themselves, while in nationalist theory every member is or should be a citizen, this requirement has in many cases only been fulfilled patchily and in recent decades. In practice, we are ready to speak of nations existing well before their mass incarnation, and what we are often referring to is the entry of the wealthier "middle classes" into the political arena, something that can be traced back to the seventeenth century in parts of Western Europe. This is a line of argument to which I shall return. (12)

The question of "mass participation" is only one of several issues that divide modernists from "neo-perennialists." Another is the issue of institutional continuity. Even modernists like Eric Hobsbawm, as we saw, are prepared to concede some value to the proposition that, in a few cases – he names Russia, Serbia, England, and France – there was a premodern basis for the modern nation-state because it could boast institutional continuity of state or church or both from medieval times; and more specifically, Hobsbawm is prepared, as a result, to speak of the possibility of Tudor patriotism in England. For John Breuilly, too, such continuity of institutions may serve as a premodern basis of modern nations, but this is exceptional. For the most part, he contends, identity outside institutional carriers (most of which, he claims, are modern) "is necessarily fragmentary, discontinuous and elusive." As for premodern ethnic identity, it "has little in the way of institutional embodiment beyond the local level." (13)

In fact, as medievalists are apt to point out, there was a good deal of institutional continuity in premodern epochs, and some of it was tied to ethnicity and religion. Susan Reynolds, for example, has drawn attention to the various barbarian *regna* which succeeded the Carolingian empire in Western Europe, and has characterized them as communities of law, custom, and descent, attached to the ruling house and its dynasty – she cites the Anglo-Saxons, Franks, Visigoths, Normans, and Saxons. Myths of descent, usually referring back to Trojan Aeneas or Noah, became important as legitimations of the claims to pedigree of barbarian chiefs and their households. But, unlike the earlier post-Roman empire period, which saw much more fluid political and ethnic processes, the tenth century and after witnessed a process of political and ethnic consolidation and the beginnings of those ethnopolitical divisions which were later to produce ethnically based national states in Western Europe. Though Susan Reynolds prefers to use the term *regna* rather than "nations," regarding the latter as too prone to teleological misinterpretation and to conflation of medieval ideas with more familiar modern conceptions of the nation, it is clear that she and several other medieval historians are referring to forms of ethnopolitical continuity, which might or might not serve as the basis for later national states. To a certain extent, this is also the case with Josep Llobera's analysis of the medieval geographical and administrative domains of Britannia, Gallia, Germania, Italia, and Hispania. For, even though he emphasizes the transient, even illusory nature of what may appear as national continuities in these domains, he is also at pains to show that modern nationalisms "are rooted in the medieval past, even if the links with it may often be tortuous and twisted." (14)

There is a further point. The term "institution" may refer not only to the economic, political, and legal forms with which we are familiar in the modern world, but also to the cultural forms analyzed by John Armstrong in his seminal work on ethnicity in medieval Islam and Christianity – forms like lifestyles, "homeland" attachments, imperial *mythomoteurs*, urban patterns, language and education, religious organization and rituals, and artistic traditions. In other words, the conception of institutions entertained by modernists like John Breuilly and Eric Hobsbawm is too restrictive, and needs to include any set of role relationships based on patterned normative and cultural expectations. (15)

A third issue that divides modernists from "neo-perennialists" concerns the role of religion. For many modernists, religion is a residual category in the modern world, and is inversely related to nations and nationalism. Even Benedict Anderson, who starts out by intimating the importance of the nation as a communion of underlying virtue able to surmount oblivion, turns his back on religion as an explanatory variable. For, as he develops his argument, it becomes clear that religion can play no part in what is ultimately a materially based cultural interpretation of nationalism. (16)

Now, while this modernist myopia about the role of religion may reflect a certain reading of the French and American Revolutions and the influence of the secularization thesis so prevalent in the postwar decades, it cannot serve as a guide either to its place in premodern epochs of ethnic and national formation or to the recent revival of "religious nationalisms," both outside and in the West. In both cases, religion and the "sacred" have played a vital part, and it is impossible to grasp the meanings of nations and nationalism without an understanding of the links between religious motifs and rituals and later ethnic and national myths, memories, and symbols. It is clearly insufficient to argue that nations and nationalism arose out of, and against, the great religious cultural systems of the medieval world. We have to recognize the complexity of continuing relations between religions and forms of the sacred, on the one hand, and national symbols, memories, and traditions, on the other hand, and the ways in which contemporary nations continue to be infused with sacred meanings. This is another issue to which I shall return in subsequent chapters.

Primordialism

Like modernists, the "neo-perennialists" seek to ground their arguments and theses in historical evidence, and are wary of interpretations that introduce other, more basic, levels of explanation. Even the most sweeping of their accounts, for example, Hastings' belief in the Christian basis of nations and nationalism, remains at the historical and sociological levels of explanation. For others, however, such methodological reticence cannot cope with the sheer pervasiveness and power of the issues raised by ethnicity and nationalism, and in particular by the question often bypassed by modernists of why so many people, relatively speaking, are prepared to sacrifice themselves to this day for the nation, as they have been for their faith.

One answer to this question lies in the concept of "primordiality." Originally advanced by Edward Shils, who distinguished various kinds of ties – personal, sacred, civil, and primordial – the idea of primordial ties was taken up by Clifford Geertz, who sought to account for the problems besetting the new states of Africa and Asia in terms of a conflict between their desires for an efficient, rational order based on "civil ties" and their continuing cleavages and "primordial" attachments to certain social and cultural "givens" – of kinship, race, religion, custom, language, and territory – which had the effect of severely dividing the new polities. Geertz himself was careful to stress that it was individuals who attributed to such primordial ties a binding, overriding, and ineffable quality. But this has not prevented some critics from denouncing "primordialism" (a term Geertz never used) as an asocial mystification of human interaction. (17)

The cudgels were taken up in defense of Shils and Geertz by Steven Grosby, who has sought to base an approach to "primordial ties" on human beliefs and cognition about the life-enhancing qualities of certain abiding features of their condition. For Grosby, two such features are critical: kinship and territory, and territory perhaps even more than kinship, because of the widespread belief in the life-nurturing and sustaining qualities of the land and its products. For Grosby, ethnic groups and nationalities exist "because there are traditions of belief and action towards primordial objects such as biological features and especially territorial location." Thus, "the family, the locality and one's own 'people' bear, transmit and protect life." That is why human beings attribute sacredness to primordial objects and why they have in the past and continue to sacrifice their lives for their family and nation. Such qualities, he seeks to show, are essential even today, and we can therefore speak of a continuing element of primordiality even in complex modern societies, which it is foolish to overlook and perverse to seek to deconstruct. (18)

It is true that "primordialism" *per se* can tell us little about the origins and cultural shape of nations (though it recognizes the processes of ethnogenesis and dissolution). This is brought home to us when we consider the work of the most radical exponent of such a viewpoint, Pierre van den Berghe. Though he has recently sought to address the question of the origin of *nations*, his basic theory of genetic reproductive drives is couched at a biological level and encompasses all extended kinship groups. Moreover, because it pertains to individuals, this approach has the effect of deflecting attention away from higher-level historical questions of nation formation. However, van den Berghe has also provided a place for culture, in the form of signs like dress, color, and speech, which differentiate between races and ethnic groups, provide cues for genetic kin, and are accompanied by myths of ancestry, which he claims mirror actual lines of descent. For all that, his main theory is articulated in terms of biological features such as endogamy, nepotism, and "inclusive fitness," and the answers to questions about the origins and forms of *nations* are necessarily general and are derived from additional external factors like the emergence of the state. (19)

The unique contribution of the "primordialists" has been to focus our attention on the intensity and passion that ethnicity and nationalism so often evoke, and which modernists, even when they condemn it, so often fail to address. On the other hand, not only does primordialism leave other questions, including the dating and character of nations, unanswered, its narrow focus, and blanket insistence on the presence of ethnicity and nationhood in the human condition *tout court*, precludes a more causal-historical analysis of the formation and shape of nations. (20)

An exception to this generalization is provided by the historical work of Steven Grosby. His scholarly explorations of the presence of "nationality" in the ancient world, and especially in ancient Israel, which I shall consider in more detail later, reveal how an interest in primordial ties can inspire and illuminate detailed historical analysis of empirical examples, in this case of ethnic communities and nationalities in the ancient Near East. For Grosby, "nationality" (as he prefers to call it) is one of several analytic categories, along with empire, city-state, and tribal confederation, and we need to distinguish it carefully from these other categories, both in general and in the often blurred empirical context of the ancient Near East. It is here that Grosby makes a fundamental point that can serve as both a guide and a warning, against the more doctrinaire assertions of modernists and their critics, insofar as it reminds us of the inherent difficulties of marrying our categories and definitions to the often sparse evidence of collective cultural identities in our historical records. For, one of the main points in his historical and sociological enquiries is to underline the fact that, even in the modern world, the boundaries which separate our categories of investigation of various historical groups are permeable. As he puts it: "Rarely does a collectivity correspond with exactitude to a particular analytic category. This is true not only for the collectivities of antiquity, but for the modern national state as well." (21)

Conclusion

This brings us back to the unavoidable issue of definition. For it would appear that in essaying to provide an answer to the apparently innocent question, "When is a nation?," Walker Connor opened up a rich seam of problems for further research – problems about elite sources, mass participation, institutional continuity, about religion and the sacred, primordiality and territory. But perhaps the most intractable of these problems is that of the very categories and definitions we employ and their uncertain relationship to the communities we seek to study. This means that we cannot evade the familiar problem of defining the concept of the nation. The question "When is a nation?" *ipso facto* demands a prior attempt to resolve the vexed and familiar sociological question, "What is a nation?" Only then can we turn to the central issue of the conditions under which nations have emerged, and examine the cultural traditions that have shaped their emergence.

1

The Concept and Its Varieties

Before we can embark on a substantive historical sociology of nations and nationalism, we must have a clear idea of the objects of our enquiry. Second, we need to examine the social processes and cultural resources of the formation and persistence of nations. Third, the question of premodern nations requires a deep historical perspective and a cultural genealogy of nations that stretches back to the ancient Near East and the classical world, if we are to gauge the traditions through which different types of national identities were formed in the early modern period. These, then, are the tasks of each of the following three chapters.

The modernist conception of the nation sees it as the quintessential political form of modern human association. For most modernists, the nation is characterized by:

1 a well-defined territory, with a fixed center and clearly demarcated and monitored borders;
2 a unified legal system and common legal institutions within a given territory, creating a legal and political community;
3 participation in the social life and politics of the nation by all the members or "citizens";
4 a mass public culture disseminated by means of a public, standardized, mass education system;
5 collective autonomy institutionalized in a sovereign territorial state for a given nation;
6 membership of the nation in an "inter-national" system of the community of nations;

7 legitimation, if not creation, of the nation by and through the ideology of nationalism.

This is, of course, a pure or ideal type of the concept of the nation, to which given instances approximate, and it acts as a touchstone of nationhood in specific cases. As such, it has become almost "taken-for-granted" as *the* definitive standard from which any other conception represents a deviation. (1)

Problems of the Modernist Conception

But closer inspection reveals that the modernist conception of the nation is historically specific. As such, it pertains to only one of the historical forms of the concept, that of the *modern nation*. This means it is a particular variant of the general concept of the nation, with its own peculiar features, only some of which may be shared by other forms or variants of the general concept.

Can we be more specific about the provenance of the ideal type of the *modern nation*? A glance at its salient features – territoriality, legal standardization, participation, mass culture and education, sovereignty, and so on – places it squarely in the so-called *civic-territorial* tradition of eighteenth- and early nineteenth-century Western Europe and North America. It was in the age of revolutions and the Napoleonic Wars that a conception of nationhood distinguished by the rationalist, civic culture of the Enlightenment, notably its later "Spartan" or "neo-classical" phase associated with Rousseau, Diderot, and David, became prevalent. As Hans Kohn documented many years ago, this conception of the nation flourished mainly in those parts of the world where a powerful bourgeoisie took the lead in overthrowing hereditary monarchy and aristocratic privilege in the name of "the nation." This is not the kind of nation imagined, let alone forged, in many other parts of the world, where these social conditions were less developed or absent. (2)

Now, if the concept of the *modern nation* and its peculiar features derive from eighteenth- and early nineteenth-century conditions in the West, then the modernist ideal type is inevitably a partial one, because it refers to a specific subtype of the generic concept of the nation, the *modern nation*, and only one kind of nationalism, the civic-territorial type. This means that a specific version of a general concept stands in for the whole range of ideas covered by that concept, a version that bears all the hallmarks of the culture of a particular time and place. It also means that the assertion of the modernity of the nation is no more than a tautology, one which rules out any rival definition of the nation, outside of modernity and the West. The Western conception of the *modern* nation has become the measure of our understanding of the concept of the nation *per se*, with the result that all other conceptions become illegitimate.

Methodological grounds apart, there are a number of reasons why such an arbitrary stipulation should be rejected. In the first place, the term "nation," deriving from *natio* and ultimately *nasci* (to be born), has a long, if tortuous, history of meaning, going back to the ancient Greeks and Romans. As we saw, its usage was not confined to geographically defined student bodies in medieval universities or to assembled bishops at Church Councils hailing from different parts of Christendom. It derived from the Vulgate translation of the Old and New Testaments, and from the writings of the Church Fathers, who opposed the Jews and Christians to all other nations, who were termed collectively *ta ethne*. Ancient Greek itself used the term *ethnos* for all kinds of groups sharing similar characteristics (not only human ones); but authors like Herodotus sometimes used the cognate term *genos*. In this, they were not unlike the ancient Jews, who generally used the term *am* for themselves – *am Israel* – and the term *goy* for other peoples, but with no great consistency. The Romans were more consistent, reserving for themselves the appellation *populus Romanus* and the less elevated term *natio* for others, and especially for distant, barbarian tribes. In time, however, *natio* came to stand for all peoples, including one's own. We cannot regard these premodern usages of *natio*/nation as purely "ethnographic," in opposition to the political concept of modern usage, for this does scant justice to the range of cases from the ancient and medieval worlds that combine both usages – starting with ancient Israel. Even though the meanings of terms often undergo considerable change in successive periods, still we cannot so easily dismiss the long history of these usages prior to the onset of modernity. (3)

A second problem concerns the modernist conception of the "mass nation." This has been partly addressed in connection with Walker Connor's thesis of mass participation in the life of the nation as the criterion of its existence, and hence the need, in a democracy, for the enfranchisement of the majority of the population as a condition for designating it a nation. But it goes beyond this particular issue. Modernists like Karl Deutsch, Ernest Gellner, and Michael Mann regard the "mass nation" as the only genuine form of the nation, and as a result treat the nation as a strictly modern phenomenon. Theorists are, of course, perfectly entitled to designate a particular phenomenon – the "mass nation" in this case – as the sole political "reality," and regard every other version as secondary and insubstantial, if not misleading. But if medieval historians can demonstrate the historical basis and importance of these other versions, which is exactly the point at issue for the neo-perennialists, the modernist stance once again becomes arbitrary and unnecessarily restrictive. This applies also to the weaker claim that the mass nation of modernity is the "fully fledged" version of the nation, and all others are lacking in some measure: does this mean that we cannot conceive of other kinds of nation from which the masses were excluded? After all, well into the modern epoch, few recognized nations could be termed "mass nations" – many members of their populations, notably the working class, women, and ethnic minorities, remained in practice excluded from the exercise of civic and political rights. So we should at least be prepared to recognize the possibility of other kinds of "nation," apart from "mass nations." (4)

A further problem stems from the common modernist assertion that nations are the product of nationalisms (with or without help from the state), and since national*ism*, the ideological movement, appeared no earlier than the eighteenth century, nations must also be modern. But, even if we accept that, as a systematic ideology, nationalism did not emerge before the eighteenth century, the assumption that only nationalists create nations is questionable; and this is true, even if we define the *ideological* movement of nationalism, along with other ideologies, in relatively "modernist" terms, as I think we must, if only to avoid confusing it with more general concepts like "national sentiment" or "national consciousness."

Now, by national*ism*, I mean *an ideological movement for attaining and maintaining autonomy, unity, and identity on behalf of a population, some of whose members deem it to constitute an actual or potential "nation."* And similarly, I think we can designate a "core doctrine" of nationalism, a set of general principles to which nationalists adhere, as follows:

1 the world is divided into nations, each with its own history, destiny, and character;
2 the nation is the sole source of political power;
3 to be free, every individual must belong to and give primary loyalty to the nation;
4 nations must possess maximum autonomy and self-expression;
5 a just and peaceful world must be based on a plurality of free nations.

In this sense, it was only in the later eighteenth and early nineteenth centuries that "nationalist" ideologies were embraced by writers and thinkers in West and Central Europe, from Rousseau and Herder to Fichte and Mazzini. As such, nationalism is a modern doctrine, and the ideological hallmark of that modernity resides in the relatively novel assumptions about political autonomy and authenticity that underlie the doctrine, and in the way these are combined with a political anthropology. (5) But this is not to deny that some elements of the doctrine go back much further. For example, ideas of the nation and a comity of nations were clearly present at the Council of Constance in 1415, and we can find many references to nations and their relations in earlier centuries, going back to antiquity, even if their interpretation poses serious problems. This means that some conceptions of the nation, which may well differ from modern conceptions of the nation, antedate by several centuries the appearance of nationalism and its particular interpretations of the nation; and as a result the concept of the nation cannot be simply derived from the ideology of nation*alism*. To confine the concept and the practice of the nation to an era of nationalism, and regard them as products of this modern ideology, is again arbitrary and unduly restrictive. (6) But perhaps the most serious defect of the modernist ideal type of the *modern nation* is its inherent ethnocentrism. This has, of course, been recognized by many theorists. Yet, they continue to treat the Western civic-territorial form of the modern nation and its nationalism as normative, and other forms as deviations. This was the basis of Hans Kohn's celebrated dichotomy of "Western" and "non-Western" nationalisms mentioned earlier. The latter, unlike their rationalist, enlightened, liberal counterparts, tend to be organic, shrill, authoritarian, and often mystical – typical manifestations of a weak and disembedded intelligentsia. Kohn's dichotomy has been followed by John Plamenatz, Hugh Seton-Watson, Michael Ignatieff, and many others for whom the popular distinction between "civic" and "ethnic" nationalisms encapsulates this normative tradition. (7)

Now, while these theorists would concede that "ethnic" nationalisms share with their "civic" counterparts such features as collective attachments to a "homeland," as well as ideals of autonomy and citizenship for "the people," they also highlight the very considerable differences. In the "ethnic" variant of nationalism, the nation is seen to be possessed of:

1 genealogical ties – more specifically, presumed ties of ethnic descent traceable through the generations to one or more common ancestors, and hence membership of the nation in terms of presumed descent;
2 vernacular culture – a culture that is not only public and distinctive, but also indigenous to the land and people in terms of language, customs, religion, and the arts;
3 nativist history – a belief in the virtues of indigenous history and its special interpretation of the history of the nation and its place in the world;
4 popular mobilization – a belief in the authenticity and energy of the "people" and its values, and the need to rouse and activate the people to create a truly national culture and polity.

This implies that, for ethnic nationalists, the "nation" is already in place at the onset of both modernity and nationalism in the form of pre-existing ethnic communities available and ready, as it were, to be propelled into the world of political nations. So, for example, in this "neo-perennialist" view, the Arab nation, descended from Arabic-speaking tribes of the Arabian peninsula, has persisted throughout history, at least from the time of the Prophet, and exhibits the classic features of an "ethnic" nation – presumed genealogical ties of descent, a classic indigenous vernacular culture (notably Qur'anic Arabic), a nativist Arab ethnohistory, and the ideal of "the Arabs" of Islam as the fount of wisdom and virtue who only need to be mobilized to achieve political autonomy. In this and similar cases, we witness the failure of modernism to include this quite different ethnic conception of the nation, which in turn derives from its theoretical rejection of any necessary linkage between ethnicity and nationhood. (8)

Category and Description

One of the main problems with the modernist conception is its failure to recognize that the term "nation" is used in two quite different ways. On the one hand, it denotes an analytic category differentiating the nation from other related categories of collective cultural identity; on the other hand, it is used as a descriptive term enumerating the features of a historical type of human community. The problem is compounded by the fact that the historical type of human community denoted by the term "nation" is cultural and/or political, or both: that is, it designates a type of human community that is held to possess a collective cultural identity or a collective political identity, or both. (9)

There is, of course, nothing improper about using terms like "nation" to describe the features of certain kinds of historical community. The problem arises when the description is such as to restrict arbitrarily the range of instances which might be included under the ideal type of the nation seen as a category of analysis. Of course, the degree to which this constitutes a serious defect is a matter for individual judgment. But my contention is that most modernists, prompted by their theoretical stance, have gone too far in the direction of arbitrary and unnecessary restriction. If they were content to describe a subset of the general category of nation, i.e., the *modern nation*, there would be no problem. But they then go on to assert that this subset stands for the whole, and this is where a descriptive historical term becomes entangled with a general analytic category. This is not to embrace a neo-perennialist approach which would make it difficult for us to distinguish national from other kinds of collective cultural and/or political identity, or to decide which instances of community and identity fell under the "national" rubric. It is exactly these kinds of distinctions that attempting to keep the analytic category of the nation separate from its use as a descriptive term may enable us to make. (10)

Given the complex ramifications of the concept of the nation, it is no easy task to separate the analytic category from the historical descriptions of the nation. The descriptive use of the term will be necessary for enumerating the features of different subtypes of the general category of the nation. But, before we can attempt such historical description, we need a clear understanding of the nation as a general analytic category differentiated from other related categories.

The first step, then, is to define the concept of the nation in ideal-typical terms, and thereby recognize the persistent nature of the analytic category as a transhistorical ideal type. Here the term "nation" represents an analytic category based on general social processes which *could* in principle be exemplified in any period of history. By differentiating the analytic category of the nation from other categories of collective identity, we may avoid designating all kinds of community and identity as "nations." At the same time, this procedure offers some chance of freeing the category of the nation from undue restrictions and offers the possibility of finding instances of the nation outside the modern period and the West, if the evidence so indicates. Thus the concept of the nation, like that of the religious community and the *ethnie*, should in the first instance be treated as a general analytic category, which can in principle be applied to all continents and periods of history. On the other hand, the content of the "nation" as a historical form of human community, exemplified in the specific features of its subtypes, will vary with the historical context. With each epoch we may expect important variations in the features of nations, but they will nevertheless accord with the basic form of the category. As at one and the same time an analytic category based on general social processes and a historical form of human community characterized by a cultural and/or a political collective identity, the ideal type of the nation is inevitably complex and problematic, and its construction is for this reason a fraught and contested task, and one which necessarily involves an element of stipulation. (11)

In this spirit, I propose the following ideal-typical definition of the "nation," as *a named and self-defined human community whose members cultivate shared myths, memories, symbols, values, and traditions, reside in and identify with a historic homeland, create and disseminate a distinctive public culture, and observe shared customs and common laws.* In similar vein, we may also define "national identity" as *the continuous reproduction and reinterpretation of the pattern of values, symbols, memories, myths, and traditions that compose the distinctive heritage of nations, and the identification of individuals with that pattern and heritage.* (12)

Three assumptions have led to the selection of the features of the ideal type. The first is the centrality of social processes and symbolic resources in the formation and persistence of nations, giving them their distinctive but flexible character. The second is that many of the features of the ideal type derive from prior ethnic and ethnoreligious symbols, traditions, myths, and memories among populations deemed to be similar or related. Together, these two assumptions address the question of "who is the nation?," i.e., the unique character of the historic nation. The third assumption is that these social processes and symbolic resources, though subject to periodic change, may resonate among populations over long periods of time. This means that our analyses of the formation and persistence of nations require, as John Armstrong has so clearly demonstrated, a scrutiny of social and symbolic processes across successive historical epochs over the *longue durée*. (13)

The insistence on analyzing social and cultural elements over the long term implies, first of all, that nations be treated separately from national*ism*, and that the formation of nations needs to be investigated independently of the rise of the ideological movement of nationalism. Second, by bringing together past (history), present time, and future (destiny), the way is opened for long-term analysis of ethnic and national phenomena across different epochs. This in turn may suggest different ways in which the social and cultural features of *ethnies* (ethnic communities) and nations can be linked.

There are three main ways in which such connections are made. The most obvious, and the one sought by most historians of nations and states, is through *continuity* of forms, if not content. Here we are usually speaking about linkages between medieval (rarely ancient) communities and *modern nations*. As we shall see, even historians of medieval and ancient communities tend to measure their degree of "nationness" by the yardstick of the characteristics of the *modern nation*, if only to deny the presence of nations in their period. This entails another form of "retrospective nationalism," in which, as Bruce Routledge puts it, the past is seen as the mirror of the present. Thus, the normal way of claiming continuity for given nations is to trace back the lineages and roots of the modern form of the nation into medieval times, in the manner advocated by Adrian Hastings and the "neo-perennialists" for Western Europe. Alternatively, one can argue that some of these modern nations have drawn on the social and symbolic features and resources of earlier *ethnies* to which they claim some kind of kinship and with which they feel an ancestral relationship – the kind of claim made by Slavophiles and others in late Tsarist Russia when they expressed a deep affinity with Old (pre-Petrine) Muscovy, or by Gaelic revivalists who identified the sources of the modern Irish nation in the Christian monastic culture of early medieval Ireland. In such cases, understandings of an ethnic past frame later conceptions of the present, as much as the latter select aspects of that past; and the task of the analyst is to attempt some kind of assessment of documented historical linkages – and discontinuities. (14)

A second kind of linkage over the *longue durée* looks to the idea of *recurrence* of ethnic and national forms, as well as their basic sociocultural elements, both at the particular and the general levels. In this perspective, nations as well as *ethnies* along with other types of collective cultural or political identities are recurrent phenomena, i.e., types of cultural community and political organization that can be found in every period and continent, and which are subject to ceaseless ebb and flow, emerging, flourishing, declining, and being submerged again, in some cases only to re-emerge (with or without the help of nationalists). Once again, we have to turn to the pages of John Armstrong's massive volume and his panorama of ethnic identities and their constituent elements in medieval Christendom and Islam to grasp both the persistence and recurrence of ethnic and national identities over the *longue durée*. (15)

Finally, linkages between pasts and presents can be effected through the *discovery and appropriation* of ethnic history. This is a familiar theme in the literature on nationalism, usually to be found in chapters on the "national awakening" or "revival." Intellectuals, as the new priests and scribes of the nation, elaborate the category of the national community, and for this purpose choose symbolic and social features from earlier ethnic cultures that are presumed to be "related" to their own designated communities and populations. This is often done by selecting significant but particular local dialects, customs, folklore, music, or poetry to stand in for the whole of the nation, as occurred in parts of Eastern Europe. The criterion here is the cult of "authenticity," in which, in order to reconstruct the community as a pure, original nation, it becomes necessary to discover and use cultural features that are felt to be genuine and strictly indigenous, untainted by foreign accretions or influence, and which represent the community "at its best." Interestingly, such cults had their premodern counterparts. Most of the premodern movements sought to create communities modeled on visions of earlier ethnoreligious cultures – such as Asshur-bani-pal's urge to recreate a superior Babylonian culture in the late Assyrian empire, or Chosroes II's harking back to pristine Iranian myth, ritual, and tradition in late Sasanian Persia. But we also find in late Republican Rome a more than nostalgic desire to return to the genuine ways and simple faith of ancestors and earlier generations, to a Cato and Scipio, in order to discover and appropriate a venerated and virtuous ethnic past. (16)

The Nation as Cultural Resource

I turn now to the second main usage of the concept of "nation" – as a descriptive term for a form of historical human community. A significant aspect of the nation as a form of community characterized by a cultural and/or political identity has been its role as a model of sociocultural organization. If at the conceptual level the nation needs to be seen as an analytic category, at the concrete historical level it can also be fruitfully regarded as a social and cultural resource, or better as a set of resources and a model which can be used in different ways and in varying circumstances. Just as the Han empire in China and Akkadian empire in Mesopotamia acted as models and cultural resources for later attempts to build empires in these and other areas, so the kingdoms of Israel and Judah, and the city-states of ancient Athens and Sparta and Republican Rome, provided models and guides for subsequent communities. This is not to prejudge the question of whether, or how far, these societies might themselves be designated as *national* communities, only to say that much later nations looked back to these examples as models of nationhood and drew from them certain resources – ideals, beliefs, and attachments, as well as of social and cultural organization.

Perhaps the best example of what I have in mind is the European reception of the biblical account of ancient Israel – a point that Hastings made, but did not really develop sufficiently. It is not only that Christianity took over the Old Testament model of a polity, the kingdom of ancient Israel, as he claimed, but that medieval rulers and elites of empires, kingdoms, and principalities in Europe from England and France to Bohemia and Muscovy, and also of churches and universities, drew on and made use of the ideas, beliefs, and attachments of the ancient Israelite community which *they* had come to understand as a "national" community. Well before the Reformation, ancient Israel had come to serve as a model and guide for the creation of their chosen communities and historic territories and for the dissemination of their distinctive cultures. (17)

How, in practice, can earlier communities be shown to provide resources and models for later ones? By what mechanisms can such influence be disseminated? The case of ancient Israel suggests the importance of sacred texts, but also of the laws, rituals, ceremonies, and offices described in those texts. Other kinds of cultural resources include customs and mores; symbols such as words and titles, languages and scripts; artifacts, like obelisks and temples, banners and insignia, icons and statues; and more generally artistic styles and motifs, such as those of ancient Greece and Rome, which were revived and renewed in subsequent epochs. Though these general resources could be used for a variety of communities other than nations, the point is that they were readily available, and some of them were associated with communities that appeared, at a distance, to resemble the later aspirant nations of Europe and could act as models for them. The messages associated with these texts, rituals, symbols, and artifacts may not have been those of their creators and original users, and the memory of them might have been fairly selective. Yet, they continued to resonate among the elites of successive generations as cultural traditions and social elements able to furnish sacred resources for the collective cultural identity of nations. (18)

The Nation as "Felt Community"

My argument so far is that we need to distinguish "nation" as a general category from the historical manifestations of the nation as a human community, one which takes different forms and reveals various features in different epochs, over and above the basic features of the ideal type. In this second usage, that of a form of human community characterized by a cultural and/or political identity, nations can be seen as sets of social and cultural resources on which the members can draw, and which, in varying degrees, enable them to express their interests, needs, and goals. This means that we may also describe the nation as an "imagined, willed, and felt community" of its members.

Such language inevitably raises suspicions of essentialism and reification, even when it is recognized that it represents a shorthand for statements about large numbers of individuals and their normative contexts. Nations, it is argued, are not enduring, homogeneous, substantial communities with fixed traits and essential needs, but simply practical categories imposed by states intent on classifying and designating large numbers of their populations in suitable ways, as was attempted and to some extent realized in early Soviet nationalities policies. In fact, according to the view advanced by Rogers Brubaker, we should not really be analyzing nations at all, only nationalisms, and treat "nations" simply as institutional practices, categories, and contingent events. (19)

But this is to throw out the baby with the bathwater. For, apart from privileging the state (itself just as much a construct), this is to miss out entirely on the understandings, sentiments, and commitments of large numbers of people *vis-à-vis* "their" nations, making it difficult to explain, for example, why so many people were prepared to make great sacrifices (including life itself) on their behalf – except in terms of mass coercion. To try to explain why, in the hearts and minds of so many of their members, their nations and their national identities appear distinctive, binding, and enduring, we do not have to share, much less use, the conceptions and sentiments of the members of nations as categories of our own analyses; nor do we have to assume that nations are homogeneous, much less that they have "substance," "essences," or "fixity." But we do have to recognize that it is these selfsame members of nations who imagine, will, and feel the community, though they do so for the most part within certain social and cultural limits. As Michael Billig has documented, because national institutions, customs, rituals, and discourses persist over generations, many people tend to accept the basic parameters and understandings of their communities from their forebears. (20)

This is not to suggest that historical nations have not been subject to considerable conflict and change, or that their "destinies" have not been the locus of elite rivalries and public contestation. Like all communities and identities, nations and national identities are subject to periodic reinterpretations of their meanings and revolutions of their social structures and boundaries, which in turn may alter the contents of their cultures. Nor should we imagine that national identities are not continually challenged by other kinds of collective identity – of family, region, religion, class, and gender, as well as by supranational associations and religious civilizations. But these caveats do not detract from the historical impact of nations as "lived and felt" communities. Certainly, at the level of the *individual*, nationality is only one of a number of identities, but it is the one that can often be critical and decisive. Individuals may have "multiple identities" and move from one role and identity to another, as the situation appears to require. But *national* identities can also be "pervasive": they can encompass, subsume, and color other roles and identities, particularly in times of crisis. Moreover, with the exception of religion, no other kind of identity and community appears to evoke more passion and commitment, including mass self-sacrifice, than the community of the nation. (21)

At the *collective* level, the role and impact of the nation are even more striking. Here, we may speak of long-term persistence through changes of both *ethnies* and nations – something that cannot be derived simply from the choices and predispositions of their members. For, just as we cannot read off the character of individual members from the political culture of the nation, so the latter cannot be deduced from the sum total of their individual preferences or dispositions, because the political cultures of *ethnies* and nations have their own norms and institutions, symbols and codes of communication. This helps to explain the fact that ethnic communities and nations may persist over long periods, despite the desertion, ethnocide, or even genocide of large numbers of their members; and why cultures can persist even in the absence of most of their practitioners. Long after the final destruction of Carthage in 146 BC and the selling of its inhabitants into slavery, Punic culture persisted in North Africa – till the fifth century AD. (22)

A Political Community?

We can now return to our starting point, the political conception of the nation proposed by many modernists, and ask: are nations to be regarded as significant only insofar as they are seen as first and foremost forms of political community and identity, or should they be seen as primarily types of cultural community and identity?

For most modernists, as we saw, the nation is a political category *par excellence*, not just in the generic sense of a community of power, but in the more specific sense of an autonomous community institutionalized in sovereign territorial statehood. Here, they draw their inspiration from Max Weber's belief in the primacy of political action and institutions in molding ethnicity and nationhood. For Weber,

> A nation is a community of sentiment which would adequately manifest itself in a state of its own; hence, a nation is a community which normally tends to produce a state of its own. (23)

In the same vein, modernists like John Breuilly and Michael Mann see national*ism* as primarily a political movement and regard its social and cultural dimensions as secondary. Since, for these modernists, nations are the creation of states and nationalisms, they are inherently political phenomena, and they become significant only to the extent that they are harnessed to states. As for their cultural attributes, these are essentially "pre-political" and of mainly ethnographic interest. (24)

Now, it is true that nations, like other kinds of collective cultural identity, are communities of power and energy, and can attract the allegiance and energies of large numbers of men and women. They may also be seen as conflict groups, united by war against other collectivities, especially other nations and national states. But, this does not mean that all nations seek states of their own, or that sovereign statehood is the focus and goal of all their endeavors. This is not the case, for example, with the Flemish and Bretons, Scots and Catalans, Welsh and Basques, despite the (variable) prominence of parties and movements among them seeking independent statehood for these nations. In each of these cases, a fervent aspiration to attain internal autonomy or "home rule" is accompanied by a commitment to remain part of the wider multinational state in which they are historically ensconced, whether it be for economic or political reasons. In fact, their aspiration to internal autonomy is in part instrumental. It provides the means for realizing other social, economic, moral, and cultural goals that are valued in and for themselves, even more than is political sovereignty. This is particularly true, as John Hutchinson has documented, of cultural nationalists bent on regenerating their national communities after centuries of lethargy and decline. (25)

Again, it is true that some nations emerged in the crucible of the state, or *pari passu* with its development. This was especially the case in early modern Western Europe, where in both England and France, and to a lesser extent in Spain, we can trace the emergence of national communities alongside the growth of the state's centralizing and bureaucratic powers. Once again, we can see how a peculiar geo-historical context has helped to condition and shape the modernist conception of the nation, to the exclusion of other historical contexts and understandings. (26)

But, equally, we should not overgeneralize from this context and its associated conception of the nation. In other historical contexts – premodern and/or non-Western – the contents of the historical community of the nation, and hence our understandings of it, are very different. There, social, cultural, and religious elements have often had a greater influence and importance than the political dimensions and conceptions favored in the West. To treat these as somehow of lesser significance betrays again that ethnocentrism which was so distinctive a feature of the modernist conception of the nation, and which has proved so detrimental to a wider understanding of nations and national identities.

It is for these reasons that historical nations which belong to different types of the general category of the nation should be seen as forms of human community characterized by a collective cultural *and/or* political identity. In other words, while some nations can be regarded as predominantly forms of political community, aspiring to or conjoined with sovereign states, others are best seen as forms of cultural and territorial community without such political partnership or aspirations, in the specific sense of claims to sovereign statehood. Their drive for internal autonomy tends to focus on social, economic, and cultural goals and aspires to their control within a given territory, without recourse to outright independence and sovereignty. We should take care not to regard such "nations without states" and their nationalisms as of less account than those that possess or aspire to states of their own, for they are often the crucibles of the future politicization of ethnicity. (27)

2

Ethnic and Religious Roots

An enquiry into the origins and forms of nations involves two different kinds of question. The first is sociological. Here we want to know under what conditions a nation comes into being, and how it is constituted. This calls for an investigation into the basic social, cultural, and political processes required for nations to come into being. The second question is historical: tracing the social and cultural "genealogy" of different forms of nations, by enquiring as to when and how the historical forms of human community which we term nations emerged, what were their specific types, and what were the factors that shaped their distinctive characters.

In this chapter, I shall explore the category of the nation in terms of the social and symbolic processes in the making of nations, particularly their ethnic and political roots and their cultural resources. In the following chapters, I shall consider some issues that arise in trying to ascertain the cultural foundations, traditions, and "genealogies" of different forms of the nation, as these are reflected in the historical record.

Social Processes of Nation Formation

A sociological enquiry into the origins and forms of nations must start by considering two issues: the various kinds of human community and collective cultural and/or political identity, of which the nation constitutes one category; and the basic social and symbolic processes that underlie the formation of different types of nations.

In the last chapter I mentioned tribal confederations, religious communities, and ethnic communities as forms of collective *cultural* identities, and city-states, kingdoms, and empires as forms of collective *political* identities. Now, while city-states and kingdoms have played important roles in the formation of nations and, more particularly, in the later rise and character of the ideologies of nationalism, it is, in the first place, to ethnic and ethnoreligious communities that we must look for the origins of many nations and the persistence of their national identities. Even those nations forged mainly on the basis of collective political identities have needed some kind of cultural underpinning of myth, memory, symbol, and tradition in order to create a deeper unity among their often diverse peoples, and these are often to be discovered in the cultural resources of *ethnies* or ethnic communities. Hence, I will start with the relationship between ethnic communities and nations, and then examine the role of some basic social and symbolic processes and cultural resources of national identity.

For most modernists, ethnic ties and identities play little or no role in a theory of nations and nationalism. In part, this reflects a desire not to confuse an already complex issue with further uncertainties, insofar as terms like "ethnic" and "ethnicity" have been used in very different ways. Ethnicity cannot be regarded, any more than nationhood, as a social and cultural given or "fixture of history." Ethnic communities are, after all, formed through processes of ethnogenesis, such as the unification of smaller ethnic categories and networks, the effects of conquest and colonization on pre-existing cultural categories, and the activities of educated strata, especially missionaries and intellectuals, in providing ethnic categories with "their" shared codes and symbols. Moreover, external factors play a large part in the subsequent crystallization of ethnic communities and networks. Perhaps the most salient of these factors has been the impact of protracted interstate wars, which not only sharpen the boundaries between states and their respective communities, but also mobilize and bring together members of different ethnic strata, and provide the stuff of heroic myths and potent memories. Other factors which help to shape ethnic communities include the impact of organized religion, and more especially the activities of the clergy in keeping records, performing rituals, and creating and disseminating a sacred canon of texts; and the competition between different kinds of elites – political, religious, economic, educational, and so on – over the significance and possession of symbolic traditions and cultural resources, as well as, of course, over organizational and material resources. (1)

Yet, however important in themselves, none of these considerations invalidates the pressing need to examine the pivotal relationship between ethnic communities and nations. For, without an attempt to grasp the nature of ethnic ties and their relationship with nations, our understanding of nations and nationalism will remain mired in the problems of modernism which I enumerated in the previous chapter, notably the arbitrary restrictiveness and unaddressed ethnocentrism at its heart.

We can, I think, reduce some of the uncertainty over the concept of ethnicity by distinguishing two current usages, the one narrow, the other broad. The narrow usage focuses on descent, actual or presumed, and translates "ethnic" as "descent-based." The broad usage, while it includes a *myth* of common ancestry (presumed as opposed to actual descent, felt rather than biological ties), stresses other shared cultural elements – of language, religion, customs, and the like. Here, I shall be adopting a broad usage, one in which "ethnic" is understood as more akin to "ethnocultural." (2)

The key concept for an understanding of the origins of nations is that of the ethnic community, or *ethnie* (to adopt the French term). By no means all ethnic identities are of this type. On the contrary, probably the most numerous type can be termed *ethnic categories*. These are constructs, often of outsiders, who group together certain populations in terms of shared cultural characteristics, usually of language, customs, or religious practices. They are generally fluid and shifting clusters of populations with an oral culture. Members of these categories share certain elements of common culture and perhaps a particular terrain, but they may possess no collective proper name, no myth of common descent and no shared memories, and little or no sense of solidarity. On the other hand, more elaborate groupings which we may term, adapting the work of Handelman and Eriksen, *ethnic associations* or *ethnic networks*, however divided in social terms, display patterns of shared activities and relations; they also tend to have a collective name, a myth of common ancestry, and some degree of solidarity, at least among the elites. Finally, there are the full-blown ethnic communities or *ethnies* whose members, over and above these characteristics, are united by shared memories and traditions, often textual, and who may display considerable solidarity, at least among the elites. Such *ethnies* can be defined, ideal-typically, as *named and self-defined human populations with myths of common origins, shared historical memories, elements of common culture, and a measure of ethnic solidarity*. Once formed, they tend to be resilient and persistent, even if they are not as stable and homogeneous as their leaders tend to portray them, since here too the membership is stratified and has differential access to scarce resources, material as well as symbolic. (3)

How are the categories of *ethnie* and nation related? A comparison of their key ideal-typical features reveals a measure of overlap, but also considerable divergences. In terms of shared features, in both *ethnies* and nations we find a high degree of self-definition, including a collective proper name, and even more important, a common fund or heritage of shared memories, myths, symbols, values, and traditions: these include myths of origin and election, memories of migration and heroic ages, and ideals and traditions of destiny and sacrifice. The differences are even more marked. Members of *ethnies* usually have a link, sometimes symbolic, with a specific territory to which they may be attached and/or from which they believe they originate, but in other cases many of their members may be scattered abroad. In contrast, most members of nations occupy and reside in historic "homelands" which possess recognized centers and clearly demarcated boundaries – lands which they claim to be "theirs" by right of indigenous origin or history or both, and to whose "poetic landscapes" they consequently become deeply attached. Second, while the members of *ethnies* share one or more elements of culture, members of nations are united by a distinctive public culture, that is, public rituals and symbolic codes, which are disseminated across the territory from one or more centers to the members of the community – a process that is usually sponsored by specialized religious, judicial, military, or educational elites, and which can be found as much in stateless nations as in those which possess their own states. And third, while we can often find some common customs among members of *ethnies*, the members of nations are united both by shared customs and common laws, which are disseminated across the homeland and increasingly observed by the members of the community – a process usually promoted, if not initiated, by religious and political elites through a single institutional framework of custom and law. (4)

These similarities and differences suggest that, from one angle, we may regard nationhood as a specialized development of ethnicity, and particular nations as territorialized and politicized developments of *ethnies*. This is not to suggest that we can always trace specific historical nations back to one or more *ethnies* – let alone to "their" anterior *ethnies*, as nationalists would have us believe. Nevertheless, as we shall see, the development of the key elements of *ethnies*, such as self-definition, including collective naming, a myth of common ancestry, the forging and transmission of historical memories, and the recognition of elements of common culture (language, customs, religion, etc.), are vital to the formation of nations. But that is only part of the story. For the concept of the nation faces, as it were, in two directions – on the one hand, towards an ethnocultural self-definition and, on the other hand, towards a territorial, legal, and political solidarity. This is where collective political identities reveal (and have historically exerted) their influence, notably through the example of the city-state and the (ethnic) kingdom. The intense bonds and often face-to-face relations found in city-states represent microcosms of the fervent loyalty and political solidarity sought by leaders of nations, and especially by modern nationalists, with the examples of ancient Athens, Sparta, and Rome serving to inspire a long line of patriot intellectuals from the Renaissance to the French Revolution and beyond. Indeed, it has sometimes appeared as though some large city-states like Athens and Venice formed embryonic nations. Equally important has been the historical model of the compact kingdom based on a dominant *ethnie*, as in late medieval and early modern France and England. As a result of their territoriality and political framework, some nations may be able to transcend their ethnocultural basis. How far this occurs in practice will depend on a variety of factors. Where such a trend is observable, the nation may become a model of legal-political community, of the kind that modernists have written into their ideal type of the civic-territorial nation; and in a state which contains a number of ethnic groups, the nation's public culture may even become increasingly distant from that of its dominant *ethnie*, though rarely without severe discord and strain. (5)

Processes of Nation Formation

These considerations suggest that nations as historical communities are both variable and subject to constant change. In the last chapter, I presented a somewhat static picture of the nation as analytic category and ideal type. Here I want to correct this, by stressing the *processual* character of nations. That is to say, nations as historical forms of human community are often in flux, even where their names, symbols, and boundaries persist, because they are the product of certain social and symbolic processes.

What can we say about the principal processes in the formation of nations? While they can appear in any period of history, there is nothing determinate about them. As *social* processes, their operation is often intermittent and reversible, depending as they usually do on human action and subjective interpretation. Nevertheless, their development and combination, and hence the formation of nations, though not confined to specific historical epochs, are likely to occur only in definite historical circumstances. These nation-forming processes include: self-definition; the cultivation of symbolic elements; territorialization; the rise of a distinctive public culture; and the standardization of laws and customs.

Self-definition

While definition of the collectivity by others may mark out an ethnic category, ethnic communities and nations require clear *self*-definition. This includes the acquisition by a given population of a collective proper name by which the community is known and recognized by themselves and by others, and the identification of the members with that named community and its symbols. This may begin negatively, as Walker Connor argues, as a process of coming to know who and what they are *not*, in opposition to others near and far, from whom the community differentiates itself. However, it is only when the members begin to know who they collectively *are*, and feel that they constitute a distinct named community, that one can speak of a process of growing collective self-definition and identification; and this will come to furnish one of the basic features in the ideal type of the nation.

We can discern such a process in both earlier and contemporary periods. For example, while the Phoenicians were named by others such as the Greeks with whom they traded, the ancient Greeks differentiated themselves through the name of "Hellene" from Persians and others whom they encountered. Similarly, the medieval English from an early period distinguished themselves from and named (and were named by) their neighbors, the Scots, Welsh, and Irish; while in the modern period, not only must all nations acquire a recognized name, if they do not already have one, but the members of these nations will differentiate themselves from self-designated groups of immigrants, as the Italians have done with the Albanians and the Germans with Turkish immigrants. In each case, a self-designating collective proper name is a vital element in this process. (6)

If collective names are vital to ethnic and national self-definition, the lack of a recorded proper name may suggest an absence of a sense of common ethnicity, let alone nationhood. This seems to have been the case among the French and Germans until the twelfth or thirteenth centuries when designations like *France* and *français*, and *deutsch*, became more widespread among populations west and east of the Rhine. (7)

Names are also essential to the exercise of power. Thus Roman generals and emperors like Caesar and Trajan felt it necessary to identify the often fluid groupings of chiefs and their followers with ethnic names which helped to map allies and enemies, and later to control the "barbarian tribes" they subjugated. How far the groups in question accepted this external nomenclature is unknown. A similar process took place under modern colonial rule, when the European powers sought to map the populations whose territories they had annexed, and traders, officials, and missionaries interpreted the different populations they encountered in terms of European ethnic classifications, sometimes accepting the categories and names given to them by the ruling ethnic community in the colony, as occurred with the Baganda in British-ruled Uganda. (8)

Cultivation of symbolic elements

The creation and cultivation of memories, symbols, myths, values, and traditions define the unique cultural heritage of each ethnic community and nation. For *ethnies*, a *myth* of origins is critical, but other myths, memories, symbols, and traditions may accumulate over time and mark out their cultural heritages from those of their neighbors, above all, where a distinct sacred literature is handed down the generations. While the possession and cultivation of such a cultural heritage is a *sine qua non* of any nation in the eyes of nationalists, it is equally to be found in various ethnic and ethnopolitical communities, from ancient Egypt to early medieval Russia. A good example is afforded by ancient Rome and its Latin League. Despite the mixed ethnic origins of early Rome under the kings, a sense of common Roman and Latin ethnicity was forged through the wars with Samnites, Greeks, and Etruscans. Perhaps the crucial moment was the encounter with Magna Graecia in the third century BC, and the great crisis of the Second Punic War, when the Carthaginians under Hannibal crushed successive Roman armies in Italy. This was the period that saw the emergence of an indigenous Latin literature in the plays of Plautus and Terence, and the prose of Naevius and Ennius, as well as a distinctive myth of austere Roman virtue epitomized in the stern figure of Cato the Censor. As a result, the Romans possessed a dual myth of descent – from Romulus, Remus, and the She-Wolf, and from Trojan Aeneas and Latium – and a complement of symbols, traditions, and memories, testifying to Walker Connor's argument that the belief in ancestral relatedness is the defining element of ethnicity, even where, as so often, the lines of descent are fictive. (9)

Even today, the sense of ancestral relatedness may persist, surfacing for example when waves of culturally alien immigrants appear to "threaten" the dominant *ethnie* of the nation and its traditional way of life. If this is so, myths of descent may not have become obsolete, even though they are less central to the definition of the community, and represent only one among several sets of traditions, myths, and memories which characterize the nation. (10)

Territorialization

A process of territorialization of communities can be observed throughout history, and is not specific to *ethnies* or nations. The attachment to specific places and the drawing of spatial boundaries to designate "home" from "outside" are, nevertheless, processes that have become characteristic of ethnicity, and more particularly nationhood. In the form of "territorialization of memories," they have proved crucial to the creation of *ethnoscapes* and the emergence of nations. One can see this particularly in the processes by which the memories and history of a community are linked to specific places, namely, the "naturalization of community" and the "historicization of nature." (11)

In the first of these processes, *ethnies* become intrinsic parts of their historic environments, perceived "natural outgrowths" of their terrains, and their monuments become "fixtures" of their landscapes and reminders of the quasi-primeval antiquity of the community, as with the pyramids of ancient Egypt or Mexico. In the second, nature itself becomes historicized: the territory and habitat of the community become inseparable from its history and culture, the place where its saints, heroes, and sages lived and died, the arena of its historic crises and turning-points, and the memorial of the heroic deeds of its ancestors. These are processes that can be observed well before the advent of modernity. We find examples in the records of the beauty of the countryside around Rome recorded in the poetry of Horace and Virgil, in the conception of the Garden of France which became increasingly popular among late medieval French writers, in the shaping of the Netherlands through their inhabitants' encounters with the North Sea, and in the early modern Swiss eulogies of their Alpine landscapes. (12)

From the eighteenth century on, the territorialization of memories and the cultivation of collective attachments to national landscapes became more self-conscious and widespread. This was largely due to Romanticism's cult of Nature, and of the appropriate expression of emotions in its presence, as with the growing fascination with the Alps. The Romantics turned territory into poetic landscapes, and made it a key component of the very conception of a nation. For nationalists, the nation is nothing if not a community of territory, where land and landscape provide both the "objective" and "subjective" bases – the very groundwork – of a genuine national community. This meant that the nation had to be unified and rendered compact within recognized "natural" borders, even if in practice its borders remained ragged; it could then take its place as a legitimate member of an "inter-national community" of nations. It could also be felt by its members to have "grown from its own soil" – even if in fact most of its members (or their forebears) had migrated to this soil from afar. The fact that so many nationalists, for all their undoubted "inventions," could build on pre-existing attachments and memories made their task that much easier. (13)

Rise of a distinctive public culture

By the term "public culture" I have in mind the creation of a system of public rites, symbols, and ceremonies, on the one hand, and on the other hand, the growth of distinctive public codes and literatures.

Whereas for *ethnies* it is enough for the members to be distinguished from outsiders by speaking a common language, observing different customs, and worshipping native gods and goddesses, for nations such shared cultural features must become common public property and serve as specific criteria of cultural differentiation. They must become part of a distinctive national public culture. Moreover, any regional variations of dialect or worship must be subordinated to this ideologized public culture, or eradicated.

Of course, neither public rituals nor codes serve of themselves to demarcate *ethnies* and nations from other collective cultural identities. The performance of public rituals has been a feature of many societies from ancient Babylonia and Egypt to medieval France, Venice, and Muscovy. Similarly, the development of distinctive public codes and literatures can be found in many kinds of societies in the ancient and medieval epochs, from ancient Athens to medieval Provence and Florence. What this means for the formation of nations is that cultural "materials" have been present for many centuries in different societies, but only under certain conditions and in certain cases, were they "brought together" and combined with other processes to create the strictly *national* type of human community.

In this respect, public rituals, ceremonies, and symbols are of greater significance for the emergence of nations than vernacular codes and literatures. The latter surface largely in the early modern period, despite Adrian Hastings' arguments for the early medieval expression of both in England and its neighbors. For the most part, literature remains the preserve of a courtly or clerical elite, at least until the early modern state "fixes" the language and its readership, and print-capitalism disseminates its products to wider circles. In contrast, not only do public rituals, ceremonies, and symbols become widespread at a much earlier date, they are perceived to be essential for impressing on large segments of the population their common sense of belonging to a wider political and cultural community, be it ethnic community, church, city-state, or kingdom, and of affirming its vitality and legitimacy. Hence the importance attached to temple ceremonies like the New Year festivals in Mesopotamia, the Panathenaic procession in Athens, and the Vestal rites in Rome; and the various ceremonies that associated the monarchy with the Church in medieval Europe, such as coronations, ritual entries into cities, and funerals. Once again, these provided models for later national*ist* rituals – of raising the flag, singing anthems, and celebrating national holidays. (14)

As we shall see, distinctive public cultures play a pivotal role in the rise of different historical kinds of nation, helping to form key elements in their shaping in successive periods. It is in large part through the rituals, ceremonies, symbols, and codes of public cultures that the main cultural legacies of antiquity have been able to forge the distinctive traditions of national community and identity that I will elaborate in chapter 4.

Standardization of laws and customs

In and of themselves, common legal systems and shared customs do not mark out *ethnies* and nations from other kinds of collective cultural or political identities. Long before the advent of modernity, lawcodes were generally associated with city-states and empires, from those of Urukagina and Hammurabi in Sumer and Babylon to the great Roman and Byzantine lawcodes. Alternatively, they were the product of great religious communities and their sacred texts, such as the Sharia or canon law.

Nevertheless, processes of dissemination of customs and standardization of laws and lawmaking have been crucial elements in the formation of both *ethnies* and nations. Most *ethnies*, once their members had acquired a written vernacular, boasted various compilations of customs, rituals, traditions, and laws, and these increasingly governed their relationships, both among themselves and with outsiders. The links between standardized lawmaking and nationhood have been even closer. Nations might even be characterized, in part, as communities of law and custom, with a sense of the common good and a set of reciprocal rights and duties for members. That is to say, even if the membership of the national community is limited, usually to adult males or heads of families in premodern epochs, their relations with each other and with outsiders are increasingly governed by common legal institutions and public codes of common laws, shared customs, and symbolic prescriptions which distinguish them from others. In fact, law, custom, and ritual may demarcate the symbolic boundaries of nations even more clearly than the looser customs and traditions that characterize *ethnies*. But no hard and fast dividing line can be drawn between them. This is clearly illustrated by the centrality accorded to the Mosaic Law by the Jews for the definition of Jewishness in the Second Temple period. (15)

More generally, we may say that the process by which ethnic communities come to be governed by increasingly standardized lawcodes and uniform legal institutions is crucial for the formation of nations, for it provides a "roof" of unity and a sense of social solidarity through shared norms and the recognition of common rights and duties for the members of the community. It is true that, for the most part, this process took place under the aegis of a state, however rudimentary, usually that of an ethnic kingdom or principality. Nevertheless, we also find complex lawcodes and legal institutions being maintained, if not generated, in the absence of a state, for example, through common religious institutions evolved in a diaspora community, such as was common among both Armenians and Jews throughout the medieval epoch. These cases suggest the need to separate the processes of lawmaking and shared customs from the purely political dimension, and especially from the modern state, with which it is so often wont to be associated by modernists. (16)

Cultural Sources of National Identity

So far, I have considered some of the social and symbolic processes involved in the *formation* of nations. But how do national communities maintain themselves, and why are they often so durable? This involves a consideration of the nature and strength of the sense of national identity in a given population and the sources of the *persistence* of nations by examining some of the nation's key cultural resources.

For the members of a community, these cultural resources are much more tangible and accessible than the general processes of the formation of nations I outlined. They are more specific, and hence more "usable" – and used, specifically, for political ends. These resources can also be chosen by individuals and groups bent on active intervention in the life of the nation, for example, by leaders seeking to revive the fortunes of the nation, or by clergy and intellectuals fashioning new symbols and narratives of the nation. (17)

But, perhaps most significantly, some at least of these cultural resources of national identity may become "sacred foundations" of the nation, set apart, revered, and treated as canonical, through a process of sanctification of key social and symbolic elements – a process in turn often derived from, if not consciously modeled on, the processes of sanctification which characterized earlier religious traditions. For, in premodern and prenationalist epochs, ethnicity is rarely separated from religion. As a result, the cultural resources which can be used, actively pursued, and sanctified by premodern ethnic or national leaders and groups come with a clear religious aura which imbues otherwise secular conceptions of the nation with a definite "sacred" quality. Even in the modern era of national*ism*, this sacred quality is rarely absent; only here authenticity takes the place of religious orthodoxy, and the cult of authenticity functions as the new core of a "political religion of the people," with its emblems and anthems, feasts and ceremonies, such as was witnessed during the French Revolution. (18)

That is why the cultural resources which maintain a sense of national identity in a population may also be regarded as "sacred foundations" of the nation, in the sense that they "underpin" the four fundamental dimensions of nationhood: community; territory; history; and destiny. Let me briefly consider these in turn.

Myths of origins and election

Two of the vital cultural resources that can be said to sustain the dimension of community in a population's sense of national identity are myths of origin and myths of ethnic election, and both highlight the dimension of community.

(1) *Myths of origin.* I have already touched on the importance of these myths. The term itself covers a broad spectrum, ranging from elaborate cosmologies and creation myths to foundation myths and myths of common ancestry. In ancient Egypt and Japan, for example, myths of divine creation were bound up with the tales of origins of a specific people, dynasty, and kingdom – tales that place the people and their rulers at the center of the universe and which are often the subject of periodic elaboration by priests and intellectuals. Alternatively, the myth of creation may be chronologically separated from that of the origin of the people, as Hesiod's *Theogony* and the first eleven chapters of the Book of Genesis testify. (19)

Foundation myths, on the other hand, are commonly associated with cities and city-states. One recalls, for example, the myth of the contest between Athena and Poseidon for patronage of Erechtheus' Athens, the subject of the sculptured figures on one of the Parthenon's pediments. Even more familiar is the myth of the She-Wolf suckling Romulus and Remus, founders of Rome, or that of the transportation of St. Mark's body to Venice, symbolized by his lion. But foundation myths can also be found in ethnic kingdoms. One of their most common forms is the royal conversion to a world religion, as occurred under Tiridates III of Armenia, Clovis in Frankish Gaul, and Vladimir in Kievan Rus'. Another is the enactment of a pact between representatives of a contiguous and co-cultural population, for example, the pact or oath of unity which originated the Swiss *Eidgenossenschaft* in 1291, the renewal of Scottish community in the Declaration of Arbroath of 1320, and, of course, the Oath of the Tennis Court in 1789. (20)

But perhaps the most familiar type is the myth of common ancestry, with its abundant genealogies and its sense of common ethnicity. Myths of common ancestry have been the most common type of origin myth in premodern epochs, and their appeal to kinship helps to account for the durability of many *ethnies*. But, as Walker Connor has demonstrated, it is not actual but *felt* history that is crucial for a sense of group identity, and so what matters is the belief in common ancestry, however counterfactual. Such myths have also provided the most fruitful model of nationhood for later nationalists, insofar as they undergird the familiar nationalist portrayal of the nation as a greatly extended family, a "super-family of families" – a self-description that undoubtedly helps to unite and mobilize the designated population for collective goals. Hence the appeal of an ethnic conception of nationhood, and of the later association of ethnicity with "purity" and "authenticity." (21)

(2) *Myths of election.* Of the many symbolic elements that form part of a community's heritage, none is more potent and resilient than the myth of ethnic election. The belief that a particular people or community was "chosen" by the deity for a special task or purpose has a long history. It can be traced to ancient Mesopotamia and Egypt, but its *locus classicus* is the Torah, brought down by Moses from Mount Sinai to the children of Israel after their exodus from Egypt. There we read of a conditional covenant: if the children of Israel will obey God's commandments and fulfill His law, they will be blessed and will possess the promised land of Canaan, both they and their descendants. But, if not, they will be punished and exiled. Their purpose is to become a holy nation, a kingdom of priests, and by this means, become a blessing to all nations. Holiness here means separation from the profane

world of the (idolatrous) nations, so that the Israelites can fulfill a moral and ritual code without the distractions and temptations of egoistic desire. (22)

Specifically covenantal myths of election have made their appearance in various communities, from the Gregorian Armenians of the fourth and fifth centuries and the "Solomonic" Ethiopians of the thirteenth to fifteenth centuries to the Calvinist Scots and Dutch of the sixteenth century, the Ulster-Scots and Puritan settlers in New England in the seventeenth century, right up to the Protestant Afrikaners after the Great Trek, and in more secular guise, the Zionists in early twentieth-century Palestine. In these cases, the quest for moral virtue and the cultivation of holiness and spirituality, often through separation and purification of their communities, were buttressed by a powerful belief in a collective covenant and in divine providence. (23)

A more common and less demanding type of election myth sees the community entrusted with a sacred task or mission, but there is no corresponding obligation, apart from continued adherence to the particular religion or tradition. There are various kinds of mission: defending the sacred realm; converting the heathen; safeguarding the true religion, i.e., orthodoxy; spreading the "truth" and morality; and being a "light to the Gentiles." This kind of missionary election myth was particularly prominent in *antemurale* kingdoms and *ethnies* – for example, among the monarchs and nobility of Hungary, Poland, and Catalonia, at the margins of Catholic Christendom. But we also find it in less exposed ethnic kingdoms – in England, France, and Muscovy-Russia after its liberation from the Tatar yoke – and in more secularized form, in their modern national counterparts, with their quests for comparative economic success, military power, and cultural fame. Nor has the missionary form of election myth been confined to the Jewish and Christian traditions. Elements of a sense of chosenness and of a belief in collective mission can be found in sixteenth-century Safavid Persia, modern Egypt with its Pharaonic movement, and in Japan from the eighteenth-century *kokugaku* movement to twentieth-century Romanticism. (24)

Homelands and poetic landscapes

One of the key processes of nation formation, as we saw, is *territorialization* – the residence of the majority of the community in the homeland, and the growth of collective memories and attachments to particular historic territories within recognized borders. In this process, *ethnoscapes* come into being through the symbiosis of *ethnie* and landscape. As I explained, this is achieved by the naturalization of ethnic history, in which the latter is seen as part of nature, and by the historicization of the natural environment, making it appear intrinsic to the history and development of the ethnic community. As a result of this two-way process, ethnic communities appear, as it were, "rooted" in "their" historic homelands, and, in Steven Grosby's words: "a people has its land and a land has its people." (25)

But this is only the start of a long-term process of the "territorialization of memories," essential for the formation and persistence of nations; and this in turn is related to the idea of "sacred territory," or the sanctification of the homeland. Whence comes this sanctification of territory, and why are its landscapes so often felt to be, not only "ours," but "sacred"? Perhaps most commonly, land that has "seen" the footsteps of the prophet, sage, and saint and "heard" their preaching becomes holy and is thereby set apart from surrounding terrains and from everyday life. This process of sanctification may be extended to the example and deeds of ethnic heroes, heroines, and geniuses, evoking reverence and emulation on the part of their descendants. And not just heroes, but the whole people may be deemed to be holy, and hence set apart, as was the case in ancient Israel, where the land became not just a promised land, but itself an object of devotion and piety as a result of the people's sanctity. Within the homeland, too, certain sites may carry a special charge of holiness, as in ideas of standing on "holy ground" or of reported miracles. These holy sites can be rivers and mountains, cities, temples and battlefields, as well as excavations and museums, but they are at their most potent in the graveyards of "our ancestors" and at the tombs of fallen patriots; for their last resting places bid us reflect on the sacredness of "our past" and "our homeland." Once sanctified in these ways, the homeland in turn becomes a powerful cultural resource for sustaining a sense of national identity. The shared attachments which it generates are often reinforced by the need to defend the sacred space, and by the many sacrifices made on behalf of the community and its homeland. (26)

Ethnohistory and the golden age

A third kind of cultural resource is found in a community's "ethnohistory." Here, successive generations of a community narrate and hand down their shared memories of the ethnic past (or pasts) of their nation. These are tales told to each other, and the ethnohistory is therefore far from uniform and unchanging; there is usually more than one narrative of ethnohistory in a given generation and community, and each of them is subject to emendation. But, in contrast to the professional historians' enquiry, ethnohistory provides a developmental story which highlights in easily memorized terms the "key events" and "turning-points" in the ethnic past or pasts of the community.

Among the most memorable of these tableaux of the ethnic past are its "golden ages." They speak of ages when the community was great and glorious in political and military terms, or when it was wealthy and prosperous, or at its most creative in intellectual and artistic, or religious and spiritual terms. If we leave aside the purely literary and mythical kind of golden age which we find in the Book of Genesis or in Hesiod, the exemplar of the historical type of golden age has been that of classical Athens, which was regarded as such already in ancient times. But it was not the first such golden era. Already in the late Assyrian empire, the court of king Ashur-bani-pal sought to emulate the culture of Old Babylonia. Perhaps the best-known case from antiquity is that of the Augustan age, where writers and statesmen looked back to the alleged virtues and pieties of early Republican Rome in the age of Cato and Scipio and contrasted them with the luxury and corruption of the empire. And in the medieval world, there is the case of Ethiopia's "Solomonic" dynasty, which sought to restore the ancient religious and "Semitic" culture of the Aksumite kingdom of a thousand years earlier, and thereby effect a radical reform of Ethiopian society and culture. (27)

The return to a communal golden age was one of the main goals of nationalist revivalisms. In practice this meant a regeneration of the community in the light and spirit of the golden age, which was seen as canonical, if not sacred. This was the way in which Greek nationalists viewed the relationship of modern Greece to its prized classical heritage, symbolized by the Parthenon; just as it was the understanding of early twentieth-century Egyptian Pharaonicists, who urged Egyptians to shake off their millennial lethargy and emulate the grandeur and heroic exploits of their great ancestors, so vividly exemplified in the massive temples of Karnak. In this and other examples, the sacred character and the functions of memories of the golden age are clearly visible. In an era of political and social change, these memories answered to shared needs for rootedness, antiquity, and continuity, as well as for authenticity and dignity. (28)

Sacrifice and destiny

The fourth and final dimension of nationhood is that of *destiny*, and it has always been closely linked to ideals of striving and sacrifice, even before the age of nationalism. Ideas of struggle and sacrifice can be found in the Bible and the Books of the Maccabees, and even more clearly in ancient Greece and Rome, where individual and collective fame and glory, for example, of the Spartans at Thermopylae and Plataea, were recorded for posterity in poetic form. There is also the powerful tradition of collective martyrdom for faith and community which arose in fourth- and fifth-century Armenia during the course of its many struggles with an expansionist Iran and its reformed Zoroastrian faith. In the Middle Ages, the ideal of martyrdom for the community comes into even clearer focus: we find it in the heroic deaths of warriors for the true faith during the Crusades, and conversely among the Ottoman *ghazis*, and in a very different mode, in the books of lamentation of the massacred Jewish communities of the Rhineland and elsewhere in this period. We have to wait till the early modern period, during the struggle of the Dutch provinces against Spain, for further evidence of this ideal, notably in the commemoration of the death of William the Silent. But it was only in the age of nationalism that the ideal of achieving national destiny through individual or collective sacrifice took root and was widely disseminated, becoming a vital cultural resource of national identity. (29)

Today this cult of sacrifice plays a pivotal role in the spread of a distinctive public culture to the members of the community. As an example of the very public celebration and self-worship of the nation, the cult of sacrifice has become closely linked to the ideal of national regeneration and revival. By the mid-nineteenth century, it was not only individual fallen heroes who were being commemorated but whole armies and all those who fell for *la patrie*. Early in this period, the Pantheon became the repository for the remains of all the great men of France, but Chalgrin's Arc de Triomphe, begun in 1806 and originally dedicated to Napoleon and his Grand Army, from the 1830s came to include all who had died for the fatherland, so that it was logical and fitting that in 1919 it should enclose the Tomb of the

Unknown Soldier. By the early twentieth century, memorials for fallen soldiers began to proliferate, reaching a climax in the huge First World War cemeteries, sepulchres, and cenotaphs. Here, the twin ideas of religious resurrection and national regeneration were fused in the cult of "The Glorious Dead" who made the supreme sacrifice on behalf of the nation, and whose memory, like the nation itself, is forever renewed. Some of these monuments became sites of choreographed ceremonies and orchestrated services for soldier-patriots and the fallen masses, transmuting the horror of mass slaughter through the uplifting ideal of national self-sacrifice. Through such rites and ceremonies, with their flags and anthems, the distinctive public cultures of modern mass nations were displayed in what George Mosse termed a "civic religion" of the masses, its liturgies and rituals modeled on preceding forms of Christian worship. (30)

Each of these cultural resources, however chosen and used, comes in time to be seen as sacred and irreplaceable. They are, as it were, the pillars of the nation, sustaining the sense of national identity through critical periods. The more of these resources, and the more developed and extensive, the stronger and more durable the sense of national identity, and the more likely to survive the dissolving effects of local fragmentation and globalizing cosmopolitanism. Their overall effect is to undergird the nation as a sacred communion of the people and to uphold and give "substance" to the "political religion" of nationalism by providing it with the cultural resources and sacred elements of ethnic myth, memory, tradition, and symbol, enacted in public rituals and ceremonies and purveyed in schools and the media. In this sense, nationalism as a political form of secular religion expresses the ideal of the nation seen as a sacred community of the citizens. For, in this image, the people are "really" at one beneath their many divisions and conflicts, and the ideal of the nation mirrors that inner unity in the sacred moment of public communion. (31)

Conclusion

In this chapter I have briefly enumerated some basic processes of nation formation: self-definition, cultivation of symbolic resources, territorialization, the dissemination of a distinctive public culture, and the standardization and observance of common laws and customs. But these provide only the necessary conditions for the *emergence* of nations. They do not in themselves explain the longevity of nations, nor the ways in which their members can survive the hazards of social existence. To ensure their durability and *persistence* requires, in addition, the cultivation of certain cultural resources of national identity: myths of origin and ethnic election, attachments to sacred homelands, memories of golden ages, and ideals of sacrifice and destiny. These cultural resources, as we shall see, are mainly derived from those of antecedent ethnic communities and ancient religious traditions. As a result, it becomes necessary to explain the persistence and the shape of nations in terms of long-standing cultural traditions that ultimately stem from certain legacies of the ancient world.

3

Community in Antiquity

Any attempt to understand the traditions through which various kinds of nations and national identities were formed in the late medieval and early modern periods cannot avoid a deep historical perspective stretching back to Near Eastern and classical antiquity, which alone can provide us with a comparative historical framework for a cultural "genealogy" of nations.

Teleology and "Ancient Nations"

However, discussion of the possibility of premodern nations requires particular care, in order to avoid, as far as is possible, any implication of a teleological reading of the historical record.

In his last debate at Warwick, Ernest Gellner quipped that like Adam, nations have no need of navels. It was only necessary to demonstrate that one nation was a modern invention to negate the nationalist belief in premodern nations or even the claim that nations have ethnic origins. And he produced his case of a purely modern invention – Estonia. Perhaps there were better choices, since the Estonians (Ests) were originally a medieval peasant people with a vernacular language and, after the Reformation, a Protestant-based literature and schooling, conquered in the thirteenth century by the Brethren of the Sword under Bishop Albert and ruled thereafter by German overlords until the early twentieth century. However, the point is a serious one, as it seeks to undermine the teleological reading of nations common to nationalists and the allied tendency of many scholars to a "retrospective nationalism," something that Susan Reynolds and John Breuilly have also castigated.

But neither the nationalist reading of nations nor the tendency to retrospective nationalism is necessary to an argument that many, but *not all*, modern nations have at their historical root ethnic ties of one kind or another which can be used as powerful resources in nation formation and persistence; or the claim that we can speak of *some* pre-modern nations, whether in antiquity or more securely and to a greater extent in the early modern period, and that this is not a purely fortuitous occurrence. Both claims are quite compatible with a moderate modernist position which would argue that most nations have, as a matter of historical fact, emerged after the French Revolution, in many cases using pre-existing cultural ties; but that in a few well-known cases (England, France, Scotland, etc.) the sense of national identity, at least among the elites, was in evidence well before that date. This is very much the claim that I wish to make here.

We also need to bear in mind that, in comparative history and the social sciences, we are dealing with possibilities and probabilities, rather than law-like propositions. Hence the more doctrinaire positions of primordial nationalists (not all nationalists, by the way) and radical modernists must be discarded in fields such as ours that admit of no great certainty. My position is to be understood as a statement of probability, not teleological necessity, which in these fields of enquiry is all that one can ask for. Hence, there is no imputation of a retrospective nationalism in enquiring into the significance of ethnic factors in the formation and persistence of nations and nationalism.

In chapter 1, I argued that as a category of analysis the concept of the nation can, in principle, span all periods and continents. Does this suggest that we might even discover historical forms of national community in our earliest records, that is, in the ancient Near East and classical antiquity?

Actually, the question suggests two kinds of enquiry, one of periodization, the other of cultural genealogy. The first concerns the criteria and evidence for the dating of the "first nations." The issue here is relatively straightforward. Either no historical records of national identity or community exist in this period, and the concept of the nation was unknown in antiquity. Alternatively, we can find at least some evidence for the presence of a national form of community and identity, as well as some of the processes of nation formation. In both cases, we need to take care not to allow our present understanding of the concept of the modern nation to determine retrospectively our assessment of that evidence.

The other kind of enquiry into cultural traditions and genealogies is more complex. It involves the investigation of the different types of collective identities prevalent in the ancient world to see how far, and in what ways, they may have provided vital cultural legacies for the subsequent formation of nations. This is the enquiry that I believe to be more fruitful and the one that I shall pursue in this and the following chapters. However, something needs to be said about the periodization of nations, and I shall also address the issues it raises. (1)

For modernists, an "ancient nation" in this sense would be a contradiction in terms. Because nations and nationalism are bound up with the more general processes of modernization, any example of nations before the onset of modernity is purely fortuitous. Ernest Gellner, in this respect the most forthright of the modernists, is unequivocal: there might be all kinds of collective cultural and political identities before the onset of modernity, but there was neither need nor room for nations. And it is true that our records of antiquity, for the most part, speak of every kind of collective identity other than that of the nation. Indeed, it is possible that the very strength and durability of these other kinds of collective identity – clan and village, city-state, religion and empire – prevented the development of just those social processes and cultural resources that help to produce and maintain national kinds of community. This is not to say that there is not considerable evidence of shared cultures and a sense of common ethnicity among the populations of the ancient Near East and classical antiquity; and even in some cases of the politicization of culture and ethnicity that comes close to the national type of identity and community. (2)

In this chapter I shall explore briefly three kinds of collective identity and community in the ancient world: empire, city-state, and tribal confederation; and show how, in each case, they have become intertwined with ethnic differences and the cultivation of a sense of distinctive ethnicity. In the following chapters, I hope to show how these three kinds of identity and community provided cultural and religious traditions that helped to form and shape different historical types of nation, mainly in Europe and the West.

Empire and Ethnicity

I start with the ideologies of ancient empires. In the royal propaganda of ancient Egypt, there was a strong emphasis on bounded ethnic groups and clear distinctions between the Egyptian elite and all foreigners. There is no doubt much truth in the view of archaeologist Stuart Tyson Smith, that this was largely a literary and rhetorical topos, a necessary part of Pharaonic propaganda directed internally, to the Egyptian elite and people. Nevertheless, on his own evidence, Egyptians clearly marked the ethnic boundary between themselves and such peoples as their Nubian neighbors in art and architecture, language and literature, dress, food, and burial practices, not to mention their respective pantheons of gods and goddesses. In his study of Egyptian relations with its southern neighbor, Nubia, Tyson Smith shows how clear were the distinctions between Egyptian and Nubian ceramics at the border fortress of Askut, and how important was the large and elaborate fourteenth-century BC Egyptian tomb of the Overseer Siamun at Tombos in Upper Nubia. This suggests that basic ethnic distinctions remained firm over several centuries, despite the frequency of intermarriage with Nubians and the large quantities of Nubian jewelry, cosmetic equipment, and female figurines, alongside Egyptian artifacts and buildings found at Askut. In other words, as Sian Jones' cultural approach to the archaeology of ethnicity had shown, constant exchange across the border served to strengthen, not weaken, the ethnic boundary, and this was continually reinforced by Pharaonic propaganda about the superiority of Egypt to the "chiefs of wretched Kush [Nubia] . . . bearing all their tribute on their backs," as an inscription of the Pharaoh Amenhotep III put it. (3)

In fact, by the Middle Kingdom, a process of Egyptianization of Nubia had set in. It was intensified by the appointment of an Overseer responsible for Kush in the New Kingdom in the mid-second millennium BC. This reconquest was provoked in part by the Pharaohs' need not to have a troublesome kingdom on a second front, while campaigning in Palestine and Syria. But it was also fed by the desire to seize precious Nubian resources of gold, ivory, and ebony, as well as captive slaves. (4)

Egypt is not alone in the divergence of its ethnic practice from its political ideology. The same duality can be found in the Neo-Assyrian empire of the eighth and seventh centuries BC. There was considerable interethnic intercourse and exchange in daily life, trade, and intermarriage.

Plate 1 Gold Mask of Tutankhamun, ca. 1350 BC (Cairo Museum).

Plate 2 Men bringing tribute from Black Africa in presentation to Pharaoh, Tuthmosis IV, ca. 1425–1417 BC (British Museum).

As is well known, the *lingua franca* of the later Assyrian empire was Aramaic, not Assyrian, there was a strong influence of Babylonian cults and religious texts in Nineveh, and Assyrian palaces were filled with Phoenician ivories and furniture. Besides, the deportation of conquered peoples made the later Assyrian empire increasingly cosmopolitan in composition. This is reflected in Assyrian sculpture where, according to Julian Reade, the different appearances and cultures of the peoples they subjugated were portrayed, and where "great care was taken in recording the dress and other distinctive characteristics of foreign peoples." (5)

Nevertheless, despite all this state incorporation and borrowing, Assyrian kings and elites never lost sight of the ultimate purpose of empire, in which, in Mario Liverani's words, beneath the veneer of a sacred form, "the kernel of the whole of the ideology [sc. of Assyrian imperialism] is a *theory of diversity as justification of unbalance and exploitation.*" (6)

Liverani lists various types of diversities – of space, time, goods, and men, and especially the opposition between the residents of the inner

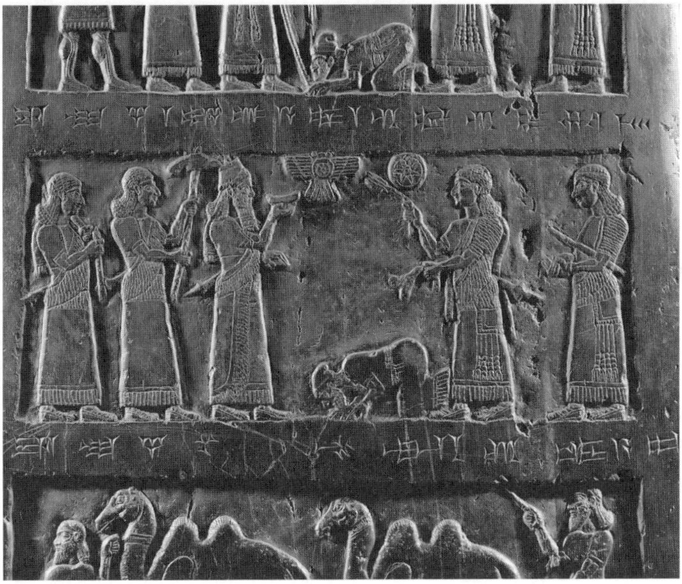

Plate 3 Jehu, king of Israel, bringing tribute to the Assyrian monarch, Black Obelisk of Shalmaneser III, ca. 825 BC (British Museum).

land and those of the periphery – between the civilized Assyrian and the uncivilized barbarian. Whereas the Assyrians saw themselves as normal, comprehensible, and fully human, foreigners appear strange, speak incomprehensible languages, and so are comparable with animals. In what is a familar pattern of relations between the dominant and subject peoples, the Assyrian ideal harked back to earlier Babylonian, Sumerian, and Akkadian models; hence the polity and society that the Assyrian kings created was essentially a hierarchical ethnic state, a state forged and organized by a dominant *ethnie*, which ruled over and exploited its subject peoples. (7)

Even under the much milder rule of the Persians, this imbalance of ethnic hierarchy was evident. In the propagandist art of the Achaemenid empire, it is true, there is none of the abasement of foreigners typical of Egyptian art, which shows aliens on their knees, or of Assyrian reliefs which depict them stooping or kissing the king's feet. Instead, in the celebrated sculptural reliefs on the staircase of the Apadana in Persepolis, we watch the representatives of various ethnic groups bringing gifts to the Great King, not bearing tribute, in a calm, dignified procession. For Carl Nylander, this expressed "a timeless idea of universal and cosmic order upheld by divine assistance and mutual loyalty between king and subjects" – a point which Josef Wiesehofer's recent study supports to some extent:

> typical products of each of the peoples, or luxury goods, are brought to the king and thus symbolise the solidarity between monarch and subjects, whether this is felt as genuine or prescribed by the monarch. (8)

On the other hand, as Darius' famous inscription of 519 BC on the rockface of Behistun testified, the Achaemenid empire was based on a clear ethnic hierarchy. Darius himself emphasizes his Persian origins, and Herodotus tells us that the empire was ruled by an absolute monarch drawn from the ranked aristocracy of the province of Persis and its tribe of Pasargadae and "the clan (*phratria*) of the Achaemenids, from which the kings of Persia are drawn." The ethnic nature of the hierarchy of imperial Persia is underlined by the fact that the Persian commoners, mainly small farmers, were exempted from the tribute (*phoros*), to which most of the subject peoples were liable, with the exception of a few peripheral peoples. (9)

Plate 4 Eastern staircase of Apadana, Persepolis, ca. 500 BC.

If we consider the royal inscriptions and sculptures, the same mixture of toleration and hierarchy is evident. On the one hand, we know of various edicts of royal sympathy with the religious and cultural autonomy of the subject peoples: Cyrus' taking the hand of Bel of Babylon, and Cyrus' and Darius' edicts restoring exiled Judeans to Jerusalem, are only the best known. On the other hand, we can read Darius' inscription in Susa about the building of its citadel with foreign labor both ways, as a boast about ethnic harmony and as legitimizing ethnic exploitation. But, even on the more favorable reading, any royal concern for ethnic diversity and cultural autonomy was counterbalanced by the political and social distance kept by the Great King and his aristocracy from the subject peoples, a distance reinforced by the closed nature of the Old Persian language and script and of early Persian "Avestan" religion. Nor did the official picture of hierarchical ethnic harmony safeguard the empire from various ethnic revolts, most notably in Egypt and Ionia. (10)

In everyday practice, there is considerable ethnic fluidity and frequent transactions across the boundary, as Fredrik Barth argued. But this is counteracted by the weight of ideology and political action. Here, ethnic distinctions are built into the fabric of the hierarchical systems of empires, and foreigners are generally treated as different, unintelligible, and often inferior. It was a model that tended to reproduce itself in different periods and continents, and in due course it was to prove a fertile source for the creation of national kingdoms.

City-State and Ethnic Identity

Already in the third millennium BC on the alluvial plains of ancient Sumer, the city-state was well developed as a focus of exclusive loyalty. In the Early Dynastic period, city-states like Eridu, Ur, Uruk, Lagash, and Nippur, each under the protection of one or more of the deities of the Sumerian pantheon, and ruled by their local lord or *ensi*, a council of elders and their temple priests, vied for supremacy, only to fall prey in the end to the ambitions of Sargon of Agade who established the first Mesopotamian empire ca. 2350 BC. After the fall of the Akkadian empire, there was a brief efflorescence of Sumerian culture under the Third Dynasty of Ur at the end of the third millennium which saw an attempt to revive the "golden age" of the Early Dynastic period, before another period of tribal invasions by the Guti, Lullubi, Tidnumites, and Elamites, followed by renewed city-state rivalry and the ultimate rise of Babylon. Throughout this period, though there was a Sumerian cultic center at Nippur, and though the Sumerian city-states formed a network of cultural and economic activity, it is doubtful how far we may speak of any clearcut sense of Sumerian ethnicity, let alone ethnic unity. Perhaps the only commonalities were cultural: the Sumerian language and its rich literature, with its myths of common origins, and the Sumerian pantheon of gods and goddesses, which subsequent Mesopotamian city-states from Akkad to Babylon adopted and supplemented. (11)

Similar rivalries beset the "Canaanite" city-states of Syria, Lebanon, and Palestine in the Bronze and Iron Ages. Again, any commonalities are linguistic and cultural, notably a pantheon of shared deities, the cults of "high places," and massive fortified cities, along with the development of a Canaanite dialect and alphabetic script. Though we hear of a "land of Canaan," a name recognized by New Kingdom Egyptians, Syrians like Idrimi and the Bible, "whether it [sc. "Canaan"] was a territorial name or designated a people, in the first place, cannot now be determined." (12)

What is certain is that the city-state was the focus of allegiance and provided the arena of political and commercial activity, notably the city-states of Ugarit, Byblos, Tyre, Sidon, Hazor, Megiddo, and Gezer. No Canaanite cultic, let alone political, center emerged to overshadow or unite the often warring city-states, and the same is true of the Phoenician city-states – it was the Greeks who termed the coastal Canaanites *phoinikes* after the purple dye used there. Neither the "Phoenicians" themselves nor the Old Testament recognized a concept of "Phoenicia"; the Old Testament speaks of "the Sidonians," the "king of Tyre," and so on. (13)

However, it was in ancient Greece that the city-state achieved its most developed form. Even among their Mycenaean forebears, city-states like Tiryns, Argos, and Mycenae, ruling over the surrounding countryside, constituted the political norm. Of course, as elsewhere, kinship ties were crucial, both in everyday life and for political rule and especially for the orderly succession of kingship. So was the tracing of genealogies in the different Greek subgroups of Ionians, Dorians, Aeolians, and Boeotians. Such cultural and genealogical divisions continued to resonate in the classical age and were even used as late as the fifth century as pretexts for the policies of the "Ionian" Athenians and "Dorian" Spartans in the Peloponnesian War. (14)

In the archaic age (eighth to sixth centuries BC), after the overthrow of aristocratic rule, the Greek *polis* developed its distinctive ethos and institutions, especially under the tyrants who were often linked to the rise of the propertied hoplite "class." In this period, any sense of common "Greek" identity was constructed through myths of origins, genealogies, and rituals by groups claiming descent from *Hellen* of Thessaly, the place where Thucydides located the first Greeks. This process may have been hastened by the new, more exclusive rights of citizenship in the emerging city-states with their growing insistence on territory and residence, but also on descent, in determining citizenship. It was certainly reinforced by the Persian Wars of the early fifth century when the stereotypical contrast between the servile "barbarian" subjects of the Great King and the "free" Greek city-state became prevalent, a contrast that already appears in Aeschylus' *Persae* (472 BC). (15)

But it was Herodotus who, once again, through the mouths of the Athenian envoys to Sparta in 479 BC, defined and articulated a sense of common Greek ethnicity, based on

Plate 5 Group of young horsemen, North Frieze of Parthenon, Athens, ca. 442–438 BC (British Museum).

> the statues of the gods and the temples which have been burnt and destroyed . . . the common blood and tongue that we Greeks share, together with the common cult places, the sacrifices and similar customs . . . (16)

And yet, for all the stereotypes of pan-Hellenic propaganda, a Greek's first loyalty was to his or her city-state. After all, not a few of the cities went over to the Persians in 480 BC, and it was their intense commercial and political rivalries, above all, those between Athens, Corinth, and Sparta, that plunged the Greek world into the long, bitter, and divisive Peloponnesian War (431–404 BC). In the following century, neither the philosopher Isocrates' pan-Hellenism nor king Agesilaus of Sparta's expedition against the Persians could unite the Greek city-states, and it took Philip's victory at Chaeronea to enforce unity, at least temporarily. Despite their many shared cultural and religious beliefs and practices – in language and literature, art and architecture, festivals and Games, as well as the Olympian pantheon – attempts to unify the Hellenes politically foundered on the rocks of an exclusive city-state loyalty and patriotism. (17)

For many Greeks, the city-state comprised a world apart, and in the case of Athens, it may actually have been more than a *polis*. In extent, population size, and the large number of its *astoi* – residents with important social, though not political, rights – Athens constituted what Aristotle termed an *ethnos*. According to Edwin Cohen, in the fifth century the Athenian *ethnos* even acquired a myth of autochthonous origins in the lineage of king Erechtheus. Does this allow us to designate Athens and its surrounding countryside, Attica, an ancient "nation" – in size as large as Iceland? After all, its members had a clear sense of collective selfhood *vis-à-vis* other city-states, with a (lately constructed) myth of common origins, a strong territorial attachment, a public culture, and standardized laws and customs. And yet, how distinctive was this public culture and how unique the ensemble of its myths, memories, and symbols? After all, many of them were shared with other Greeks, notably with city-states in their own Ionian ethnic subgroup. Certainly, Pericles in his famous Funeral Oration, as transmitted by Thucydides, tried to instill in his fellow-citizens a sense of Athenian cultural primacy and political leadership of Greece, as well as the ideal of noble sacrifice of life itself on behalf of their city in the Peloponnesian War. But, the war in which these Athenians fell was an intra-Hellenic war, not one fought against the Persians, and the leadership to which Pericles' Athenians aspired was very much at the expense of their allies in the Delian League. Besides, Pericles did not say that his fellow-citizens should "fall in love" with Greece or the Hellenes, but with the city-state of Athens alone. (18)

But, whether or not we agree with the contention of Edwin Cohen and Aviel Roshwald that Athens might be seen as a nation and a national state, the ancient Greek *polis* left a vital cultural legacy for later ages and states. This was partly due to the way in which Alexander and his successors used it as a model for the hellenization of the Near East, and partly because the fierce loyalty to the *polis* was framed by wider shared cultural and religious Hellenic networks. As a result, the ideal of political solidarity and liberty of the *polis* became part of the wider literary and artistic heritage of ancient Greece, which was transmitted through Arab and Byzantine scholars to medieval and early modern Western Europe, offering a model of republican community based on an intense kind of citizen equality and patriotism. With the return to classical antiquity and the Greek revival, this model became an inspiration for those ideals of autonomy and unity that modern nationalists were to make into central tenets of the new secular religion of the people. As a result, the city-state, far from being diametrically opposed to or obstructive of ethnic and national community, actually came to serve as one of the nation's most widespread pillars and molds, providing it with some of its enduring features and its most significant historical forms.

Ethnic Identity and Tribal Confederation

Our third type of collective cultural and political identity, tribal confederation, might appear at first sight to have much more affinity with ethnic and national forms of community. For some, in fact, "tribe" and "ethnic group" are closely related, if not interchangeable, terms. But, if we adhere to a meaning that sees the tribe as not just a cultural group but as the political expression of segmented lineages, then we can see that tribes and tribal confederations could also undermine, and obstruct, a sense of wider ethnic identity, let alone the emergence of nations – as the frequent tribal feuds suggest.

An early example of such a confederation, the *Amurru*, or "Amorites," first appears in northern Syria in Akkadian and Sumerian documents of the late third millennium BC. Immigrant workers in the cities of Sumer and Akkad, they were known as Martu in Sumerian and by their wanderings were felt to be a threat to civilized life. These semi-nomads are described as

> the Martu who does not know houses, who does not know cities, the uncouth man who lives in the mountains, . . . the Martu, people of raiders, with animal instincts, like wolves. (19)

Subsequently, the Amurru penetrated the defensive wall built near Babylon to keep them out, and individual Amorites took power in the Sumerian cities, with Hammurabi of Babylon taking the title of "lugal Amurru," king of Amurru. But in this period, the "Amorite" tribes are recorded individually as Haneans, Suteans, Amnanu, Rabbu, and so on; and it is clear that, scattered in villages, and working as peasants and semi-nomadic shepherds, they failed to coalesce in a pan-Amorite confederation; and, apart from a fourteenth-century kingdom of Amurru in central Syria, their name became merely a memory or geographical term in the Assyrian annals.

We are on firmer ground with the later Aramean confederation. In the early first millennium BC, various Aramean kingdoms are documented, the most important being Aram-Zobah, Aram-Damascus, and Arpad in Syria, Aram-Naharaim, Bit-Adini, and Bit-Zamani in north Mesopotamia, and Bit-Dakuri and Bit-Amukkani in southern Babylonia near the Persian Gulf. If they constituted a threat to Assyria in the eleventh and tenth centuries, and to the kingdom of Israel in the ninth century, their great geographical spread and heterogeneous organization appear to have precluded a stable cultural, let alone political, unity. Even successive Assyrian onslaughts on the Aramean kingdoms in Syria from the ninth to seventh centuries failed to mobilize a pan-Aramean sentiment, though they did unite segments of the Arameans under the dominant city-state of the period – Damascus in the ninth and Arpad in the eighth century. (20)

This is not to say that the Arameans did not share common cultural practices. There was, after all, a common Aramaic language and script. There was also the growing importance of the cult of the Aramean storm-god, Hadad, at least in Syria. And then there were the repeated alliances of the Aramean kingdoms against Assyria. For these reasons, according to Steven Grosby, the Arameans of Syria may have constituted an incipient nationality; this is a not unreasonable inference from the wording on the Sefire stele of ca. 750 BC recording a treaty between two Aramean kings, Mati-el of Arpad and Bir-Ga'yah of KTK (an unknown kingdom), which speaks of "all-Aram," including perhaps "upper Aram" and "lower Aram." (21)

On the other hand, it has to be said that the common Aramaic language and script became so widely diffused as to constitute the *lingua franca* of the Near East in the first millennium, partly as a result of the large-scale deportations of Arameans by the Assyrian kings, and it was often used by Assyrian rulers to address their subjects. Hence, rather than help to define an Aramean *ethnie*, some have argued that the forcible mingling of peoples and their assimilation to a common language was instead one of the key facets of the rise of an *Assyrian* national state. Be that as it may, neither a common Aramaic language nor the precedence of the cult of Hadad could forge a wider unity and overrule the pre-eminence of local Aramean city gods – or prevent frequent border disputes between the several Aramean kingdoms. (22)

There is perhaps stronger evidence for regarding the semi-nomadic Edomite tribes as a cultural, if not a political, unity. In the biblical account, as Grosby points out, the Edomites appear as a unified kingdom blocking the path of the wandering Israelites after the Exodus. The book of Numbers refers to a people called *'edomi* (Edomites) and a territory, *kol 'edom* (all Edom) with borders around Mount Seir (Numbers 20:16, 23). We also know that in the ninth century BC, they engaged in political alliances and conflicts with Hamath, Tyre, and Sidon, as well as with Israel and Judah. Again, there seems to have been a supreme god, Qaush, of perhaps a pantheon that included a goddess called Edom, but just how important worship of Qaush was to the identity of an Edomite is unknown. For the biblical authors, Edom and Edomites were close to Judah, in terms of both territory and tribal genealogies, and there are hints that the worship of Yahweh originated in Edomite lands – though they were much later forcibly converted to Judaism by the Hasmoneans. But how far they constituted a separate ethnic community (*ethnie*) with a shared myth of origins and common memories and culture is unclear. (23)

The Case of "Ancient Israel"

It is only when we turn to the Israelite tribal confederation that we have sufficient evidence to enable us to make a judgment about the degree to which we can legitimately speak of an ethnic, or a national, community and identity. Sufficient perhaps, but not decisive, as the many conflicting opinions about all aspects of "ancient Israel" testify. On the other hand, the long-term significance of the ancient Israelite and Judahite experiences for the subsequent formation of nations is difficult to overestimate.

The name "Israel" is first found on the stele of the Pharaoh Merneptah (ca. 1210 BC), which lists the places and ethnic groups in Canaan that he claims to have conquered or destroyed. But it is not clear whether Israel is on this occasion a territorial or ethnic designation, or both. "Israel" appears next on the stele of king Mesha of Moab (ca. 830 BC) and in the Assyrian annals as that of the biblical northern kingdom, alongside the southern kingdom of Judah. In the biblical books of Joshua and Judges, we read of a series of conflicts between Israelite tribes and various Canaanite "tribes" and city-states, and with the Philistines, Edomites, Ammonites, and Moabites. This would suggest a measure of political unity, perhaps even a league of the kind once proposed by Martin Noth. But the Book of Judges also emphasizes the divisions between the various Israelite tribes, those in the south, those in the east across the Jordan, in the central hill country, and the rather separate northern tribes – with the central cult of Yahweh at Shiloh appearing to exert little political influence. (24)

The question of the origins of Israel and of its unique faith in Yahweh – a question that continues to divide scholars – is bound up with the origins and nature of the Covenant that marks out the Israelite tribes from others, and which was to have such a profound influence on the subsequent formation of nations. Even if "Israel" originally designated an ethnically mixed group of Aramean nomads from the east and Canaanite peasants fleeing to the hill country in the wake of the breakdown of Egyptian rule after 1300 BC, the centrality of the hill tribe of Ephraim, to which Joshua, the servant of Moses, belonged, and the gradual assimilation of the cult of the Canaanite high god, *El*, by that of Yahweh, marks the beginning of a long process of growing ideological if not always political unification. Moreover, while some scholars like Gosta Ahlström treat the Exodus and Moses narratives as secondary, others like Irving Zeitlin find a broad accord between the biblical account in the Pentateuch and Near Eastern custom and usage in this period. Despite these disagreements, the fact remains that by the time of Saul (ca. 1000 BC), the Israelite hill tribes, together with Benjamin and Judah, had realized a fair degree of political unity, which has led at least one scholar to claim that a number of Israelite tribes did already acknowledge a fairly close relationship, and even a "fairly close union of a national type based on religion" – though without clearly defining the meaning of the term "national" in this, or any, period. (25)

The scholarly debates over the United Monarchy are equally divisive, with some scholars dismissing it as post-Exilic propaganda, while others, on the basis of the biblical account and some disputed archaeological evidence, are prepared to accept a scaled-down version of the narrative in the first Book of Kings. Again, it is the subsequent myth of a glorious kingdom, of the valiant David and the wise Solomon, reputed authors of many of the psalms and proverbs, that is significant. The United Monarchy came to represent a "golden age" that was rendered so much more poignant by the bitter subsequent division into the kingdoms of Israel and Judah. Yet, from the start, kingship in Israel was viewed ambivalently – as sacred, even messianic, but also as deeply suspect and corrupting, as the prophets make abundantly clear – an ambivalence that would re-echo and haunt Western civilization. (26)

Despite the subsequent divisions, by choosing Jerusalem as the capital and building the Temple there, David and the United Monarchy did provide a basis for the rise of territorial attachments and a distinctive public culture centered on the worship of Yahweh. While the northern kingdom of Israel saw a continuous struggle between the dominant Baal cult of Phoenicia and worship of Yahweh, as recorded in the cycle of Elijah stories, the smaller southern kingdom of Judah, though also troubled by foreign cults, was able to pursue a more consistent policy of religious unification based on the Temple worship and the ideal of the Covenant. Even there, only after the destruction of the northern kingdom by Assyria in 722 BC and the flight from the north of many refugees with their religious traditions to Judah, could a thoroughgoing process of religious reforms be inaugurated. From the reign of Hezekiah in the late eighth century to that of the late seventh-century king Josiah, the kingdom and people of Judah appear to have become a more self-consciously monolatrous society and ethnic community, with a clearer sense of origins and shared historical memories. This development was aided by four factors: the influence of favorably minded kings like Hezekiah, the impact of prophetic activity from Isaiah and Micah to Jeremiah and Ezekiel, the discovery of the Deuteronomic lawcode in the Temple in 621 BC, and the probable editing of Deuteronomy and the historical books. Above all, it was the result of the rise of a textual culture disseminated from the court and Temple in the capital, following the rapid urbanization of Jerusalem in the wake of the Assyrian destruction of Samaria in 722 BC and Sennacherib's invasion of Judah in 701 BC. The desire of the royal court to project its power and legitimacy by founding a library, as in Egypt and Assyria, and the associated increase in literacy, helped to record and shape the memories, myths, and traditions of both the refugee northern and the southern tribes into a coherent ethnohistory centered on the Davidic golden age. (27)

For many scholars, the reforms of king Josiah (639–605 BC) are regarded as crucial for the shaping of the Bible and the rise of a Judahite ethnic consciousness. Though archaeologists are divided about the "fit" between many of the geographical and ethnic observations in the Pentateuch and the expansion of Josiah's kingdom in the wake of Assyria's retreat after 628 BC, there is little dispute about the significance of Josiah's religious campaign against the foreign cults and high places (*asherot* and *bamot*), the discovery of the Deuteronomic lawcode in the Temple, and the public reading of it which king Josiah organized in front of

> the priests and the prophets and all the people, both small and great: and he read in their ears all the words of the book of the covenant which was found in the house of the Lord. (II Kings 23:2)

For Steven Grosby, these events attest the growth of a sense of national community and identity. There is the involvement of the populace, the dissemination of a public culture, observance of common laws and customs, and growing attachment to a common territory "from Dan to Beer-sheba," which Josiah sought to reclaim. (28)

Even if we concede Grosby's claim that an idea of nationality can be discerned in this period, we need to exercise caution. To begin with, it was probably an elite affair, and one that was confined to Jerusalem and its immediate environs. The persistence of idolatrous cults in the countryside reveals the limits of any sense of national community based on shared religious observance. Second, its manifestation was all too brief. After Josiah's death in battle in 609 BC and the deportation of Judean elites to Babylon by Nebuchadrezzar in 597 BC, and finally with the fall of Jerusalem in 586 BC, the remaining rural population almost certainly continued with their former idolatrous cults. Once again, the survival of a sense of Judean ethnic identity and religious monotheism was confined to the elites who collected and edited the pre-Exilic writings in Babylon and some of whom returned to rebuild the Temple in Jerusalem several years after Cyrus' edict of toleration in 538 BC. However, the small and desolate Persian province of Yahud around Jerusalem was only revived through the intervention of Nehemiah as the king's emissary and the reforms of Ezra the scribe, especially his ban on intermarriage with the surrounding populations. But it was Ezra's public reading of the Torah and his elevation of the Mosaic law that helped to define, as Peter Ackroyd put it, membership of the community:

> There are marriage limitations imposed; there is an emphasis on purity, the defining of the community in terms of its acceptability to the deity – foreign marriages and hence alien religion represent a threat to community life. (29)

While this evidence points to a revived ethnic community defined in religious and ritual terms, and one that continued to collect and collate myths of origin and sacred ethnohistories and enact rituals in the sacred Hebrew language, can we speak of a (renewed) national community, however small and precarious? Unfortunately, there is scant evidence for the Persian and early Hellenistic periods, except in terms of inferences from later Pharisaism to the earlier Men of the Great Synagogue. Only with the split between Hellenizers and *Hasidim* in Jerusalem under the Seleucids in the early second century BC, and the subsequent revolt of the Maccabees in 167 BC against Antiochus IV Epiphanes' misguided attempts at religious and cultural conformity by installing the worship of Zeus in the Temple, can we begin to discern the lineaments of a national community, albeit one that was divided and subject to conflicting pressures. Centered on monotheism, Torah, and Temple, and beginning to define Jewishness in both religious and ritual terms, the Jews were increasingly recognized as a separate nation with a distinctive public culture, law, language, and territory, even though they shared much of their material culture with the Hellenistic world around them. (30)

Nations in Antiquity?

From this all too brief survey of selected cases of collective cultural and/or political identities and communities in the ancient world, we can now ask to what extent a sense of common ethnicity was prevalent, and whether it makes sense to speak of "nations" in antiquity. Here I can only suggest some provisional conclusions.

It appears, first, that the most common and widespread forms of collective cultural and political identities, above the level of the clan and village, were the city-state and the tribal confederation. Even imperial identities originated in one of these two kinds of community – city-states in Mesopotamia and tribal groupings in the case of the Medes and Persians – and continued to be based on them. To this generalization, Egypt stands as a partial exception, though cities like Memphis and later Thebes afforded bases for successive dynasties.

Second, unless one adopts a definition of the concept of "tribe" that equates it to that of an ethnic community or *ethnie*, ethnic ties rarely formed the basis for a complete and exclusive society in the ancient world. Instead, we find them generally intertwined with each of these types of cultural and/or political identity and community. Besides, quite often, ethnicity seems to have been ascribed by others, and was not necessarily self-ascribed, as in the case of the "Phoenician" city-states, discussed above.

Third, where ethnic ties are visible, we can distinguish three levels of community. In the first, which I termed an *ethnic category* in chapter 2, we find a loose aggregation of groups with some similar cultural practices from a particular area, a named territorial and cultural category recorded by outsiders, like the Guti and Lullubi who helped to overthrow the Sumerian dynasty of Ur around 2000 BC. In the second, which was designated an *ethnic network*, these groups, usually tribes or city-states, form a field of cultural activity exhibiting a degree of cultural commonality, but rarely any political unity; here I cited the Aramean tribal confederations and the Sumerian city-states. It is not always easy to distinguish ethnic networks from ethnic categories, but, unlike the latter, elite members of ethnic networks tend to possess myths of common origins and shared memories, if little solidarity.

What, I think, distinguishes the *ethnie* is its elaboration of shared memories into a composite "ethnohistory" of the kind that we encounter in ancient Greece, in the writings of Herodotus and Thucydides, and in ancient Israel. In the ancient Greek case, despite the centrifugal forces of city-state loyalty, the Greek-speaking and Olympian-worshipping communities were conscious of their relatedness and myths of common ancestry (despite the many variations) and proud of their difference from, if not superiority to, non-Greek *barbaroi*, something that clearly marked off their colonies from the neighboring Mediterranean peoples. It was for this reason that Moses Finley, following Meinecke, termed the ancient Greeks a *Kulturnation* – in my terms an *ethnie* with shared ancestry myths, common historical memories, a common culture, and a degree of solidarity – because of their lack of political and territorial unity. Similar considerations apply to the Israelites. For a time, tribal disunity was overcome in the face of the Philistine invasions, but after David had removed the threat, north–south differences resurfaced and the kingdom was divided. However, this did not destroy the close cultural links between them. The histories of the kingdom of Israel were recorded along with those of Judah, and both were included in the Books of Kings. (31)

But, finally, can we speak of "nations" in the ancient world? Can we discern at least some of the processes that encourage the formation of communities approximating to the ideal type of the nation? If we accept the definition I proposed in chapter 1, a named and self-defined human community whose members cultivate common myths, memories, symbols, values, and traditions, reside in a historic homeland, disseminate a distinctive public culture, and observe common laws and customs, then I believe we can show that some of these basic processes were operative, and that in a very few cases they encouraged the formation of nations, at least for some periods of their existence. To this end, four cases can be considered from the ancient world, three empires and a kingdom: the Neo-Assyrian empire, the Persian empire, ancient Egypt, and the kingdom of Judah, and later of Judea.

It may seem strange to suggest, given their logical opposition, that an empire might also constitute or be an extension of a nation, or vice versa. But we are quite happy to allow, for example, the nineteenth-century French nation "its" empire, or more precisely to say that a French state that acquired an empire had become, or was becoming, a national community. Might not the same be true in the ancient world? (32)

The Neo-Assyrian empire

To describe the Neo-Assyrian empire as a nation could mean either that the Assyrians constituted a nation in their own right, while ruling over a number of other communities, or that the whole Assyrian empire, in its later stages, had become or was in the process of becoming a single nation.

Earlier, I underlined the hierarchical and exploitative nature of Assyrian rule. But what of the Assyrians themselves? They were a named and self-defining community, with an aristocratic myth of origins from the city of Assur and its eponymous god, shared memories of their kings' exploits recorded in the royal annals, a common language, and, among the nobles, a status pride and sense of superiority to their own commoners on their estates and to the subject peoples. Given this elite solidarity, we may legitimately speak of an Assyrian ethnic community.

On the other hand, evidence of special feelings towards an Assyrian homeland or sense of sacred territory outside the "land of Assur" itself is scarce; nor was there a single capital. Second, beyond some cults of the Assyrian deities, and palace art and royal propaganda, there appears to have been little effort to disseminate an Assyrian public culture across the empire. Captives or visitors to Nimrud or Nineveh might be overawed, but we hear little of a distinctive Assyrian public culture being purveyed to Assyrian commoners, let alone to the foreign subject peoples. Moreover, as mentioned earlier, Neo-Assyrian culture was greatly indebted to the religious cuneiform texts and Akkadian literary culture of Babylon, which was regarded as canonical and a golden age to be revived. As for standardizing common laws and customs, apart from regular tribute, military conscription, and some royal edicts, the mass of the subjects who remained in their lands were implicitly allowed to retain their local customs and laws. (33)

Alternatively, could we describe the territory annexed and the society created by the Neo-Assyrian empire as a nation-state, at least in its later stages? This is the thesis recently propounded by Simo Parpola. With the American model in mind, Parpola argues that the two processes of regular deportations and cultural assimilation helped to forge a new, more compact and homogeneous society. By forcibly mingling the peoples of the ancient Near East, granting many of them citizenship rights, and assimilating them through a common language, Aramaic, and a common script, the Aramaic alphabet, the Assyrians were for the first time in history consciously forging a nation-state. It is an attractive thesis. There is no doubt that these trends did help to promote a new, more cosmopolitan society by breaking down the isolation of peoples in the ancient Near East. On the other hand, the American parallel is misleading. The United States was, and is, an immigrant society, which the individual members of its various ethnic groups chose to enter and in which they voluntarily adopted the American way of life while retaining many of their own customs, beliefs, and habits. Besides, from the first the United States was a popular republic, based on the civic national ideology of its founding fathers. No such national ideology can be found in Assyria, immigration was highly coercive, and the relationship of the Assyrian rulers to the subject peoples was, as we saw, generally exploitative. Essentially, the Neo-Assyrian empire remained a case of ethnic hierarchy based on military force and economic domination. The almost universal jubilation that greeted Assyria's downfall, and the near total disappearance of the Assyrian *ethnie* along with its state, confirms the failure of the Assyrian "national" project, if such it was. (34)

Achaemenid Persia

Many of the same considerations apply to Achaemenid Persia. We can concur in describing a Persian *ethnie*: a named and self-defining human community, with a myth of common ancestry attached to the ruling house in which the nobles shared (tracing the lineage of the leading clan of Achaemenes, of the Pasargadae tribe), shared memories of the king's exploits and battles won (as Darius boasts on his epitaph at Persepolis), a common Old Persian language, and a common belief in the blessing of Ahura-Mazda on the Persian kings and nobles, in a timeless and harmonious cosmic order.

But, once again, this describes an ethnic hierarchy at odds with the idea of a national community. Thus, though it was praised for its rich agriculture, the land of Persis in southwest Iran, the seat of Achaemenian power, held no special or sacred status, nor was there a single capital in the two centuries of the empire. Its public culture, too, was largely reserved for the Persian nobles and important foreign emissaries, and again there was a linguistic division, with Aramaic, the *lingua franca*, used for public communications with the subject peoples. Though Persian rule was certainly less brutal, the role of the subject peoples was well portrayed, as we saw, in the processions of ethnic groups bearing gifts to the Great King on the Apadana staircase at Persepolis, or in the royal inscription at Susa, which lauded the labor and resources of the subject peoples. Both convey the sense of majesty and distance between rulers and ruled in a far-flung empire. The only difference from earlier empires was the more explicit toleration of local laws and customs, stemming from Cyrus' policy, and hence a less overt desire to integrate the subject peoples in a single multiethnic community. The later attempts by Parthian and Sasanian dynasties to hark back to the model of Achaemenid Persia provides an interesting contrast with the fate of Assyria. (35)

Ancient Egypt

The case of ancient Egypt is more complex. Isolated by its geography and united by the Nile, an Egyptian community and identity evolved for nearly a millennium under the unitary state of the Old Kingdom. This aided the development of myths of origin, in their various creation myths, but the relative lack of contact with others before the

Middle Kingdom may have delayed a clear sense of self-definition. But, as we saw in the case of relations with Nubia, by the early second millennium the aristocracy had developed a clear conviction of Egyptian superiority to foreigners, along with many myths, memories, and symbols, and a nostalgia for the golden age of the glorious Fourth Dynasty in which Amenemhet I chose to set his propagandist tract known as *The Prophecy of Nerferti* to justify his usurpation of the throne in 1991 BC. Perhaps more telling is the Egyptian attachment to the Black Land nourished by the Nile. In the well-known fictional *Tale of Sinuhe* in the same period, a high official of the court who had fled to Syria to avoid being wrongfully accused of being involved in the conspiracy to murder Amenemhet recounts his flight, his long sojourn in exile, and his desire to be buried in Egypt in the land of his fathers according to Egyptian burial rites, which were later accorded him. At one point, Sinuhe laments:

> I am even so a foreigner whom none loveth, any more than a Bedouin would be loved in the Delta . . . What is a greater matter than that my corpse should be buried in the land wherein I was born?

From a later period, one might also cite the desire of Kamose, Pharaoh in Thebes, to "save Egypt which the Asiatics have smitten," and the clear sense of Egyptian rulers of Egypt's historic boundaries, from the Delta to Elephantine in the south; though how far the land was held to be not just blessed but sacred is unclear. (36)

That ancient Egyptian elites created a distinctive and enduring public culture of rituals, ceremonies, and symbols, supported by a language and hieroglyphic script, and a system of education, is undeniable. It was perhaps the most impressive and all-embracing of public cultures. At its center was an ideology of divine kingship, which claimed that the Pharaoh was the incarnation of the falcon-god Horus and son of the sun-god Ra and that it was his duty, through the performance of public rituals and wise government, to ensure that *Ma'at* (justice or truth) prevailed in the world of men. According to Barry Kemp, this ideology was

> continually reinforced in provincial association by ritual and by the iconography of ritual which, for example, made the king responsible for the ceremonies of the provincial temples.

Though the children of nobles and scribes had a separate education, men from lower classes could be admitted into the culture that supported this ideology. And though we cannot gauge how far it was disseminated outside the elites, it is worth recalling that this was the only type of public culture to which Egyptians were exposed for two and a half millennia (with the exception of the short interlude of Akhnaten's "heresy"). (37)

Ancient Egypt is often depicted as a highly regulated society. This may have been the result of a long tradition of centralized authority developing early on, when Egypt was largely free of external threats and could therefore forge a more integrated community in which standardized law and bureaucratic regulation played a large part, because of the need to harness the effects of the annual flooding of the Nile. To some extent, this model was carried into Palestine and Syria, when Egypt acquired an empire under the New Kingdom; at the same time, the subject peoples there appear to have been able to retain some of their local customs and laws. Perhaps because for so long Egypt was a self-contained society, without an empire, it came to approximate more closely the national type of collective identity and community, even if that identity was most clearly carried by its elites. Here the basic processes of self-definition, cultivation of myths, memories, symbols, and values, territorialization of attachments, dissemination of a distinctive public culture, and development of standardized laws and custom were most evident. On the other hand, some key cultural resources were lacking. The Egyptians failed to develop a myth of ethnic election – as opposed to divine favor for the Pharaoh and his dynasty; and though the elites of later periods harked back to earlier "golden ages," they failed to develop a purposive ethnohistory, or a sense of Egyptian collective destiny demanding struggle and sacrifice on the part of its members.

Judah and Judea

Just these cultural resources were slowly developed in certain periods of the ancient history of Israel – or to be more precise, of the kingdom of Judah and the later commonwealth of Judea.

Earlier, I sought to show the growth of an ethnic community in the kingdom of Judah by the late eighth or seventh century BC. Here was a named and self-defined human community with shared ancestry myths, elaborated historical memories, and a common Hebrew literary culture based on the centrality of the worship of Yahweh, the Torah of Moses, and the Temple. Under strong reforming kings like Hezekiah and Josiah, and powerful prophetic calls to purification, this heritage encouraged among the political and religious elites a strong ethnic consciousness, bound up with the ideal of the divine Covenant, at a time when Assyria was menacing Judah's independence.

But can we go further and see in ancient Judah an early instance of the national type of community, perhaps indeed the prototype of the nation, as claimed by Adrian Hastings? It is difficult to ascertain the degree of attachment to the territory of Judah. Certainly, it remained the Promised Land, and some scholars argue that it was only in this period that the land became sanctified through its occupation by a chosen people. We have a celebrated record of just such a fervent attachment, composed later, in exile "by the waters of Babylon." And in the psalms and oracles of the prophets, we can see something of the joy and love of the land and its features – the mountains of Carmel, the beauty of the Sharon valley, the hills of Judea, and especially the sacred city of Jerusalem itself, the one and only capital of Judah – of the bounded territory, whose borders were set down in the Torah. (38)

Many scholars would also concur in the increasingly distinctive nature of Judah's public culture. Yet, given the persistence of idol worship in the Judean countryside, even in Josiah's days, it is likely that a strong national consciousness, if such it was, was confined to Jerusalem and other towns nearby. There, as we saw, the assembled people participated in renewing the covenant of the Book of Law found in the Temple in 621 BC and in the accompanying religious reforms of Josiah. Certainly, the king tried to extend the reach of his reforms by tearing down the high places and idols in the countryside. In this case, the distinctive public culture was both the Word of God and a code of Law, applicable to one and all. The problem was to secure its widespread observance; and here Josiah's early death in battle cut short his programme of reform. Only in the Babylonian exile could the programme be partly resumed, by further editing of the laws and histories of the Pentateuch and Deuteronomic books; and only in the post-Exilic community of Jerusalem and its Temple could Ezra and Nehemiah begin to lay the basis for a renewed and purified national community. (39)

All of which goes to support Steven Grosby's characterization of late seventh-century Judah as a "nationality" – I would say "nation" – but one that was quickly wiped out. Nevertheless, the model had caught on. Even without their own kings and under foreign rule, the Jews of Jerusalem began to build an autonomous ethnoreligious community under its own religious authorities centered on the Temple and its public culture, and harking back to a golden age of the Mosaic Covenant. The moment that circumstances opened the way for a degree of independent political activity, a new note of struggle and sacrifice for the Torah and community was introduced in the successful Maccabean revolt of 167 BC, and leaders like Simon sought to combine their military position with the religious status of high priest, through the ratification of the assembled people. In the succeeding century, we see a renewed emphasis upon the extent of the land of Israel, the efflorescence of Temple culture, supplemented by the growth of synagogues, and a wider observance of the Torah. Despite the secession of the Essenes and the conflict between Sadducees and Pharisees, the Roman occupation only strengthened the processes that encouraged the formation of a national community among the Jews in this period, with the Pharisees and the Zealot party expressing the heightened national sentiment prevalent among large numbers of the Jewish residents of Roman Palestine. (40)

Conclusion

Though any conclusion about the presence of nations in the ancient Near East can only be very tentative, it appears that, while ethnic ties and networks were widespread, only in ancient Egypt and Judah might there be enough evidence to allow us to speak of nations in antiquity. Only in these cases had the necessary social and symbolic processes become sufficiently developed to create the right conditions for these communities to approximate to the ideal type of the nation, and only at certain periods in their histories. In the Neo-Assyrian and Persian cases, on the other hand, only some of the relevant processes were operative, sufficient to encourage the emergence of self-defining *ethnies*, but not to create the conditions for nations. Moreover, when it came to the cultural resources of election myths, golden ages, and destiny through sacrifice, resources which help to maintain a sense of national identity, these were only really well developed in the example of Judea; and this may help to account for its continuing relevance and influence over the *longue durée*.

Two further conclusions may be drawn. The first is the vital importance of politics and polities. Each of the cases considered emerged within the matrix of a political system – bureaucratic empire or patrimonial kingdom – and it was political ideology and political action that were crucial to the formation of *ethnies* and, more particularly, nations. In ancient Greece, on the other hand, the weakness of an overarching Hellenic ideology and lack of a single political framework in the face of the exclusive patriotism and solidarity of the *polis* militated against the formation of an ancient Greek nation – and *a fortiori* of a Phoenician or Sumerian nation. Hence, the centrality of political ideology and institutions in the formation of nations must be underlined.

But, by the same token, so must religious ideals and cults. While, of course, the Persians and Assyrians possessed their own cults and ideals, they either failed to unite the subject peoples round them or openly tolerated the presence of local gods and cults. Either way, religion could not act as the cement of social solidarity. In Egypt and Judea, on the other hand, religious conceptions, ethics, and rituals provided the binding elements of national consciousness and social cohesion. It is true that, in Egypt, the common people were in later periods of foreign rule distanced from the temple religion and language of the priesthoods and nobles, with the result that in the Roman period rival religions like Christianity could make massive inroads at the expense of traditional Egyptian religion, which depended on the power of the divine Pharaoh. In Judea, on the other hand, the original religion of God, Torah and Temple, married to the ideal of the Covenant with its myths of ethnic election and the Promised Land, could be continually renewed through varied reinterpretations and increasing inclusion of the populace, especially after the Maccabean revolt and the rise of the Pharisees. It was this self-renewing religion that, in the shape of all three monotheisms, was to exert so powerful an influence on the later development of nations.

4

Hierarchical Nations

If the ancient Near East yielded little in the way of nations, it was nevertheless rich in cultural legacies to succeeding communities and epochs. Nor does the lack of processes and resources conducive to the formation of nations allow us to dismiss the social and cultural experience of the ancient Near East and Greek antiquity as of little interest and no consequence. Far from it. This experience was vital both in the example and model of ethnic community that was developed in that epoch, and for the formative cultural legacies it bequeathed. As we saw, ethnicity was widespread and had a twofold role. On the one hand, it was interwoven with other kinds of collective identity and community; on the other hand, it became an important, even primary, type of identity and community in its own right, often developing out of "tribal" confederations. I have discussed the ethnic bases of nations elsewhere. So here I want to focus on the second aspect of the experience of antiquity: its "legacies" of communal culture which have been so influential for the formation and shaping of nations in subsequent epochs.

Three Types of Public Culture

We can start by distinguishing three main kinds of communal public culture: hierarchical, covenantal, and civic-republican.

Hierarchy, in the generic sense of a form of sacred order, can characterize most kinds of community and state, but in its more specific meaning it denotes a sanctified order insofar as it is believed to mirror and embody the celestial order on earth. There are two subvarieties of this kind of sacred order. In the first, the ruler is himself a god, and he is assisted by orders of priests and nobles who share some of his sanctity. The prototype here is ancient Egypt: the Pharaoh was regarded as a god and embodied *Ma'at*, the Truth, and over long time spans the priesthoods, notably that of Amun-Ra, exercised immense influence over Egyptian society. In the second and more common subtype, the king is god's representative on earth, receiving his authority to rule from a god, and issuing commands in his name, though he might subsequently be accorded divine honors. This form of hierarchy was characteristic of the successive empires of Mesopotamian society from Sargon of Akkad to the Achaemenid Persians, and is symbolized by the celebrated stele of Hammurabi where the Babylonian monarch is shown receiving his code of laws from the sun-god, Shamash. (1)

It would be a mistake to imagine that a society governed by the principle of hierarchy was static. Even in the Egyptian case, there was an oscillation between epochs of strong, centralized administration and "intermediate" periods of weak, central rule, often with rival dynasties and fragmented authority vested in the governors of the nomes. Moreover, epochs of strong, dynastic rule could generate expansion; the concept of hierarchy was infused with a vigorous sense of Egyptian ethnicity, particularly among the elite, which took the form of economic expansion and even conquests, in Nubia and Palestine. The same was true, as we saw, in Mesopotamia, where the Assyrians, in particular, combining hierarchy with a strong sense of common ethnic identity, were able to expand their territories, while their elites greatly increased their economic resources and cultural development, mainly through cultural borrowing and adaptation. In both cases, we can discern a growing belief in an elite ethnic and political sense of superiority, at least as justification for conquest and exploitation of foreigners, though in the long run it was insufficient to secure the survival of this form of ethnic state and civilization. Nevertheless, the hierarchical principle was to prove an important form of ethnic public culture in later epochs, and a vital influence on the shaping of nations. (2)

Covenantal public cultures introduce a more egalitarian conception of the social order, and a more intimate form of sacred communion between the members of a society. In this conception, predominantly associated with the monotheistic traditions, the deity chooses a community to carry out His will by separating it from others and requiring that its members perform certain rites and duties in return for His favor and blessing. While the tasks varied, they generally involved the regulation of the members' lives through a moral and ritual code of law which sanctified the community and the world. Here, too, there is more than one form of covenantal public culture. In those cases where it is combined with a hierarchical structure, the recipient of the covenant is a church or brotherhood acting on behalf of the whole community. This was the case in fourth- and fifth-century Armenia, whose Holy Apostolic Church effected the Covenant between Christ and His people, a relationship greatly enhanced by the close kinship between the missionary founder, St. Gregory, and the ruling Arsacid house, and by his successors' attempts to retain unity among Armenia's great landed magnates. The Armenian version of the Covenant was greatly indebted to Old Testament and Maccabean models of ethnic election and popular martyrdom for faith and country, as recorded by early Armenian historians like Elishe and Paustos Buzand. (3)

But the covenant may also be effected directly with the kin community as a whole. This was the case with the Covenant made between God and "the people," the Israelites, at Mount Sinai. Moses may have acted as the intermediary, but the whole people are said to have witnessed the presence of the Lord and to have agreed to His will and Torah:

> And he [Moses] took the book of the covenant, and read in the audience of the people; and they said, All that the Lord hath said will we do, and be obedient. (Exodus 24:7)

The purpose of this covenant was to create out of the Israelites "a kingdom of priests and an holy nation" (Exodus 19:6), and for this reason the Covenant was made with the whole community and its Law pertained to every member. Even here, a hierarchical element made an early appearance, for, after the people betrayed their God by worshipping the golden calf, Moses appointed Aaron and his descendants as high priests, and instituted the Levites to guard the sanctuary and the ritual code, thereby paving the way for the Temple priesthood. (4)

Medieval Ethiopia affords a particularly revealing example of the ways in which a covenantal principle can be fused with a hierarchical public culture. The successive Ethiopian kingdoms and dynasties were typical of the hierarchical form of public culture in a Christian Monophysite kingdom with a dominant ethnic Tigrean culture. But the inauguration of a new Semitized "Solomonic" dynasty in 1270 marked

Plate 6 Moses receiving the Law and teaching it to the Israelites, Tours Bible, 834 AD (British Library).

something of a break with this tradition. For while it retained and intensified the hierarchical principle, it looked for its legitimation to the much earlier Christian kingdom of Aksum, and for its *mythomoteur* to the legend of the Solomonic succession. According to this dynastic myth, first recorded in the fourteenth-century national epic the *Kebra-Negast* (Book of Kings), the first king of Ethiopia, Menelik, was the son of the Queen of Sheba and Solomon. Whereas in the biblical text (I Kings 10:1–14) the Queen of Sheba visits Solomon to question him and, on being convinced of his wisdom and prosperity, marvels and returns to her country, in the *Kebra-Negast* she conceives a son, Menelik, by him, who many years later returns to Jerusalem as an adult and carries off the original Ark of the Covenant; and with its departure for Ethiopia, the Lord's blessing on Israel is also transferred to the new chosen people and land of Ethiopia. This myth was used by the powerful kings of the new dynasty both to expand Ethiopia's borders and to underpin a series of major cultural and social reforms, and thereby effect a thorough cleansing of Ethiopian society in line with the covenantal Judaic elements of Monophysite Christianity. (5)

The third main form of public culture, the *civic-republican*, is most closely associated with the ancient Greek *polis* and its Roman successor. At first glance, it stands in stark contrast to both the hierarchical and covenantal types, for the idea of a self-governing commune, however restricted the franchise, and an autonomous regime, answerable to no outside power, marked a new stage in the development of collective political community. Yet, in many ways, this was an ambivalent type. On the one hand, the citizens of the commune were bound by a secular compact, not a covenant with God, and their ideal was liberty under a secular law, not the self-discipline of a quest for holiness, much less obedience to a sacred dynastic order. From this compact flowed civic duties and public responsibilities, based on laws allegedly handed down by ancient founders and lawgivers like Lycurgus, Solon, and Numa Pompilius. In the classical democracies, especially, aristocratic hierarchies were supplanted by principles of civic freedom and legal equality, with residence and ethnic ancestry replacing noble birth as the criteria for citizenship and office. On the other hand, the republican type was also a form of sacred community based on a civic religion. Each city-state had its own tutelary deities and myths of sacred origin, and most of them boasted their own peculiar rites and ceremonies, such as the Panathenaic festival in ancient Athens or the Isthmian Games at Corinth. The temples, statues, and cults of the city gods were, as we saw, central to ancient Greek and Roman self-definition, as well as to the Greco-Roman civilization in which they were enveloped; and their communal oaths were framed in religious terms, and witnessed by the city's gods. (6)

Rome and Judea

Although it marked a radical break from the dominant hierarchical form of public culture, the civic-republican model was rarely free of hierarchical elements. This is most strikingly confirmed by the history of Rome. Starting out as a small city of the Latin League, ruled by a succession of kings, Rome soon fell within the Etruscan orbit and adopted many elements of Etruscan culture. But, in 510 BC, its last king was expelled and the city was henceforth ruled by a patrician senate and consuls, in uneasy rivalry with the tribunes of the *plebs*. For later historians like Sallust, Livy, and Tacitus, this was an almost legendary period of "republican heroes" such as Brutus the consul, Cincinnatus, Mucius Scaevola, and Curius Dentatus, whose virtues of courage, honesty, frugality, and simplicity so starkly contrasted with the luxury and corruption of the late republic and early empire. Over the next two centuries, Rome achieved military pre-eminence in central and south Italy, a position confirmed by its successful resistance in the early third century to the invasion of Pyrrhus of Epirus and its subsequent defeat of the Carthaginians in the first Punic War (265–241 BC). At the same time it encountered the more sophisticated culture of Magna Graecia in the south, an encounter that helped to shape its sense of collective identity and its Trojan ancestry myth. This was followed by the epic wars against Hannibal, Rome's triumph over Carthage in 202, and its eastward expansion in the following century to become the dominant power in the Mediterranean, before it fell prey to the ambitions of rival generals and their armies. (7)

Throughout these centuries, the city was periodically riven by conflicts between patricians and plebeians, and tensions between the rival principles of hierarchy based on birth and landed wealth, and of popular participation and civic liberty under common laws – tensions which gave rise to serious popular uprisings under their tribunes, the Gracchi brothers. Later ages nevertheless looked back with nostalgia to its civic and republican ethos, and downplayed the factional and class conflicts, a sentiment intensified by the uneasy transition to the early principate. Partly in response, Augustus was careful to preserve the civic institutions, rituals, and symbols of republican public culture, while his poets annexed the rhetoric of Roman and Italian "freedom" and patriotism – as opposed to the Oriental "luxury" and "slavery" of Antony and Cleopatra. Yet, already in Virgil, the idea of Rome's imperial "mission" made its appearance: Rome's destiny is to topple the proud and spare the subjugated. At the same time, a new kind of imperial hierarchy enveloped, and soon eroded, the city's republican ethos, while preserving its vestigial forms. Though the emperor was simply *primus inter pares*, his and his family's dominance within the state reflected Rome's mastery of the peoples of her empire.

Although in moments of dynastic crisis the praetorian guard and rival armies dispensed power, for long periods the empire was unified by a hierarchical public culture centered on the symbols and rituals of emperor worship and deification. (8)

Both Roman models, the republican and the imperial, were to be taken up by different collective actors in various periods of European history; and, given Rome's enduring prestige, were to have significant consequences for the shaping of nations. Broadly speaking, the imperial model predominated during the Middle Ages, whereas the Renaissance saw a marked revival of the civic-republican form of public culture. But this is only an approximation. In medieval Italy, as well as in the northern European communes from the twelfth century, there was a conscious harking back to a republican ethos and civic institutions, including the office of consul, within a largely hierarchical feudal order and a dynastic Christendom. On the other hand, during the early modern period when cities and their burghers experienced a huge increase in their wealth and powers, the principle of absolutism appeared to embody a far more strenuous form of hierarchy, buttressed by the idea of the divine right of kings. Both kinds of public culture were to contribute to the shaping of different forms of national community, in different periods. (9)

Rome was not the sole source of public cultures that helped to shape national communities, nor the only one to bequeath a dual legacy. More than one ideal emanated from the biblical traditions. After the fall of the kingdom of Judah, the dominant form of public culture of ancient Israel, based on the Mosaic Covenant, had been reinstituted by the post-Exilic reforms of Ezra and Nehemiah and was, in the fourth and third centuries, kept alive through the Men of the Great Synagogue and the Pharisees. When the Covenant, along with the Temple, was placed in grave jeopardy by the Hellenizers and the edicts of Antiochus Epiphanes in 167 BC, the Maccabean party not only restored Temple worship but upheld the laws of the Covenant and secured a measure of independence for their Judean state under the Hasmonean kings. In this period, Jews were generally united around a belief system that centered on the one true God, His Torah, and the Temple. But they also kept alive the messianic tradition of Davidic kingship, as the anointed saviors of the people, and only partly accepted the Hasmoneans; hence the efforts of Simon to secure the high priesthood by popular acclaim in 140 BC. (10)

When in the late first century Jewish independence was curtailed, first by Herod and his family, and then by successive Roman procurators, to be finally extinguished after the fall of Jerusalem in 70 AD, the covenantal ideal and Torah were preserved by the rabbinic successors of the Pharisees, in their academies in Javneh and Galilee. But the messianic and Davidic traditions, espoused among others by the Zealots, became of necessity more muted and symbolic, especially after the failure of Bar-Kochba's revolt in Judea in 132–5 AD. At the same time, elements of both the covenantal ideal and the messianic tradition of Davidic kingship entered into the mainstream of early Christianity along with the Hebrew Bible, which the early Church accepted as the "Old Testament" and reinterpreted to accord with its own theology. In particular, the Church took over the role of the chosen people, seeing itself as *verus Israel*, now that God had withdrawn His favor from the Jewish people because they had rejected the messianic claim of Christ. But, lacking in the New Testament a clear political model of community, the Church, not to mention later Christian princes, fell back on an ideal of anointed, sacred kingship, particularly after Constantine and his successors had adopted, and adapted, Christianity as the dominant religion of the Roman empire. Hence, it was to be mainly through Christianity that these biblical traditions could be utilized in the construction of medieval public cultures and communities. (11)

As we have seen, the covenantal model did not stand alone. That it could be fused with hierarchical traditions is clear, but could it also be combined with a republican form of public culture? In principle, there seemed to be an unbridgeable gulf between the divine covenant found in ancient Judah and the secular compact of the citizenry characteristic of the republican model. But, in practice, different communities have been able to forge public cultures based on more than one principle. Already in ancient Israel and Judah, the idea of a double covenant, between God and His people, and between the king and people, made its appearance, to be taken up some two thousand years later in early modern Europe. This idea could be extended to compacts between citizens and rulers, for example in the many autonomous communes within the Holy Roman Empire. Similarly, intercantonal oaths in the Swiss *Eidgenossenschaft* had a sacred dimension and, as we shall see, even modern republics did not entirely dispense with sacred covenantal elements. (12)

Plate 7 Christ, Emperor Constantine IX Monomachos, and Zoe, Zoe Panel, mosaic, 1028–34, 1042–55 AD (East wall, south gallery, St. Sophia, Constantinople).

But, even if the three main forms of public culture are not mutually exclusive, and most of the historical cases that we encounter have been of a "mixed" type, the analytic distinction remains helpful in an initial classification of cultural forms of the nation, for it orients us to the dominant characteristics of each case. Thus, despite these caveats, it is possible and useful to speak of "hierarchical nations," "covenantal nations," and "civic-republican nations," and to locate their predominance in certain periods, even if few instances exemplify the pure type, and even if a given type of public culture cannot be confined to a specific period of history. In this chapter I shall concentrate on the hierarchical form of public culture, and ask how far we may begin to speak of "hierarchical nations" in the medieval, as opposed to the modern, epoch. In succeeding chapters, I shall explore the rise and character of covenantal and republican nations in later periods, and the role of nationalism in nurturing both.

Hierarchy and Nation in the Near East and Russia

In the Near East, late antiquity saw a long-drawn-out struggle for dominance between the Hellenistic powers and Parthia, and thereafter between the Roman empire and Sasanian Iran. These are all classic aristocratic empires based on clear hierarchical principles, and as such seemingly far removed from any concept of the nation, whether ethnocultural or political. But, even here, we can discern the development of a few of the processes underlying nation formation, albeit to a very limited extent and only in certain periods.

In an inscription from Hajjiabad, as in that on the rock relief at Naqsh-i Rajab, the great third-century Sasanian monarch Shapur I sets out clearly the hierarchy at the apex of his empire:

> This is the range of the arrow shot by US, the Mazda-worshipping god Shapur, the king of kings of Eran and Aneran, whose origin is from the gods, the son of the Mazda-worshipping god Ardashir, the king of kings of Eran, whose origin is from the gods, the grandson of the god Pabag, the king. And when we shot this arrow, we were shooting before the kings [landholders; *sahrdaran*], the princes [*vaspuhragan*], the grandees [*vuzurgan*], and the nobles [*azadan*].

Apart from the explicit hierarchical principle, echoed in the fourfold stratification of clergy, warriors, scribes, and commoners, Shapur distinguishes his rule from that of his father and predecessor, Ardashir, in terms of the extent of his empire. Whereas Ardashir's rule was confined to Iran (*Eran*), his own empire included non-Iran (*Aneran*), i.e., other provinces. As Wiesehofer points out, this is the first time that the customary title of the Iranian ruler, "king of kings," was linked to Iran (*Eran*):

> The Sasanians created the idea of Eranshahr ("Empire of the Aryans") as a political concept, one of whose aims was to establish their legitimacy as heirs of the earlier great Iranian empire of their "forefathers" (the Achaemenids), as successors of the ancient mythical kings, and as followers of the Zoroastrian creed which had its roots in Iran. A further aim was to create a new "identity" for themselves and their subjects by using this concept of Eranshahr as the political and cultural homeland for all who lived there and by anchoring it in a very remote past. (13)

Eran is not an ethnic concept, rather a territorial and political designation, but, even so, it is not clear how far this reflected a degree of "territorialization" of memories and attachments. At the same time, the need to link their rule with the mythical kings and the Achaemenids suggests a Sasanian concept of their own historic territory within the ensemble of conquered provinces and peoples. There is also some sense of collective self-definition, although only on the part of an elite, and an attempt to cultivate myths, symbols, and memories of the heroic past. The latter was especially prominent under the later Sasanian monarchs. Thus Chosroes I (531–79) sponsored an antiquarian revival, as well as books of protocol and rules of aristocratic behavior, alongside his bureaucratic consolidation at the expense of the great nobles. Richard Frye thinks it highly probable that "the lays and legends of ancient Iran were gathered together" in his days and that the national epic of Firdausi "was much the same then as now." Yet, "the past which was revived in epic, in traditions and in customs, . . . was a heroic past of great and noble families and of feudal mores, not of a centralised, bureaucratic state which Chosroes wanted to establish." It was at this time, then, that the various cycles of ancient legends, many of them of East Iranian origin, were adapted to contemporary ideals to become the basis for Firdausi's later *Shah-nameh* (Book of Lords). (14)

Under the later monarchs, too, there was growing legal standardization, in line with state centralization. But, as far as one can see, this extended equally to all the provinces and peoples of the empire, as did the public religious culture of the fire temples of orthodox Zoroastrianism after the reforms of the late third-century chief *mobad*, Kartir. The latter seems to have been a missionary, insofar as he tried to institute fire temples and orthodox Zoroastrianism among the Hellenized Magians and pagans outside Iran. Nevertheless, under Kartir, according to Joseph Wiesehofer,

> Sasanian Iran was Zoroastrianised to a greater extent than ever before in the country's previous history. The religious influence on legal culture, literature and pictorial symbolism, as well as funerary customs of the period (exposure of the body and burial of the bones) bear witness to this fact. Religious authorities were present at many places, from the village and its local centre of worship to the royal court, to watch over "divine service," execution of rites and preservation of religious traditions.

This suggests that Iran held a special place in the state religion and the empire's religious public culture, and that, within Iran, the southwestern region of Persia, through its sacred sites, its "forefathers" of the Sasanians, and the memories preserved by the Zoroastrian clergy, was singled out, if only to a limited extent. Quite clearly, we cannot speak of nationhood or national identity under the Sasanians. Yet, both in terms of public culture and the cultivation of Iranian myths, symbols, memories, and traditions, an ethnopolitical basis for much later national developments of a collective Iranian identity under Persian cultural leadership was forged during this period. (15)

Can the same be said, *mutatis mutandis*, of the Byzantine empire? On the face of it, this purest example of the hierarchical principle was as far removed from the concept and practice of national community as can be imagined; in the words of Cyril Mango, "there never existed a Byzantine 'nation.'" The inhabitants of Byzantium were known as *Romaioi* and felt that they belonged to the Eastern Roman empire; but they defined themselves primarily in regional and/or ethnic terms, and even more as Christians. The empire of which they were part was an Orthodox polity, in which state and Church complemented each other in an ideal harmony under the Holy Emperor, God's vice-gerent on earth, reflecting a divinely ordained global order. Covering a profusion of ethnic and religious communities in far-flung and culturally variegated territories, the empire was united by loyalty to the Emperor and through an official state-backed faith. Moreover, as in Sasanian Iran, the clergy of the state religion were loath to tolerate, if they did not persecute, the various religious minorities within the borders of their empire. (16)

Nevertheless, developments in later centuries, following its defeat by the Seljuq Turks at Manzikert in 1071 and the Sack of Constantinople in 1204 by the Crusaders, brought a much truncated Byzantium after its restoration in 1261 towards a growing sense of Greek ethnopolitical identity and political community. For Alexander Vasiliev, this last flowering of Byzantium brought "the rise of patriotism among the Greek people, accompanied by a turning back to the glories of ancient Greece." John Armstrong speaks of a "precocious nationalism" in this period, based on a sense of election and protection by God in a time of trials and adversity. As *verus Israel*, the Orthodox Church and community enjoyed God's special favor, and this was reinforced by the bitter antagonism of the Greek-speaking clergy and people to both the heretical Latins and the infidel Turks. In fact, Greek culture and language had been revived in the court and bureaucracy already in the ninth century, at a time when Greece itself was being recovered from the Slavs and Albanians; and it became ever more critical to Byzantine Orthodox identity and community as the Near Eastern and Western provinces were conquered by Bulgars, Slavs, and Turks. Of course, Orthodoxy was by definition universal in its scope and mission. But, as ethnic churches flourished in the former Balkan territories of the empire, and because the Greek New Testament was reinforced by an Orthodox Greek liturgy, Greek language and culture became the necessary vehicles and provided an increasingly significant identity for the remaining Orthodox Christians in the severely contracted Byzantine empire. At the same time, it was a city rather than a historic territory, and a universal public culture rather than an ethnopolitical repertoire of symbols, myths, and memories, that formed the basis of this cultural community. Only after the fall of Constantinople, under centuries of Turkish rule, and reinforced by the *millet* organization of the Ottoman empire, was the cultural and religious identity of the Greek-speaking population of the former East Roman empire in the Balkans (and the diaspora) gradually refashioned to furnish the basis for a Greek ethnopolitical community. (17)

The Russian Exception?

Byzantium's offshoot and spiritual successor, Muscovite Russia, traced its lineage back to Kievan Rus', a feudal state founded in the ninth century by a combination of Scandinavian Ryurikid overlords and Slav peasants, which looked to Byzantium both for its dominant hierarchical principle and for its ideological self-definition. Vladimir's conversion to Orthodox Christianity in 988, according to the Russian Primary Chronicle (*The Tale of Bygone Years*, composed ca. 1115), had been prompted by Russian admiration for the beauty of Orthodox liturgy and ritual, though geopolitics and trade were probably more decisive. Nevertheless, Orthodox symbolism underpinned the power of the Grand Dukes of Kiev and Orthodox ritual gradually helped to unify Russian society, while its Christian theology of suffering and redemption was soon married to a strong conviction of ethnic election. For the author of the Primary Chronicle, writing of their suffering in the year 1093, the Russian people had been chosen by the Lord, but it had sinned and was therefore chastised by defeat and captivity:

> He has all the more unleashed his anger upon us insofar as, being more favored than any, we have sinned worse than others. For being more enlightened than the rest, knowing the Lord's will, we have scorned it and all that is beautiful, and we have been punished harder than others.

This Orthodox theology of ethnic suffering and salvation was extended to the countryside by the fourteenth-century monastic movement, led by missionaries like St. Sergius and St. Stephen, for whom the pursuit of the saintly life defined a specifically Russian ideal, and provided a foil to the growing union of the Orthodox Church and dynastic power, centered now on Muscovy. For, in the succeeding century, the fall of Constantinople encouraged an ever closer union of state and Church, together with the idea of Russia as the last bastion of the true faith. So, just at the moment when the Russian Church achieved the status of a national autocephalous Church, and the religious community became identical with the political community, the state itself turned increasingly autocratic and hierarchical, and its rulers consciously adopted such Byzantine titles as *autocrat* and *tsar*, as well as Byzantine court ceremonial and symbols like the Byzantine two-headed eagle. (18)

It was only to be expected that, in these circumstances, theological conviction should give rise to political doctrine. At the Church Council of 1504, Abbot Joseph of Volokolamsk monastery affirmed the principle of autocracy and the supremacy of the tsar who received his scepter from God. But the ideal of Orthodox Russia as the "Third Rome" received its classic expression in a letter of 1506 from Abbot Philotheus of Pskov to the ruler, Vasilii III, which, after declaring that the first Rome had fallen because of its heresy, the second to infidel Turks, concluded:

> Two Romes are fallen, but the third stands fast; a fourth there cannot be. Thy Christian kingdom shall not be given to another.

The hierarchical principle received its fullest expression in the elaborate Byzantine ritual of Tsar Ivan IV's coronation in 1547, and its exclusive Orthodox basis was visible in the ensuing crusade against

Tatar Kazan in 1552. This was complemented by Church Councils like that of Stoglav in 1551, which enforced greater discipline in the Church, and by the composition of books by the Metropolitan Macarius that dwelt on the themes of the Third Rome and the tsar as ruler of the Orthodox – ideals which were disseminated to large segments of the people through the daily liturgy and royal ceremonies. (19)

But only at the end of the century, during the Time of Troubles (1598–1613), did the expression "Holy Russia," applied to the land and people of Russia, become common as a symbol of the piety and devotion of a suffering people, especially during the invasions of Swedes and Poles. Yet this ethnic myth of the "Russian people" never freed itself from the more powerful ideal of a righteous tsar, the father of his people, and hence of a dynastic myth of election. In the subsequent Great Schism of the 1660s, the ethnic Russian myth seemed to describe better the settlements of the Old Believers, while the dynastic myth became increasingly divorced from it and attached to the growing Russian empire, especially after Peter the Great and his successors. (20)

From this brief discussion, we gain the clear impression that the empires of late antiquity and the Middle Ages were far removed from the idea and practices of nationhood, and that few of the processes which are necessary for the formation of nations were present during their long histories. For this reason, too, we cannot expect to find any sense of national identity among their populations. This was especially true of Byzantium and Sasanian Iran. Certainly, the elites of both empires possessed a sense of their collective identity *vis-à-vis* significant others, as well as myths of origin, but that identity was either purely religious – Orthodox or Zoroastrian – or political – it pertained to a conglomerate state rather than a unitary nation. Both empires also cultivated elaborate repertoires of myths, memories, traditions, and symbols, and in the Byzantine case a keen sense of divine election, though it was one that attached to a religious faith and a holy ruler rather than to a people or a land. Perhaps most important, there is little evidence of a territorialization of memories and attachments. A vague sense of the primacy of Iran, and within Iran of Fars, existed among the Sasanian elites, but the empire was really a coalition of provincial princes and noble estates, and such territorial loyalties as existed were regional. The same was true of Byzantium, as we saw. Alternatively, it was the city of Constantinople that generated a sense of territorial belonging.

But this is not the whole story. As we saw, there were attempts to disseminate a religious public culture in both Eranshahr and Byzantium; and the clergy in both cases were active in opposing other religions and stamping out heresies. Since religion was often associated with ethnicity, this tended to privilege the dominant *ethnie* at the expense of ethnocultural minorities. Moreover, the empire's public ceremonies and rituals of worship were those of the dominant faith and were determined by its clergy, though, once again, in Byzantium we are dealing with a universalizing religion. In these empires, the dissemination of laws and customs followed ancient Near Eastern traditions, but in the Byzantine case also built on the heritage of Rome, notably under Justinian.

The Russian case is rather different. Not only was there early on a clear self-definition of the community, as well as the cultivation of many Russian myths and legends, traditions and memories. There was also a strong attachment to a Russian homeland. Of course, Russian-speaking settlements were spread out over a large area, stretching northwest to Novgorod and northeast to Vladimir, Suzdal, Tver, and Moscow. Such a slow process of uneven territorialization lacked the clearcut borders of the "compact nation" that was to become the Western nationalist ideal. But, on the emotional level, it furnished an ample basis for the cultivation of ethnoscapes and ultimately, in the modern period, a national identity tied to a specifically Russian "nature" and landscapes. (21)

Moreover, the Muscovite period, as we saw, witnessed the development of an Orthodox public culture which, after the fall of Byzantium, became an exclusively Russian religious culture of the only surviving kingdom of the "true" faith. On the other hand, it is doubtful whether, or how far, legal standardization developed in the sixteenth and seventeenth centuries, given the extent of the empire, the customs of its various ethnic communities, and the large holdings of the aristocracy. Only after the Petrine reforms was a centralized bureaucracy established with sufficient powers to disseminate uniform laws across this vast area, though a sense of Russian community had by then become somewhat attenuated by the inclusion of neighboring peoples in an ever-expanding empire. Nevertheless, from the fifteenth to seventeenth centuries, we can perhaps discern the outlines of a hierarchical nation, centered on the tsar, the Church, and the Orthodox community, and combining a vivid attachment to a homeland with a public Orthodox culture on the threshold of the early modern period. (22)

Premodern Nations in the Medieval West?

It is in vain that we search for the elements of nationhood in the aftermath of the breakup of the Western Roman empire, as nineteenth-century nationalist histories presumed when they traced the origins of European nations to a Clovis, Arminius, or Hengist. True, our sources record a rapid succession of ethnic groupings on the move, but, with a few exceptions, their sense of self-definition appears bewilderingly fluid and their myths of origin often fleeting. Patrick Geary has argued that these myths and symbols were mostly the creations of war lords and tribal chiefs seeking to legitimate their position through a noble lineage, while the fragile coalitions they led were often reported by the Romans' informants under tribal names, with the result that the Romans were prone to attribute to these shifting and often subdivided ethnic categories and regional groupings a greater objectivity and solidity than they warranted, in line with their own ethnic models and expectations. Nor, again with some well-known exceptions, do we encounter much in the way of territorialization of collective memories and attachments, or the development of a sentiment of homeland. As for the other key processes of nation formation, the dissemination of a public culture and the standardization of legal practices, these seem to have been largely the preserve of Rome's imperial successors in the Carolingian and Holy Roman empire, and of the growing power of the Papacy. (23)

The exceptions to this general picture in the second half of the first millennium in Europe have been the subject of vigorous debates. Susan Reynolds has argued that some of the more stable medieval kingdoms that emerged in the ninth and tenth centuries, notably the Anglo-Saxons, Franks, and Normans, "corresponded to a 'people' (*gens*, *natio*, *populus*), which was assumed to be a natural, inherited community of tradition, custom, law and descent." Labeling them *regna*, as opposed to (modern) nations, and their sentiments of loyalty *regnal* rather than national, Reynolds takes the older view of Hugh Seton-Watson to task for positing a teleological view of political development, in which a pre-existing nation is seen to move inevitably through the attainment of "national consciousness" to the end-state and boundaries of the nation-state. This kind of perspective prevents us from understanding the ideals and sentiments of medieval communities for what they were, unclouded by modern and often national(ist) presuppositions. (24)

More recently, however, Reynolds has claimed that "the concept of the nation that lies at the heart of all forms of nationalism was widespread long before the eighteenth century," though it was generally felt to be self-evident and did not require an ideology or movement such as we encounter in the modern period. This concept combined the idea of a natural community of descent, custom, and culture with the notion of a political community with political rights, even if it was not independent. Moreover, when a collective name persisted, as between the Franks and France, myths of origin tended also to persist, in this case, that of Frankish/French descent from the Trojans – and that despite considerable change in the population and boundaries. For Susan Reynolds, nations and nationalism are concepts that belong in the realm of political theory, or better of popular ideas which are self-evident to the participants and hence barely figure explicitly in the historical record. But, for modernists like John Breuilly, this is not enough to support an argument for the existence of premodern nations, let alone nationalism. These ideas may well have been current in medieval Europe, and they may well have been political as well as ethnographic, but we need other direct evidence before we can be sure that people in the Middle Ages felt that they belonged to a nation; and by "people" here is meant most of the members of a polity's population. (25)

England: The First Nation?

In many ways, England provides the test case for premodern nations. Adrian Hastings had indeed argued that England was the first in the column of premodern nations (Armenia and ancient Israel were prior but isolated cases), pointing out that fourteenth-century texts reveal a concept of the nation that is very similar to modern concepts, and that, given the flowering of English literature and the use of English language in court and administration which coincided with an upsurge of "nationalism" in the Hundred Years' War, we are justified in regarding the English as a medieval nation. But Hastings also regarded late Anglo-Saxon England from the tenth century as a fully formed "nation-state." In this he followed the maximalist view of historians like James Campbell and Patrick Wormald, who claimed that, while Bede only proposed the vision of an English Christian nation (despite his own strong loyalty to Northumbria), it was Alfred who, by his government, laws, and literary and educational achievements, gave Bede's ideas institutional substance, and began the process of welding several kingdoms and peoples into a single nation. Yet, only in the tenth and eleventh centuries did his successors, notably Athelstan and Edgar, manage to consolidate the idea and reality of an English nation and unite its various groups and polities into a single kingdom. (26)

Against this view, Krishan Kumar has argued for the absence of any real sense of English national sentiment in this period, even if Anglo-Saxon England

> had become one of the most, if not the most, integrated and centralised states in Europe, an achievement usually credited in the main to Alfred the Great. William the Conqueror inherited a well-ordered state with a uniform system of administration, a highly developed structure of royal law, a centralised coinage and an effective system of taxation.

Yet, Kumar contends, this is quite different from an integrated *nation*, or a developed sense of *national identity*. The attempt to resuscitate the Mercian kingdom in the tenth century, the internationalism of the Roman Church, the links with Scandinavia, and the factionalism of the English nobles belie any real sense of national identity among the upper classes in this period. Each of these, taken singly, might not be so serious; after all, in modern times, there is more than one accepted nation whose Church has ties beyond its borders, whose members possess links with other areas, *ethnies*, or states, is racked by factionalism, and so on. However, taken together, these limitations do seem to undermine the case for English nationhood in this period, even if we need to question Kumar's key modernist (and circular) objection that Anglo-Saxon England failed to exhibit "some sense of a relationship between elites and the commonalty, the ordinary people of the community. A nation composed of elites and expressing only elite-consciousness is not a nation in the accepted sense of the word today." (27)

On the other hand, whether we accept a maximalist view of an Anglo-Saxon *state* under the *rex Anglorum* before 1066 or not, a separate case can be made for the creation of a sense of shared Anglo-Saxon ethnicity. By the tenth century, texts like the epics *Exodus* and the *Battle of Maldon*, the *Anglo-Saxon Chronicle* and Bede's earlier *Ecclesiastical History of the English People*, strongly suggest that, in addition to a named and self-defining English community with a myth of common origins, Anglo-Saxon elites possessed a fund of common myths, memories, symbols, and traditions, notably a providentialist myth of ethnic election, modeled on the Old Testament ideal of a covenanted people. Moreover, a common Anglo-Saxon language did provide an effective means of communication with other classes, as well as giving birth to a rich and diverse literature. Common language also aided the dissemination of royal laws and institutions across most of the kingdom, even if, as Breuilly argues, we have no direct "independent evidence" that people using shire courts, for example, thought of them as "English" institutions and became attached through them to an "English" nation. However, what seems to have been lacking, except for brief periods, was a high degree of territorial cohesion and unity. And, although the sources speak of insular attachments to *Engla lond*, it is not clear how far this applies to (roughly present-day) England or to Britain as a whole – something that continues to bedevil analysis to this day. As for a common and distinctive public culture, we cannot be sure how far it was disseminated in this period, even by the Church, although, as Wormald argues, it was in and through local government (shires and shire courts) that "the mutual dependence of the king and a decidedly broad political nation" was realized. (28)

The implication of Wormald's argument is that the Anglo-Saxon kingdom, like others in Northern Europe, was essentially non-hierarchical, depending as it did mainly on local assemblies for its cohesion. In contrast, the Normans appear to have imported a markedly hierarchical character to their rule, both in terms of manorial feudal ties and through their superimposition of a class of French-speaking knights on an earlier English social order. Moreover, their interests were decidedly European. Most of the Norman kings of England spent much of their time abroad, defending or expanding their possessions in various parts of present-day France, while the archbishops were often from the Continent. The elite culture of this period was also continental; in its architecture, language, and literature, it was either French or a derivative from French culture. On the other hand, by the late twelfth century, the Norman rulers styled themselves kings of England and their knights had intermarried and assimilated to a considerable degree. By this time, too, they were clearly differentiating themselves from both the Welsh and the Irish, whose culture and customs they regarded as "degenerate." Moreover, twelfth-century historians such as William of Malmesbury, John of Worcester, and Orderic Vitalis, along with Henry of Huntingdon, helped to revive Anglo-Saxon history and a sense of the English past, if only to legitimize Norman rule, and they also appear to have sought reconciliation between the English and the Normans. Moreover, in adopting the vision of Geoffrey of Monmouth's *History of the Kings of Britain*, the English kings, notably Edward I, were staking an English claim to rule over the whole of Britain, in the manner of the pre-Saxon legendary Briton "emperor," Arthur. (29)

This suggests that an English (Anglo-Norman) *ethnic* identity was being revived, with a new self-definition, myths of origins, and shared history linked to a particular territory, clearly differentiated from the Welsh and Irish. On the other hand, a *national* identity was only beginning to emerge in this period. There is little in the way of a distinctive public culture and language (Latin remained the official language, while French was spoken at court), and only some degree of territorial cohesion (the north, in particular, remained largely separate). What did develop in this period was a relatively strong English state, with centralized finances, a single English written law, controlled by the court, and a system of assize courts with trial by jury, staffed by professionals. As Rees Davies remarks: "By the thirteenth century, English law was regarded as one of the distinctive hallmarks of Englishness and as an integral part of English political culture." (30)

Things began to change in the later fourteenth century, when we witness elements of a distinctive public culture, such as the rise of sacred kingship and its political symbolism in the reigns of Richard II and Henry V, the establishment of the two Houses of Parliament, the growing use of English by the clerks of Chancery, and the beginnings of a (Middle) English literature in the poetry of Gower, Langland, and Chaucer, and in the vernacular translations of the Bible in the age of Wyclif. Chaucer's decision to write mainly in English undoubtedly cut him off from a European readership, but it also brought him close to a specifically English consciousness, which suggests that "he saw his readers *as* in some important ways English." (31)

These developments had their roots in the preceding century, in reports like Wendover's of 1233 against the Poitevins, which places native-born Englishmen before foreigners, or poems like the *Song of Lewes* celebrating English liberty in the barons' victory of 1264. But it was the succession of wars against Wales, Scotland, and France, culminating in the Hundred Years' War, which, though mainly motivated by dynastic interests, increasingly stimulated sentiments of national loyalty to the person of the king, as symbol of the nation – and especially to Henry V. For, even putting aside Shakespeare's idealized and biblically inspired portrait of Henry, we are left with a monarch who sought to promote the English language, overcome the deep splits in the English aristocracy generated by his father's usurpation, and integrate the various ethnic groups and classes fighting under his banner. It is, of course, possible to see in his actions merely the use of national sentiment for dynastic and imperial ends, as Krishan Kumar suggests, but this presupposes the existence of some degree of "national feeling" in the first place. Besides, several medieval historians claim that it was in just these two centuries that a sense of national identity was to be found, at least among the elites, but perhaps also among the yeomen. (32)

All this suggests that many members of the upper and some in the middle classes were developing a sense of national identity in late medieval England. Though they continued to feel the power of other collective identities and loyalties, both local and Catholic, the ideal of an English ethnopolitical nation and its fate within roughly its present borders had begun to exercise a greater hold, now that the royal possessions in France were being challenged and lost. A distinctive public culture centered on the monarch and a more centralized legal system help to account for this trend. On the other hand, without some of the sacred resources of golden ages, sacrifice, and the like, an English identity lacked the "religious," and hence binding and self-sustaining, quality that we associate with the nation; it took some time for the sacrifice of the crusader on behalf of Christendom to be transferred to the *patria*. What does re-emerge is a conviction of English ethnic election. Thus in 1377, the chancellor, Adam Houghton, delivered a speech at the opening of Parliament praising Edward III's victories and the prosperity of the kingdom which "showed that England enjoyed God's favour, that the English were the new Israelites and their kingdom the *heritage de dieu*." Nor was this an isolated expression of missionary chosenness. Accompanying hopes of an Anglo-French crusade, there was also a considerable degree of English "territorial patriotism," notably during the victory celebrations after Agincourt. (33)

France: The Most Christian Kingdom

"Saint royaume de France": Joan of Arc's celebrated description summed up a long tradition of hierarchical monarchy in France based on a pronounced sense of French ethnopolitical community. The sanctity of the French kingdom derived from the virtuous ancestors of her kings and the cult of St. Louis, from the piety and devotion of her people, the number and quality of her saints, especially St. Denis, the quantity of her relics, the number of her martyrs and holy corpses, her many churches and cathedrals, priests and universities; above all, from the purity of her people's faith, their lack of heresy and their ceaseless support for the Church. No wonder that the French kings, from the time of Philip IV, around 1300, styled themselves "the most Christian king," and saw their people as the most chosen part of *verus Israel*, the Catholic Church, which had replaced the original chosen people. And, for all his antagonism towards the incumbent Pope, Boniface VIII, Philip IV regarded himself as "the shield of the faith and the defender of the Church." (34)

The claims of the French kings rested on a pedigree every bit as ancient and noble as that of the English kings. Stemming from Clovis' unification of the Roman province of Gaul and his conversion to Catholic Christianity in 496, in opposition to the Arian Visigoths, their claims harked back to the superiority of

> the illustrious nation of the Franks, chosen by God, valorous in arms, constant in peace, profound in wisdom, noble in body, spotless in purity, handsome without equal, intrepid, quick and fierce, newly converted to the Catholic faith, and free of heresy

as the eighth-century prologue to the texts of the earlier Salic Law put it. Not long afterwards, at the Council of Soissons, where Pepin, son of Charles Martel, was anointed with holy oil by the bishops, with papal blessing, the Frankish kingdom was declared to be a new kingdom of David and its people similar to ancient Israel in the divine order – a position confirmed at Charlemagne's coronation as emperor by the Pope in 800. (35)

This belief in the sacral primacy of a French kingdom was revived in the early twelfth century under Louis VI, when the cult of St. Denis, the royal patron saint, was established. The saint's praises were sung in the *chansons de geste*, and his *oriflamme* was raised in battle. But texts of this early period applied the term "most Christian" to the French people rather than the kingdom or territory, much less to the kings, since none before Louis VII had gone on the Crusade. This began to change in the early thirteenth century, when Philip Augustus had recovered Normandy and the "Franks" were providing the leadership of the Crusades, the Capetian kingdom was becoming known as the *regnum Franciae*, and the phrase "defense of the realm" became increasingly common, with kings like Philip Augustus and Philip IV invoking it to justify their wars. (36)

However, from the mid-thirteenth century, belief in divine protection of the French kingdom and the elevated status of its monarch and people was encouraged by the cult of the saintly Louis IX and by the clerics of great abbeys like St. Denis and Fleury. In 1239 and 1245, St. Louis was addressed by the papal chancellery as "the most Christian prince, ruler of a most devoted people," while educated Frenchmen began to see themselves as a *beata gens*, faithful to Church and Papacy. This was also the epoch of the *Grandes Chroniques de France*, translated into French from earlier Latin texts, which lauded the fervor and purity of French Catholicism and the piety of its kings. Of this period, Joseph Strayer writes that the Capetians "had to invent the France which they claimed to rule. They had to make men proud of the country as well as loyal to the king; they had to expand the idea of France to make it match the expansion of their own power." To this end, argues Strayer, two ideas were conjoined: the holy king and the sacred country, their fusion helping to speed the emergence of a centralized French state around 1300. (37)

For Colette Beaune, too, territory, people, and monarch were seen as equally holy from the time of Philip the Fair. In 1302 Friar Guillaume de Sauqueville first referred to the French as the people of God, chosen by Him as Israel had been, the land of the new covenant, the promised land, the holy land: "God chose the kingdom of France before all other people." Nogaret's propaganda also asserted that God had chosen France as his own special kingdom: "the kingdom of France was chosen by the Lord and blessed above all other kingdoms of the world." This was echoed by the contemporary papal bull, *Rex Glorie*, which stated that:

> The King of Glory formed different kingdoms within the circuit of this world and established governments for diverse peoples according to differences of language and race (*divisiones linguarum et gentium*). Among these, like the people of Israel (*sicut israeliticus populus*) . . . , (so) the kingdom of France, as a peculiar people chosen by the Lord to carry out the orders of Heaven, is distinguished by special marks of honor and grace. (38)

Later, Georges Chastellain gave this sentiment Mosaic expression: "God shines his countenance upon you, the hand of God rests on the people he has chosen." This was witnessed by the special signs of grace: the holy ampulla for anointing kings, the lily, and the *oriflamme*. Beaune's comment is worth quoting in connection with the idea that a hierarchical concept of the nation does not link the elites with the mass of the people:

> The kingdom's sense of nationhood was formed early in its history; in consequence it was inspired far more than other nations to draw its worth from its faith and its conformity to divine will. The term "most Christian" was applied without distinction to the French king, the people and the territory. (39)

In the next two centuries, the concept of France expanded in various ways. At first it had been a political concept, Philip Augustus' *regnum Franciae*; by the mid-thirteenth century, it had expanded to include the whole of the kingdom, "a specific territory, a land in which the race of Franks had lived since time immemorial." Thereafter, she became personified: sweet, beautiful, free (from taxation), valiant, loyal, faithful, learned, most Christian *domina Francia*. For Alain Chartier, writing ca. 1420, the person of France constituted an ensemble of natural and cultural attributes, towards which everyone had the same duty as a child to its mother. By 1484, the chancellor of France could take up the theme of France as a garden, and assert that "the beauty of the country, the fertility of the soil and the healthiness of the air outdo all the other countries of the world." This was accompanied by stirring calls for her defense. In the 1490s, in the *Doctrinal de*

Noblesse, we read that "Everyone should devote himself to the defense of his land. Honor and true glory crown those who die for their country. Nothing is too difficult to save the place of one's birth." And, lest this might be mistaken for a call to defend solely one's native region, Beaune quotes the contemporary prayer for the lord Jean de Bueil:

> Priez pour moi bonnes gens,
> Pour les sires de Bueil occis a la grant guerre,
> En bataillant pour la France et pour vous.
> ("Pray for me, good people, / For the lord of Bueil killed in the great war, / Fighting for France and for you.") And Colette Beaune adds: Mort pour la France. (40)

Not only was a concept of France familiar and widely diffused among the educated classes, it pertained to a kingdom, a land, and a people, and as such embodied the hierarchical principle of a unified social order in a given territory. But hierarchy did (and does) not entail isolation of elites from the majority of the population. In spite of the regional differences in the French kingdom, and the very different culture in the south, knowledge of and attachment to a wider concept of France was gradually, albeit fitfully and unevenly, disseminated from Paris and the Île de France to other regions through the various processes of nation formation: the definition of a collective French identity through opposition to external powers, notably the English state; the circulation of myths of (Trojan) origins, memories, and symbols of the French kingdom; the growing territorialization of memories and attachments to *la France*; the extension of laws and customs from the center to various regions; and the creation and diffusion of a royal and Christian public culture, including the coronations, entries into cities, healing power of the king, and the role of parlements. (41)

What helped to consolidate a French national identity by the early sixteenth century was the forging of some sacred cultural resources. Undoubtedly the most important was a powerful myth of ethnic election, focused on the monarch, but also attached to the land and people of his kingdom. How far this conviction was shared by ordinary people, particularly those in the countryside, we shall probably never be able to ascertain. But, by the fifteenth century, protracted fighting against English and Burgundian enemies may have encouraged many townspeople and perhaps some of the villagers to sympathize with Joan of Arc's call to defend the holy kingdom of France.

Scotland

We find similar combinations of hierarchy, territorial attachment, and wider participation elsewhere. The kingdom of Scotland, during and after the Wars of Independence, is a case in point. The prime evidence here is the Declaration of Arbroath (1320). But that document is only one of a series of diplomatic moves designed to counter the claims to overlordship of Scotland by the English monarch, Edward I. Edward I's assertion of his perceived rights was countered by the Instructions sent to the Scottish representatives at the papal court of Boniface VIII at Anagni in 1301, and by subsequent documents like the Declaration of the Clergy of 1309 and the Irish Remonstrance of 1317, culminating in the Declaration of Arbroath. According to Edward Cowan, the recipients of these pleadings could not have failed to understand that they "emanated from something more than the mouths of renegade English subjects or feudal rebels disenchanted with their mighty ruler. What was being articulated was the voice of a nation." (42)

In each of these documents there is reference to the "community of the realm," and sometimes to "the consent of the whole people" (*consensum populi et plebis*). Thus the 1309 Declaration of the Clergy speaks of the whole people suffering servitude, torture, and slaughter, as do the Irish Remonstrance of 1317 (in even more extreme terms) and the Declaration of Arbroath. But is this anything more than the conventional terminology of the period? The prolonged wars against Edward seem to have brought to the fore a class of freeholders beneath the thirty-nine earls and barons who affixed their seals to the Declaration. A Scottish Parliament also emerged in this period, though it never attained the centrality and importance of its English counterpart. If so, the frequent appeals to the *gens* and *natio Scottorum* represent a widening of the political nation within a typical aristocratic social order. (43)

Nevertheless, the question remains: can we infer a sense of Scots national identity in this period from these well-argued, professional documents, beyond a small baronial elite? In fact, we know very little about how the common soldiers felt, except for the fact that, as Bruce

Webster reminds us, "they did fight, like their leaders, in circumstances when it would have been simpler and safer not to do so." (44)

Moreover, all the above documents utilize the rhetoric of tyranny, and claim that the peeple have elected a prince who, like Judas Maccabeus, is the instrument of the Lord to drive out tyranny and free the people from servitude. The 1301 Instructions drive the point home by likening Edward to Antiochus IV, who by defiling the Temple sparked the Maccabean revolt. Much of this rhetoric about *libertas* and tyranny was, of course, shared by others in Europe, and stemmed in part from such tracts as the *Policraticus* of John of Salisbury writing in the twelfth century, but mainly from the Old Testament and Apocrypha. In the Scottish case, and particularly in the Declaration of Arbroath, there is also a strong classical influence: well-known passages about dying for freedom hark back almost verbatim to Sallust's *The Conspiracy of Catiline* (63 BC). (45)

Hence, to argue with Kumar that the events and documents of this period "had the character more of a civil war than a national war in the Border region" between the Balliols and the Bruces, and that "what was true of the Border region was true of the two countries as a whole," is to miss the point that the wars against the three Edwards also helped to forge a Scottish political identity. True, this is not a national identity as conceived by German Romantics or Slavophile intellectuals, though the Celtic inheritance was cultivated at this time. Nor did it involve the whole population, though more than the aristocracy participated. Granted, too, that much of lowland Scotland's culture and language was heavily Anglicized, and cross-border influences were all-pervasive. At the end of the day, most of the Scottish nobles fought against the English (some of them rather fitfully) and resistance was mounted, armies fielded, and myths and memories of battle and liberty created and handed down the generations. That is the nub of the matter. As so often, it is what later generations would make of the wars (and much later the Declaration) that mattered. (46)

In fact, it is the period around 1400 that saw the elaboration of a sense of Scottish national identity. Already in the 1370s John Barbour's epic, *The Bruce*, had laid out an anti-English history of the Wars of Independence and lauded freedom as the goal and meaning of Scottish identity. This was taken up by John of Fordun's prose history shortly afterwards, which elaborated the myth of Scota, the migration from Pharaoh's Egypt to Spain and thence to Scotland, and the history of the unbroken line of Scottish kings. This was followed by Andrew of Wyntoun's *The Orygynale Cronykil of Scotland* in the 1420s, a long verse chronicle of the history of the world and of Scotland, and in the 1440s by the most popular early account of Scottish history, Walter Bower's *Scotichronicon*, which aimed to underline the importance of history for Scottish identity and that of a strong monarchy to bolster that identity. This flowering of poetic and prose "histories" became the basis of subsequent assertions of Scottish identity, and fed the popular hostility to the English which culminated in the disaster of Flodden in 1513 and the death of James IV. Nevertheless, the fifteenth century had seen the elaboration of a distinct Scots identity based on the origin myth and the narrative of Scottish history. (47)

Hierarchical Nations?

Do these three cases provide sufficient support for the emergence of premodern nations in the fourteenth and fifteenth centuries? Do they allow us to speak of "hierarchical" nations?

Of course, by the criteria laid down by modernists, these cases hardly meet the standard of *modern* nations. Their members are not citizens; most of them do not participate in political life. It is not even clear that they feel they belong to a particular nation; but then again, it is not clear that they do not. We simply do not know. (But then, we do not know how many members of quite a few modern nations feel they belong to "their" nations.) Moreover, they are not "nationalist" nations, in an ideological sense. On the other hand, the medieval kingdoms of England, France, and Scotland conform well to some of the other modernist criteria. They were territorialized communities; they were legal-political communities; and they were autonomous, indeed fully sovereign communities. They were also participants in an "international" system, a *de facto* system of alliances and antagonisms which took shape in the later Middle Ages.

Even more important, in terms of the social and symbolic processes of nation formation, they were well advanced. Their elites had a clear sense of collective identity, of named self-definition *vis-à-vis* significant others. They also possessed familiar and well-rehearsed myths of origin and ancestry, along with a panoply of other myths, symbols, memories, and traditions which they cultivated and which distinguished them from their neighbors. From the thirteenth century onwards (earlier in the English case), these monarchical communities had become increasingly territorialized. Though local and regional attachments remained strong, these kingdoms had a political center, a large, bounded, if at times fluctuating, political space, and a sense of territorial possession, along with memories and increasing attachments, at least on the part of elites, to the kingdom's territory. This period witnessed, too, a rapid growth in the centralization and standardization of legal codes and legal institutions, and repeated attempts to apply a single code of observance of law and custom across the provinces and regions of the kingdom, with varying success. Finally, in all three kingdoms, there was a clear development of a distinctive public culture. This included the political symbolism of sacred kingship, the rituals of parliaments, estates, and assemblies, the rise of vernacular linguistic codes in legal and political affairs, the emergence of a vernacular literature, and the close association of public ritual and symbolism with Christian belief and liturgy.

It may seem rash to base an argument for premodern hierarchical nations on just three examples – though, as we shall see, there were other, less advanced, cases in Europe – but in terms of the criteria for forming nations that I outlined at the outset, these three monarchical communities provide ample grounds for regarding them as premodern nations by the fifteenth century – so long as we clearly differentiate them from later historical examples of the category of nation. We are confronted here by a type of nation that differs in many respects from Western democratic nations, one that is characterized by hierarchy rather than equality, and tradition rather than modernization. But then, many modern nations are undemocratic, and not a few cling to long-standing traditions.

Once we accept that "nationhood" and "modernization" are only contingently related, then we can see that not only may there be nations which radically differ from the standard Western concept, but that our modern Western concept of the nation is in need of considerable revision. That concept has been wedded to the idea, propounded and pursued by some (though not all) nationalists, that the nation is or must be culturally homogeneous, and that historic internal divisions must be erased. Clearly, such regional and cultural subdivisions were, and continued to be, a normal feature of hierarchical nations. In fact, they have often persisted to this day. For all its fierce centralism, the

Revolution failed to abolish the historic regions of France, while the division of Lowlands and Highlands persists in Scotland to this day, not to mention the *Länder* and cantons in Germany and Switzerland. We have also become much more accustomed to think of the nation as an overarching community housing, but also binding together, through a common symbolism and institutional network, different cultures and ethnic communities. In this respect, at least, the hierarchical nation may have pointed the way to a looser, "post-modern" type of national community.

5

Covenantal Nations

For modernists, nations and nationalism emerged in the late eighteenth century, at the earliest. Even if they do not accept Elie Kedourie's judgment that nationalist ideology originated with the German Romantics, notably with Fichte's *Addresses to the German Nation* (1807–8), many of them would date the genesis of nationalism to the French Revolution, the aftermath of the American Revolution, and the last Partition of Poland. However, when it comes to the emergence of nations, modernists display greater ambiguity. If it is nationalism and the state that, as Gellner and Hobsbawm argue, engender nations, then clearly their emergence must be placed firmly in the nineteenth century, perhaps even later. If, on the other hand, nations are held to form over a longer time span, then they are more usefully seen as products of eighteenth-century Western European conditions; these include the commercial and military rivalry between its states and the formation of bourgeois associations and reading publics in growing opposition to bureaucratic absolutist states. (1)

The issue of "national identity" raises fresh questions. Here, modernists are divided. One tendency is to regard everything before 1700, including any evidence of national sentiment, as of no consequence for the subsequent development of nationalism and nations, on the grounds that nations are essentially a product of the scientific and technological revolutions associated with early industrialization. Others, while accepting this general position, concede the presence of national ideas and sentiments in premodern periods, but regard them as largely descriptive and lacking the political dynamism of later nationalisms. Only in one or two cases, notably early modern England, are they prepared to allow a more persistent and widespread premodern national sentiment. In a footnote to his *Nations and Nationalism*, Ernest Gellner concedes "the early emergence of national sentiment in England" some two centuries before the advent of industrialism which, in his opinion, may be the result of the rise of individualism and a mobile spirit. Similarly, Eric Hobsbawm, in his *Nations and Nationalism since 1780*, after telling us that "proto-national" bonds of region, language, and religion have no *necessary* connection with the rise of the modern territorial national state, admits that membership of a historic state, as in Russia and Serbia, may act directly "upon the consciousness of the common people to produce proto-nationalism – or perhaps even, in the case of Tudor England, something close to modern patriotism." (2)

In this chapter, I shall be arguing that in parts of early modern Europe we witness the rise of both an elite sense of national identity (and not only in hierarchical states) and in a few cases a wider "middle-class" national sentiment. Second, I want to put forward a more specific thesis, that this period saw the rise of a form of ideological nationalism, which in turn helped to consolidate both the identity and the community of the nation.

Early Modern National Identities

We already saw some evidence of a restricted elite sense of national identity, based both on ethnoreligious and political cores, notably in Western European states. The German case is usually cited as a prime example of the lack of any sense of national identity, indeed of its impossibility until the nineteenth century. A population with a babel of vernaculars, not to mention dialects, and an imperial institution of rapidly diminishing power after the death of Frederick II, hardly seems to qualify for that sense of community required by a sense of nationhood. Yet, even on this unpromising terrain, Len Scales has argued, there existed among the educated classes of the fourteenth and fifteenth centuries a sense of German identity among German language speakers tied to an Empire with specifically German roots. Even earlier, Italians referred to the followers of the Saxon and Salian emperors as Teutones and Teutonici, and with the Investiture Contest and the doctrine of papal translation of the Empire to the Germans, formulated by Innocent III in his decretal *Venerabilem* (1202), a sense of German identity bound up with a predominantly German Empire became widely accepted and was reinforced by the German literature of the Minnesangers. This identification was aided by the myth of Trojan origins of both the Franks and later of the German people as a whole. The ethnic character of the Empire can be found, according to Scales, in documents from the imperial chancery, but even more in "vernacular and Latin chronicles and annals, and in the political songs and verses in which the thirteenth and fourteenth centuries were so rich." However, it is in the political treatises, pamphlets, and tracts of the period that we find the fullest expression of a sense of common German ethnicity, even as the central German power waned, and their writers were generally middle-class provincials. It was in and through this political culture that a sense of German national and political identity was projected, even in the absence of real unitary power. By the fifteenth and early sixteenth centuries, particularly after the recovery of the manuscript of Tacitus' *Germania*, humanists like Konrad Celtis, Ulrich von Hutten, and Lorenz Fries could extol the originality and purity of the German language and the excellence of German culture, linking both to a glorious German imperial past. (3)

In Eastern Europe, too, there is evidence of fervent national sentiments, at least among the urban, educated classes. In Bohemia, the Hussite crusade brought popular Czech national sentiments to the fore. In the early fifteenth century, the association of Bohemia with a holy land and the Czechs with a holy nation – addressed as *sacrosancta natio bohemica*, *sancta natio*, and *sacrosancta communitas*, in the reiterated words of Master Jerome of the University of Prague in 1409 – became an intrinsic component of the Hussites' reforming zeal. This culminated in the call in 1420 to the Czechs "to rally to the defence of the 'most Christian' kingdom of Bohemia, assisted by their patron, St. Wenceslaus." (4)

Similarly, in fifteenth-century Poland, after the unification of its crown with that of Lithuania and the defeat of the Teutonic Knights, the court and gentry became increasingly wedded to the idea of an exclusive national Polish community, against both German and Jewish traders. Despite the protection of the latter by the kings, increasingly exclusive laws were passed against Jews, stimulated by the clergy and also by a sense of *antemurale* Catholic mission against Tatars and Muscovite Orthodoxy. But in the following centuries, with the inroads of Protestant churches, though the Polish Catholic Church continued to play a vital role in the kingdom, Catholicism became, in fact, the religion of just under half of the population of Poland-Lithuania. (5)

Spain is sometimes cited as a case of early statehood and national identity. But in the long-drawn-out centuries of the Reconquista it is hard to find a consistently Spanish, as opposed to Castilian, Portuguese, Navarrese, or Aragonese, national sentiment, even though some later Spanish historians have given these centuries of confused loyalties and intermingled (Christian, Jewish, and Muslim) cultures a framework of peninsular Catholic identity, as enunciated at times by the kings of León. Given the very different structures of these four kingdoms, it is hardly surprising that the rare moments of united action, as in the crusade that led to the victory of Las Navas de Tolosa in 1212 over the Almohads, failed to stimulate a wider Hispanic political identity. (6)

By the fifteenth and early sixteenth centuries, on the other hand, a sense of conditional Castilian chosenness which atoned for the sins of the Visigoths and their punishment at the hands of the Muslim invaders was increasingly tied to a "sacred geography" which saw "their land as a special gift of God." In the Aragonese kingdom, too, messianic prophecies of "the New David" who would come from Spain, rebuild "the citadel on Mount Zion," and reconquer Jerusalem were seized on by the Trastamara monarchs, culminating in the many prophecies of Ferdinand's reign. How far this trend was responsible for an increasingly exclusive and ethnic sense of Spanish identity aimed at the new *conversos* which ultimately led to the expulsions of Jews and Moors by the united monarchy is difficult to assess. What seems certain is that, beyond a very small elite, a Spanish identity, enveloped as it was in the monarchy's imperial role, was unable to develop and challenge the existing patriotic sentiments of Spain's traditional kingdoms and ethnic communities. (7)

Italy presents a particularly fascinating example of the rise of an elite sense of national identity, which was again unable to challenge, let alone encompass, the strongly rooted traditional regional identities of its kingdoms, duchies, and city-states. For some like James Stergios, this plethora of loyalties and sentiments left no room for a sense of Italian national identity; indeed, terms like *nazione* and *patria* referred almost exclusively to the city-state and regional communities into which the peninsula had long been divided. For intellectuals like

Machiavelli, the term *nazione*, in particular, signified place of birth or geographical area – though this designation also included the German, Italian, French, and Spanish "*nazioni.*" The use of the more heroic *patria*, too, which had earlier been associated with the ideal of *virtù*, also declined during the sixteenth century in favor of the state and its amoral *raison d'état* ("*ragione di stato*"). (8)

But this is only part of the story. Discussing the issue of *italianità*, Josep Llobera points out that during the Renaissance there was a growing awareness of the cultural and historical unity of Italy, based on the consciousness of the Roman heritage. On the other hand, a sense of belonging to "Italia" was largely confined to humanist intellectuals, and was less salient and intense than devotion to one's city-state – be it Milan, Florence, Rome, Naples, or Venice. Similarly, Anders Toftgaard, while agreeing that terms like *nazione* are used as synonyms for *gente* and *popolo* and relate to genealogical and geographical origins, reminds us that Italian humanist intellectuals like Ariosto and Pietro Bembo frequently spoke of "Italians" and "Italia." Though he agrees that we cannot, of course, speak of an existing Italian nation, such common expressions clearly tell us that ideas of Italy and Italians were not simply modern inventions. (9)

Thus, in his temporarily lost treatise on the Italian language of 1304–5, *De Vulgari Eloquentia*, Dante reveals

> a clear concept of territory called Italia with inhabitants sharing some sort of culture. These inhabitants, called *latini* or *Itali* by Dante, share a common culture, a common heritage and a common language and are thereby different from other peoples, such as the French and the Hispanic. Dante argues that Italy is culturally united and should seek to become politically united. This "Italian" community is, however, only one of the communities imagined by Dante, who loved the city-state of Florence but also, in his *Monarchia*, pleaded for the recreation of the Holy Roman Empire. (10)

Here we see both the fluidity of medieval political identities and the imagined presence of a national identity. In fact, the concept of a national Italian character, one among many such national characters based on common language and origins, but also on its current oppression and occupation by outside powers, was common currency among many Italian Renaissance intellectuals in their debates about the nature and desirability of an Italian literary language, as it was to most outsiders. This means that in the early modern period there was a long-established discourse of Italian national identity, which, because it lacked a unitary political framework, could only much later provide cultural materials for the political movement to unite Italy in the Risorgimento. (11)

In sixteenth-century France, that political framework was already several centuries old. From the thirteenth century, the France of principalities had been gradually united under the crown and its "most Christian" king, though several regions retained their customs, laws, and cultures, especially in Brittany and the south. In the next century, some of the intellectuals and lawyers began to separate the kingdom and nation from the person of the king, and by the fifteenth century they were conceiving *la France* as a person: in Alain Chartier's *Quadrilogue invectif*, she is a royal lady, a sorrowful mother upbraiding her three children (the quarreling estates), while for Gerson, as we saw in the last chapter, France is like a secluded garden, fertile and beautiful. By the later fifteenth century, under the influence of Italian humanism, the idea of the *nation* of France was increasingly fused with the classical concept of *patria*; and both were given cultural and literary, as well as political, content. Already in the 1370s, French humanists like Jean de Hesdin had disputed Petrarch's assertion, on the return of the Papacy from Avignon to Rome, that outside Italy it was unnecessary to search for poets and orators. A century later, Robert Gaguin, moved by love of his country, produced an inventory of French literary figures going back to the Gallo-Romans and Gregory of Tours. Nevertheless, for these writers, Latin remained the supreme language for serious works. It was only with Jean Lemaire des Belges' *La Concorde des deux Langaiges* of 1511 that a French literary language began to be viewed as the equal of its Italian counterpart; hence the need to write in (literary) French. In this text, France is conceived as a nation encompassing subnations (of Brittany, Hainaut, Burgundy, etc.), much like Italy and its subnations; but in the French case, political unity underpinned the desired revival of French language and culture. (12)

A similarly political stance is evident in Joachim Du Bellay's *La Deffence et illustration de la langue francoyse* of 1549. The medieval idea of *translatio studii*, the transfer of learning from Athens to Rome, and thence to Paris, was now united with growing political and military power: in Du Bellay's essay, France was to witness an efflorescence of cultural power in tandem with its political power, and *amor patriae* was paralleled by *amor linguae patriae*. In the subsequent Wars of Religion, when anti-Italian feelings ran high, especially on the Protestant side, the French term *patrie* became widespread, and was used instead of, or alongside, the older term *pays*, to include the whole population of the kingdom of France. And while, for Du Bellay, *La Deffence* was a cultural project for the select few, designed to appeal to the new king, Henri II, its arguments for cultural parity with Italy and its aggressive eulogy of the French and their superior manners and customs nourished the state-sponsored elite affirmation of national identity and attachment to the French *patrie*. (13)

The Wars of the Roses in mid-fifteenth-century England and the loss of possessions in France would hardly seem a propitious moment for the display of English national sentiment, let alone an assertion of English national identity. But conflict and division can also foster national sentiment, and the fact remains that, for all the decades of confusion and carnage wrought by battling Yorkists and Lancastrians, the English kingdom held together and emerged more centralized and powerful under the Tudors. Moreover, the long retreat from the Continent actually helped to encourage a sense of specifically English identity, which had already become evident in the stereotypes of foreign nations with whom the English kingdom came into conflict. Of course, we are dealing with a hierarchical form of national identity, as in much of Europe, and one confined to a small elite. Nevertheless, this included the political class, for whom the realm of England represented, in Henry VIII's words, "an empire," independent of papal or (Holy Roman) imperial control. As Llobera points out, "there is evidence of a strong identification of monarch with nation, but this is to be expected from the period"; and he quotes with approval Hans Kohn's judgment that the accession of the Tudors "laid the foundations for that national homogeneity which was the necessary condition for the later development of nationalism" in the seventeenth century. (14)

"Homogeneity" is rather too strong a term, and even "unity" in such a stormy period seems hardly apposite. But then it is difficult to think of any period in the nineteenth or twentieth centuries – the era of modern nationalism – where unity, let alone homogeneity, could be said to characterize most nations. What we have in early modern

England is evidence of a growing sense of national identity among a small minority of the population, but one that gradually percolated outside the ruling elite to the towns. This sense of national identity was, even more than before, centered on a powerful monarchy, especially after Henry VIII's split with Rome and his assumption of the supreme governorship of the Church of England. For this reason, Krishan Kumar, in his critique of Liah Greenfeld's thesis that Tudor England "invented" national*ism*, argues that what we have at this period in France, as in England and elsewhere, is a "crown-centered patriotism," not national*ism*. He rightly disputes Greenfeld's view that sixteenth-century England witnessed the emergence of a popular, and even democratic, nationalism based on a social revolution of the newly mobile. But, in dismissing an early English national*ism*, Kumar also refuses to admit the possibility of a growing sense of English "national identity" in this period – something he had already half conceded in his analysis of late medieval England. Throughout, Kumar oscillates between a sense of "national identity" and "nationalism" – neither of which terms he formally defines. Certainly, there is no evidence of an ideological movement of nationalism in England during the sixteenth and early seventeenth centuries. But this does not entail the absence of a sense of English "national identity" or of English "national sentiment," albeit one confined to a minority. As we saw, the elites of a hierarchical community may be imbued with a sense of national identity, and even national sentiment; and that, I think, is what the many, often intense, expressions of Englishness during this period suggest. For, though they were centered on the crown, they often included a generalized expression of "love of country" and nation, in opposition to other nations. (15)

The Dissolution of Christendom

What may we glean from this brief survey of the presence or absence of "national identities" in late medieval Europe? Can Marcu's earlier thesis of a wave of sixteenth-century European national*isms* be sustained? Little evidence of an ideological movement for autonomy, unity, and identity for a population deemed to constitute a nation can be found in this period. What we have instead are elite expressions of national sentiments, and a sense of national identity among some of the humanist intellectuals, lawyers, and bureaucrats, feelings and attitudes that could and sometimes were cultivated or manipulated by rulers when it was to their advantage. (16)

It is easy to dismiss these early expressions of national identity. But, as we saw in the cases of Italy and France, they provided concepts and a discourse of the nation which could be used by the later nationalists to authenticate the objects of their aspirations and mobilize their co-nationals. But they were also important in their own right. Ideas and sentiments of national community, across several parts of Europe, attested to the growing importance of delocalized but bounded territory, and the exercise of sovereign jurisdiction within it, in the face of imperial or papal claims. This is a process that had been underway since at least the thirteenth century, notably in France, and it was hastened by the loss of authority of the Holy Roman Emperor after the death of Frederick II in 1250 and the Captivity of the Papacy and Great Schism in the fourteenth century. By the time of the Council of Constance (1414–18), the rivalry of kingdoms and territories intruded into the deliberations of the Church. From the mid-fourteenth century the Church had been divided for administrative purposes into four geographical regions: Italia, Germania, Hispania, and Francia. When the Spanish delegates were temporarily absent from the Council of Constance, the English were allowed to form a *natio*, as they had been at the earlier Council of Pisa. But, when the Aragonese delegates arrived, demanding the status of a nation, this provoked serious disputes over the meaning of the term "*natio*." The French delegates argued that the English be reduced, once again, to being part of the German nation. But they also introduced the idea of principal nations and lesser nations or kingdoms, of the size of England – at a time when the Hundred Years' War was at its height. Not unexpectedly, the English delegates replied that the English nation possessed as much force and authority as the renowned nation of Gaul,

> whether a nation be understood as a people marked off from others by blood relationship and habit of unity, or by peculiarities of language, the most sure and positive sign of a nation in divine and human law and the essence of it . . .
> (*sive etiam sumatur ut gens, secundum cognationem & collectionem ab alia distincta, sive secundum diversitatem linguarum, quae maximam & verissimam probant nationem, & ipsius essentiam, jure divino pariter & humano*)

What this and the various arguments at these Church Councils reveal is not that Romantic linguistic nationalism surfaced in the Middle Ages long before Herder, but rather that the old unity of Christendom had been undermined, and that a new principle of territorial kingdoms, legitimated in terms of "nations," was beginning to take root. Of course, the definition of the nation was still fluid; it could embrace a kingdom of one language (France), or of several language groups ("England or Britain"), or just a province (Florence or Gascony). Indeed, the English delegation argued that theirs was more of a nation than the French, because only one language was spoken in the main in France, whereas

> the renowned nation of England or Britain includes within and under itself five languages or nations, no one of which is understood by the rest . . .
> (*Natio tamen inclyta Anglicana, alias Britannica, in, de & sub se quinque linguae habet, videlicet nationes, quarum unam aliam non intelligent*) (17)

But this was more than a simple ethnographic dispute. As the maneuvering at the Councils made clear, it was also a political principle and an instrument for gaining influence on behalf of kingdoms. It is not that the kingdoms themselves were new; what is novel was the fragmentation of Christendom, and its dual authority, spiritual and temporal, of the realm of Church and Empire, with the result that ever greater power accrued to its consituent parts, the principalities, kingdoms, and city-states. (18)

With the loss of restraining ecclesiastical influence, the rivalries of the European states grew more intense and extensive, particularly when the voyages of discovery opened up vast new realms for European exploitation and conquest. Within Europe, not only England and France, but Denmark and Sweden, Spain and the Netherlands, and later Poland and Russia, came into increasing conflict, with a divided Italy and Germany providing cockpits for Great Power intervention. Such prolonged warfare demanded a much greater concentration of resources by the princely states, with more professional armies and modern technology; and that in turn required more long-term financing, mainly by the new merchant bankers like the Medici and Fuggers. Politically, it also required a greater degree of control by the kings over their domains, and hence in the first place a strengthening of the patrimonial state, of the kind that occurred in England under Henry VIII and Russia under Ivan IV. Anthony Marx goes even further, arguing that to keep their hold on power in the face of often determined opposition from powerful nobles and clerics, kings had to bolster their rule not only through ideas of sacred monarchy and divine right, but also by mobilizing their subjects on behalf of the state. This in turn meant pursuing policies of homogenizing the population of the kingdom; and since religion was the main axis of unity and cleavage in early modern society, the kings sought to exclude all those who did not adhere to the dominant and majority religion of the state in the hope of making their societies more cohesive through the principle of an exclusionary "nationalism." Hence the expulsion of Jews and Muslims from Spain and Portugal at the turn of the sixteenth century, the Wars of Religion in France and eventual expulsion of the Protestants after the revocation of the Edict of Nantes in 1685, and the continual hostility to and intermittent persecution of Catholics in England from the late sixteenth to the eighteenth centuries. (19)

At first sight, this is an attractive thesis. It appears to tie in well with the various manifestations of an elite sense of national identity that we saw emerging in various parts of late medieval and early modern Europe, and it captures well the needs and strategies of ruling elites in this period of religious turmoil and political fragmentation. It also underlines the growing territorialization of attachments and power, as well as the different outcomes in the three states – Spain, France, and England – that Anthony Marx analyzes. Certainly, some at least of the processes of nation formation, including the formation of distinctive public cultures and the cultivation of various myths of descent and election, were well advanced by this era. But Marx's claim that all this bred an "exclusionary nationalism" for the first time, two centuries before the French Revolution, is less plausible. For one thing, exclusion of minorities, whether schismatics or Jews, was nothing new: medieval Europe was from the time of the Crusades rife with persecutions and expulsions. Mobilizing the passions of the religious majority also had a long history; and it could serve a variety of political ends – for the king, the Church, the nobles, the urban traders, and the peasants. For another, the cases Marx compares are quite different in their contexts and outcomes. Spain, in particular, seems not to have achieved national "homogeneity," nor even much unity after the expulsion of Jews and Muslims, and the expulsions themselves do not seem to have fueled a greater sense of national identity and cohesion in a peninsula so long divided between historic kingdoms and ethnic communities. This may also have something to do with the rapid acquisition of an empire by the ruling house *before* a widespread sense of national identity could take root among the elites. (20)

But there is a more serious objection to Marx's thesis. He defines nationalism as "a collective sentiment or identity, bounding and binding together those individuals who share a sense of large-scale political solidarity aimed at creating, legitimating or challenging states," adding that this is often "perceived or justified by a sense of historical commonality which coheres a population within a territory and which demarcates those who belong and others who do not." This essentially civic and political definition ties popular identities and sentiments to the state, not the nation, since for Anthony Marx – as for many modernists – nationalism is only important insofar as it is linked to a state, whether supporting or challenging it. But, whereas the concept of the state refers to a set of autonomous *institutions* exercising a monopoly of legitimate authority over coercion and extraction in a given territory, the concept of the nation signifies both a category of collective cultural identity and a historical form of (imagined, but also felt and willed) *community.* As a result there is something far more dynamic, inclusive, and purposive, as well as more richly varied, about nationalism than Marx allows. This suggests that we need to search for additional ideological factors, over and above state competition and elite strategies, or state competition for overseas markets, to account for the dynamic vision and mobilizing power of nationalism. (21)

Reformation and Covenant

Where shall we look for these ideological factors? For some theorists, they are to be located within the traditions of the Christian faith. Elie Kedourie argued that the subversive, revolutionary power of nationalism could be traced back to its medieval millennialist heritage, to the antinomian movements of Christian apocalyptic prophecy, from Joachim of Fiore to the Anabaptists. The problem here is that millennial movements tend to flee this world and are too short-lived to have produced the ideology and culture of a this-worldly nationalism. Adrian Hastings, on the other hand, sought the origins of nationalism in the sanction that Christianity gave to the vernacular, notably through translations of the Bible, as well as in Christianity's tendency to adopt the political model of a monolithic nation from the Old Testament, which it had, after all, accepted and adapted to its own purposes. Yet, for most of the Middle Ages and beyond, Christian rites were, with some exceptions like the Armenians and the Georgians, performed in the medium of universal languages, Latin and Greek; and it was only in the later medieval era that translations of the Bible began to appear in the West. (22)

However, Hastings' invocation of the Old Testament political model, though he did not develop it, is more to the point. The spirit of the Gospels is, after all, universalistic and the Christian Church transterritorial. For much of its history, it was purveyed by supranational clerisies, liturgies, and languages. Nations and nationalism, in contrast, are founded on principles of cultural diversity, individuality, and sacred territory, and they require different sources and models, notably in the early stages of nationalism. This means that we need to go back beyond a universalizing Christianity to its specifically Jewish root in the Hebrew Bible.

This is where the Reformation inaugurated a new stage in the processes of nation formation – and ultimately the emergence of the ideological movement of nationalism. Although it began as an apocalyptic European movement in opposition to the Papacy, and its central message was one of individual justification by faith through grace rather than by man's works, the Reformation's later development, particularly under the influence of Calvin and Zwingli and their Reformed churches, witnessed a much greater engagement with the world and a quest for election through signs of communal fellowship, collective moral discipline, and public works. (23)

The later Reformation provided the context for a return to the Old Testament, and more especially to the narratives and laws of the Pentateuch, on the part of many members of the non-Lutheran Reformed churches, notably the Zwinglians and Calvinists, and a revaluation of its place in the Christian canon. Simon Schama contrasts the "wholly sacred" character of the New Testament with the "this-worldly" nature of the Old, in the eyes of the Reformed churches, and argues that:

> The result of all this was to rescue the Old Testament from its position in Catholic theology as a necessary preface, a "second stage" in the teleology of original sin and eventual redemption, and to restore to the relation between the two books a kind of complementary symmetry. In the world view of the Catholics, the exemplary nature of the Old Testament was overshadowed by the distinction between Christians and, as it were, incipiently deicidal Jews. In the Calvinist mentality, the eventual Messianic chronicle *could only* be comprehended by the history of the Jews, through whom the Almighty had worked his will. (24)

What was this exemplary nature that so appealed to members of the Reformed churches? It is not as though the Old Testament heroes had been neglected. There had been plenty of references to Abraham, Moses, Joshua, David and Solomon, and the Prophets, whether in literature, political texts, or medieval art: witness the many stained-glass windows and sculptures of the biblical heroes in abbeys, cathedrals, and parish churches. But this was in many ways part of the hierarchical tradition, and where it sought to sanctify kingship, it became increasingly a key element in the symbolism of monarchical nations and "crown-centered patriotism." Not a few English kings from Alfred to Henry VIII and Elizabeth sought to model themselves on the kings of ancient Judah; perhaps too they were mindful of their dependence on the divine wrath, as expressed by the prophet Hosea:

> I gave thee a king in mine anger, and took him away in my wrath. (Hosea 13:11)

Sacred kingship was not a significant component of the Old Testament heritage of the Reformed churches, though from time to time they had to seek the protection and leadership of Protestant princes like William of Orange. What really drew them to the Hebrew Bible was the narrative of the Exodus and the revelation at Mount Sinai, together with the journey to the Promised Land and the prophecies of redemption to which it gave rise. In other words, they were drawn to the Jewish Torah and the Prophets, and to the Book of Psalms, all of which attested to the election of the ancient Israelites, their travails in the wilderness, and the promise of redemption in their land. (25)

Now, central to the Torah as expounded in the Pentateuch was the conviction of a special Covenant between God and His people, involving the chosenness of the Jews, that is, God's choice of the Jews and their deliverance from slavery in Egypt through His miracles and outstretched arm. What was of special interest to the Reformers was the conditional type of Covenant, in which God promised Moses on Mount Sinai that, if the children of Israel kept his laws and statutes, they would prosper in the land of Israel, and if they forsook his Law for the idols of their neighbors, they would be punished and expelled from the Promised Land. Here, God's purpose, as we saw in earlier chapters, was to create "a kingdom of priests and an holy nation" (Exodus 19:6); this was to be achieved by separating the children of Israel from their idolatrous neighbors, and forbidding them to have any intercourse with them lest they be tempted to engage in their "abominable" practices, so as to make them walk in the way of righteousness and lovingkindness. (26)

This kind of conditional covenant came to have a particular appeal to the Reformed churches, because it seemed to mirror their lot. As both the Pope and Emperor moved swiftly to condemn, ban, and finally burn Protestant "heresies" and heretics, so the Reformers frequently had to flee and find refuge in autonomous cities like Geneva and Zürich, Emden and Amsterdam. Their plight seemed to echo all too vividly the wanderings and tribulations of the original chosen people. Nor was this just a metaphorical, if comforting, analogy. The idea of Covenant figured prominently in the thinking of Zwingli and his successor, Heinrich Bullinger, in Zürich, while the hope of "election" was, after all, a central concern of all the Reformers. It sprang from their belief that, in view of man's utter sinfulness – the legacy of St. Augustine and his reading of St. Paul's Letter to the Romans – not works but faith in Christ alone could hope, through God's grace, to avert the awful decree of eternal damnation. For Calvin, indeed, God's providence became ever more significant. For, despite the decree of double predestination, whereby human fate had been foreordained from birth or before, there was always the possibility that one might be chosen to be saved by God's grace, and become one of the elect. (27)

Of course, "election" in the Calvinist theology did not possess the same meaning as the biblical concept of "chosenness." But, in time, external pressures, not to mention inner anxieties, brought it closer to the biblical ideal. For one thing, the Reformers, and especially Calvin, saw in the holy scriptures, the Old as well as the New Testament, the whole Word of God. In other words, it was only through close reading of the Word of God, as revealed in the Bible, that the true Christian could understand the world and maintain his or her faith; and that obviously included the sacred history of God's dealings with His chosen people. Calvin himself was drawn to the analogy of ancient Israel as a mixed covenanted nation, one that contained those who had listened to God's word and those who rejected it. By repenting of their sins and living a life of faith and devotion in a community obedient to God's Law as revealed in the Pentateuch, the members of the Reformed churches might hope to find signs of God's favor and even of election. Besides, those who thought themselves to be of the elect would, out of gratitude and love of God, want to perform good works. Thus the life of the Covenant could deter people from the antinomianism that stalked a predestined order, and answer the troubling question of why it was necessary to do good at all. For another thing, what was originally a reformation addressed to the faith of the individual became increasingly also a task of creating reformed communities – churches, conventicles, cities, even nations – the result, as I said, of the persecutions and trials that the Reformers and their churches frequently faced and which seemed to parallel so closely the sufferings and tribulations of the ancient Jews, recorded in the Pentateuch. Hence the increasing interest in collective election, and in the status of an elect nation, even if the latter was only what Calvin termed a "general election," and even if within that nation, only the godly might achieve "a second, more limited degree of election." Yet, here too, there was clear biblical precedent. Had not the prophets of ancient Israel and Judah inveighed against the sins of the people and spoken of the redemption and restoration of only a remnant who would escape God's wrath because they were deemed to be righteous? From this, the Reformers inferred that, while all the people might enter the promised land, only those who strictly kept God's law and submitted to a public code of moral discipline might hope for signs of the more "limited" election. (28)

Covenant and Reform in Scotland and England

This became very much the position of more Calvinist-oriented Reformers in the late sixteenth and seventeenth centuries. For example, the first Covenant in Scotland was formed in late 1557, but it was not until 1559–60 that, under the influence of John Knox, the Reformation succeeded in carrying through a revolution against the government of the absentee Catholic Queen, Mary Stuart, and adopting the Calvinist Confession of Faith and the Book of Discipline. For Knox, in his *History of the Reformation in Scotland* of the 1560s, the Scottish Church was "the purest and best reformed of any Protestant church." On the other hand, he bemoaned the failure of Protestant England and Scotland to unite under a godly prince like King David, using the analogy of the decline of ancient Israel which split into two kingdoms, Israel and Judah. (29)

Yet, it was not till the 1580s and 1590s that a theology of covenant came into its own, with the political writings of Robert Bruce and John Davidson. A more theological and Calvinist version was advanced by the principal of Edinburgh University, Robert Rollock, with his "covenant of works." In these decades, too, a National Covenant was renewed several times, and in the following century it became a standard feature of Scots political life. Thus, in 1638, in response to Charles I's attempts to harmonize religious practice in Scotland and England, the National Covenant was renewed with a very public oath to stand to the defense of the king "in the defence and preservation of the aforesaid true religion, liberties and laws of the kingdom." At the same time, everyone who swore the oath was to behave "as beseemeth Christians who have renewed their covenant with God." (30)

Perhaps the best known of its many renewals was the Solemn League and Covenant, which was part of a treaty concluded with the English Parliament in 1643 during the Civil War, to preserve the reformed religion "according to the Word of God and the examples of the best-reformed Churches." This was to be achieved by extirpating Popery and Prelacy, and preserving peace between Scotland and England, the parties "acknowledging their own shortcomings and professing their desire to amend their lives." By the later seventeenth century, the king had become bound through a double national Covenant, between God and people and king and people, as laid down in the Old Testament. (31)

The process of reform was rather more tortuous south of the border. What had begun as a Tudor matrimonial dispute escalated by the mid-1530s into a full break by the English kingdom from Rome and the assumption by the monarch of supreme governorship of the Church of England. Yet Henry VIII was no Puritan; he had, after all, written a book in defense of the (Catholic) faith. His was an assertion of Royal Supremacy, both political and economic, through enrichment of the crown by the dissolution of the monasteries. In fact, his last years saw an attempt by Henry to steer a more conservative path in the face of growing, if often covert, Protestant sentiment.

It was in the reign of his son, Edward VI, the Protestant-tutored boy-king likened by many to king Josiah, that reformers like Cranmer were able to sweep away many Catholic rituals and substitute their own Reformed vernacular Book of Common Prayer in 1552, though not without mass resistance in parts of England. In this way, England became for a time part of the European Protestant movement, and a haven for Protestant refugees. The return to Catholicism under Mary and her persecutions of what was at the time still a Protestant minority laid the foundations of a sentiment that saw in England a beleaguered Protestant kingdom, summed up in the prayer of an anonymous pamphlet of 1554:

> O lord, defend thy elect people of Inglond from the handes and force of thy enemies the Papistes.

But the despair of the Marian exiles was counterbalanced by a self-confident religious conviction of England's unique identity and mission, to the extent that John Aylmer, future bishop of London, was able in 1559 to enter a marginal exclamation that "God is English." (32)

Of course, this was the year of the Elizabethan Settlement which saw the return of the exiles. Among them was John Foxe who in 1563 published the first edition of his highly influential *Acts and Monuments*, generally known as Foxe's *Book of Martyrs*, a book whose popularity in England was second only to the Bible. Contrary to an earlier interpretation which saw it as a quintessential work of English religious nationalism in which England was portrayed as *the* elect nation, recent historians have pointed to the international character of his apocalyptic record of Protestant martyrdom, as befitted a work of the European movement of Protestant reform. At the same time, Foxe devoted much space to the sufferings of English Protestant martyrs against the background of the Protestant struggle against the papal anti-Christ. For many in England this was the most significant aspect of his work, and in the words of Diarmaid MacCulloch, Foxe's "massive and repeatedly expanded compilation became one of the cornerstones of English Protestant identity, a potent reminder of the militant character of the English Reformation." (33)

By the latter part of Elizabeth's reign, a series of Catholic plots against the queen, and finally the attempted invasion by the Spanish Armada in 1588, created a more favorable environment for the Puritan minority, which in turn became more Calvinist in its orientation and organization. Its leaders continued to nurture the belief that England could become *an* elect nation; thus John Field's *A godly Exhortation* of 1583 tells us that "God hath given himself to us," while Thomas Cartwright's *An Answere unto a letter of Master Harrisons* declares that "The Lord is in covenant to that people to whom he giveth the seals [i.e., sacraments] of his covenant," as "he doth to our assemblies in England." (34)

Despite the suppression of the Puritan leadership in the 1590s, Puritanism continued to grow throughout James I's reign, encouraged by anti-Spanish and anti-Catholic sentiment, especially after the discovery of the Gunpowder plot. By the 1630s, a growing number of the gentry began to identify their English national sentiment with strong Protestant conviction, partly as a result of the attempts by Charles I's government to impose "Arminian" policies, which were seen as a Trojan horse "ready to open up the gates to Romish tyranny and Spanish monarchy." This fusion of religion with English national sentiment became widespread in the 1642 Parliament; subsequently, in the words of Anthony Fletcher, "Civil War was a forcing house of national identity." (35)

What kind of nation did the Puritan godly seek? Theirs was a Commonwealth: after 1649, they rejected any concept of hierarchy. But it was a republic that owed more to the Old Testament than to classical models, and it was based on the power of a militant and victorious God-fearing army, marching into battle with the psalms on their lips. The "Bible" carried by Cromwell's armies consisted of a series of those quotations which bore most on warfare and the spirit of soldiery; and as one might expect, the vast majority of the extracts were drawn from the Old Testament, especially the books of Deuteronomy, Psalms, and Chronicles. Cromwell's New Model Army fought the Lord's battles, in the dual cause of God's England and England's God, to establish the sovereignty and dominion of the Puritan English Commonwealth. As Cromwell exhorted Parliament in 1653:

"Truly you are called by God as Judah was, to rule with Him, and for Him." Cromwell did not distinguish between the interests of Christians and those of the nation; they were "the two greatest concernments that God hath in the world." (36)

John Milton's worldview, for all its internationalism, was also thoroughly imbued with national sentiment and Old Testament imagery and ideals, especially that of a chosen people. In a well-known passage, he dwells on the proximity of England to its God:

> Consider what Nation it is whereof ye are, and whereof ye are the governours; a Nation not slow and dull, but of a quick, ingenious and piercing spirit, this Nation chos'n before any other . . . [When] God is decreeing some new and great period . . . What does he then but reveal Himself . . . as his manner is, first to his English-men? (37)

Of course, Milton's Protestant vision was also European. He saw England leading the Reformation and the movement for civil liberty, as *an* elect nation, a "Nation of prophets, of Sages and of Worthies"; and he returned to the episode in the Book of Numbers when Moses rebuked Joshua for wishing to silence Eldad and Medad for prophesying in the Israelite camp in the wilderness, and exclaimed in quasi-prophetic language:

> For now the time seems come, wherein Moses the great Prophet may sit in heaven rejoicing to see that memorable and glorious wish of his fulfilled, when not only our seventy elders, but all the Lord's people are become Prophets.

Nevertheless, his hopes centered on the great experiment of the Reformed English republic, and the expectation that God would uphold his special people – usually England, but sometimes including the Scots in "Britain." In other words, England, like ancient Israel, was a covenanted nation; and here, Milton and Cromwell spoke for many in the camp of the godly. And for a decade, they were able to impose their Puritan nationalist vision of England on the people, and try to create a new "covenantal nation" on the basis of a long-established elite English national identity, broadening it out through pulpit and print to a larger, if mainly urban, segment of the population. (38)

A New Israel in the Netherlands

England was not the first example of an emergent covenantal nation, nor perhaps the most successful. Certainly, it was rivaled in intensity of expression by the United Provinces in the seventeenth century. Already, in the early heroic phase of the Dutch revolt against the Duke of Alva's Catholic Habsburg armies in the late 1560s and 1570s, the identification of the rebels with ancient Israel was clearly expressed. This can be seen in "beggars' songs" (*Geuzenliederen*) which compared William of Orange to Moses and David, and the king of Spain to Pharaoh. The Dutch people were described as "God's elect" and "God's people," while the Spanish were dubbed the arrogant and cruel "foreign nation." In the official proclamations of prayer and fast days (*biddagsbrieven*) of the 1570s, the God who was invoked was the God of the Old Testament. An example cited by Philip Gorski is William of Orange's proclamation of 1575:

> His Excellency, following in the footsteps of Christian Princes, who, in times of danger and distress have sought refuge in the Almighty God, and together with their people, have humbled themselves before His almighty hand and have repented and turned away from their previous and sinful lives . . . (knowing that) God has never left his people in their moment of need, but has always stood by them and delivered them. (39)

In their plight, the Dutch turned back to the Exodus narrative, as we see in another *biddagsbrief* of 1580 which begged God to

> turn away the horrible plagues, the great destruction and the long-lasting war from these lands . . . and liberate these lands and their good inhabitants from all which leads to their rule and from this accursed and eternal slavery. (40)

Appeals to the Exodus and Mosaic motifs were even more numerous in the following century, and their example was copiously invoked by Dutch preachers, rhetoricians, writers, and artists. Many Dutch Protestants had had to flee the Duke of Alva's persecution and the advance of his armies in the southern parts of the Netherlands, crossing the water barriers to the free republics in the north. Hence the flight of the Israelites across the Red Sea and their deliverance by

God from Pharaoh's armies provided a striking analogy. In 1612, the greatest Dutch dramatist of the period, Joost von Vondel, published his play *Passcha ofte De Verlossinge Israels uit Egypten*, in which he compared William of Orange to Moses:

> O wondrous fate that joins Moses to Orange
> The one fights for the law, the other beats the drum
> And with his own arm, frees the Evangelium
> The one leads the Hebrew through the Red Sea flood
> The other guides his people through a sea . . . of tears and blood. (41)

Several Dutch artists also took up these themes, along with many others from the Old Testament, notably the Patriarchs, David, and Esther and Mordechai. Hendrik Goltzius, Abraham Bloemart, Cornelis van Harlem, Ferdinand Bol, as well as Rembrandt, all portrayed dramatic episodes from Moses' life, including the receiving of the Covenant and the breaking of the tablets. The popularity of the Exodus and wilderness narratives in the Pentateuch was undoubtedly, as Simon Schama points out, a reflection of the parallel which the Dutch perceived between the plight and formation of the ancient Jewish people and their own, as they were molded and separated out as a distinct people by the brutality and fanaticism displayed by Alva and his master, Philip II of Spain, together with the long years of war and adversity. (42)

Biblical themes of Exodus and Covenant are also vividly expressed in the concluding prayer of the Zeelander Adriaan Valerius' *Nederlantsche Gedenck-Clanck* (The Netherlands Anthem of Commemoration) of 1626, part of which reads:

> O Lord when all was ill with us You brought us up into a land wherein we were enriched by trade and commerce and have dealt kindly with us, even as you led the Children of Israel from their Babylonian prison; the waters receded before us and you brought us dry-footed even as the people of yore, with Moses and with Joshua, were brought to their Promised Land. O Lord, you have performed wondrous things for us. And when we have not heeded you, you have punished us with hard but Fatherly force so that your visitations have always been meted out to us as a children's punishment. You have not counted the sins of your people against them but have freed us from the yoke of the Moabites even as it was with Deborah and with Barach whose power went before

> us in the field and that of stout-hearted Gideon who fought against the violence of the Midianites. (43)

Accompanying the text is an engraving of the seven sister-provinces and the princes of Nassau-Orange kneeling in reverence and prayer before the Dutch hat of liberty on a pole beneath a banner inscribed with the biblical holy tetragrammaton in a cloud of glory. By this time, the patriotic equation of "Netherlands–Israel" had become a staple of Dutch politics, and was widely disseminated to the public through prints and cheap pamphlets. By mid-century, the Calvinist party, with the support of the House of Orange, had formulated a covenantal nationalist political programme which included not only freedom from alien domination, but also the unification of society through religious conformity and strong moral discipline, including strict Sabbath observance and sumptuary laws, a free church, and a strong government committed to carrying on the war with Spain and its other enemies in Europe or overseas and to cleansing the republic of its enemies within. (44)

England, Scotland, and the Netherlands were by no means the sole examples of the Reformation feeding a dynamic "covenantal" form of nationalism. We can find other examples among the Ulster-Scots settlement in northern Ireland, in the northern American colonies, and much later, among the Afrikaners after the Great Trek. Of particular importance was that part of the Swiss Confederation that included Zürich, Berne, and Basel, where the idea of the Covenant chimed so well with the Swiss traditions of compacts for mutual defense between cantons going back to the late thirteenth century, and where the Ten Commandments and the Mosaic Law were held in great respect. Nevertheless, both here and in Germany, Poland, and Hungary, the Reformers only succeeded in taking over parts of the linguistic and political society, in some cases only temporarily, while in Bohemia and France they were ultimately defeated and expelled. (45)

Elsewhere, it was the less political Lutheran wing of the "magisterial reformation" that took hold. In Scandinavia, the initiative rested with the kings, Frederick II and Christian III in Denmark and Norway, and Gustavus Vasa in Sweden. As one might expect, this resulted in a stronger assertion of the Royal Supremacy and an absolutist state. But it was matched on the ground by, in Denmark, a rapid acceptance of evangelical Lutheranism, assisted by the translation of the Bible into Danish in 1550, and in Sweden, by a more gradual educational Lutheran movement headed by Olaus Petri and Laurentius Petri, whose religious writings and church ordinances of 1562 and 1571 paved the way for the ratification of Lutheranism as the national religion at a general Church Council in 1593. (46)

Covenanted Nations, Covenantal Nationalism?

By the early seventeenth century, the various processes of the formation of nations were well developed in Northern, Central, and Western Europe. These included self-definitions and recognition of established names of kingdoms and genealogies of their peoples; the cultivation of memories, symbols, myths, and traditions in varying degrees; the growing territorialization of ethnic memories and popular attachments to territorial kingdoms and provinces; the creation of a public elite culture and its rudimentary dissemination to other strata; and the development of shared customs and standardized law-codes across individual kingdoms and provinces. As we saw, these processes had already given rise to a certain degree of national identity and sentiment such that we could begin to speak of hierarchical nations, but it was limited to ruling and intellectual elites.

The sense of national identity was now intensified and extended among a broader elite through the assertion of the Royal Supremacy in states that broke with the Pope and the Catholic dispensation and adopted one of the varied forms of Protestantism. Even in states which took up a less politicized evangelical doctrine and liturgy, the populace at large could hardly fail to be involved and to some extent mobilized, both for and against the doctrinal and liturgical changes, and on behalf of or against particular Protestant kings and princes. Thus, in Denmark, as intimated, large numbers of rural folk as well as townspeople were swept by fervent adherence to the Lutheran ideas and practices emanating from the contiguous North German cities as early as the late 1520s; and it was this movement which helped first Frederick II and then Christian III to break the power of the Catholic nobles and clergy and assert the Royal Supremacy, thereby laying the foundations for the later absolutist state. (47)

In cases like Denmark and to a lesser extent Sweden, the effect of the Reformation was to intensify and expand the hierarchical nation without engendering any large-scale middle-class or popular movement for autonomy, unity, and identity on behalf of a Protestant nation. However, in other cases like Scotland, the Netherlands, northern Switzerland, and Transylvania, the adoption of a more radical Reformist version of Protestantism, whether of the Zwinglian or Calvinist varieties, involved a much greater degree of popular mobilization amounting, in some cases, to a definite movement of Protestant nationalism. This was due to a number of factors: the earlier formation and struggles for national autonomy, the character of the ruling and governmental apparatus, the nature of competing elites, and the place of the kingdom, city-state, or province(s) within the interstate network of rival polities and economies. But perhaps the crucial factor in generating a wider popular Protestant nationalism was the political activism of the Reformist churches, which resulted from both the repression they experienced at the hands of kings and the Roman Church and the inspiration they derived from a return to the Old Testament, with its narratives of the Exodus and the Covenant with ancient Israel.

The biblical history of the ancient Israelites and Jews not only revealed God's dealings with His chosen people, but also provided models of political community – with or without a godly king. As a result, two versions of the covenanted nation emerged in the seventeenth century, one monarchical, the other republican. The first is represented by Scotland and England in the earlier part of the seventeenth century, the second by the seven United Provinces after the Union of Utrecht (1579), but more especially from the truce with Spain from 1609, and by the English Commonwealth of the 1650s. In the first type, the nation was united around the ideal of the double covenant, between God and people and king and people; in the second type, a single covenant bound the community to God in all its assemblies. In fact, there was some overlap between these types, as the Scots example shows. After all, the National Covenant coexisted with, and aimed to underpin, the monarchical covenanted nation, that is, the covenant between king and people; and despite many conflicts, something similar could be found in the Netherlands in respect of the princes of Orange. Both types of covenanted nation, albeit in varying degrees, introduced a popular element into the political community, something that was excluded in the earlier hierarchical type. To be sure, in practice, usually only the wealthier burghers and traders were able to secure entry to the political nation, alongside the nobility, clergy, and gentry; and again in practice, there was little in the way of choice for the covenanted – as there had been none for the children of Israel, after the initial agreement at Sinai. Moreover, again in practice, a tacit ethnic criterion operated: the covenanted belonged to a distinct ethnopolitical community with some sense of at least elite national identity – the desire of the seven northern provinces to recover the southern provinces of the Netherlands owed as much to ethnopolitical history as to religion or the immediate political struggle against the Habsburgs. (48)

Perhaps more important than the social extension of the covenanted nation was the intensity of the bonds that its religious beliefs and practices fostered. So strong were these bonds in some cases that we may truly speak of the impact of a "covenantal nationalism" in this period. I am not simply referring to the creation of commonwealths through pacts and oaths, important though these were. Rather, it is to the sustained and intensive movements for autonomy, unity, and identity that emerged in this period that we must look for the earliest examples of national*ism*. The significance of these movements for our understanding of the cultural traditions and genealogies of nations is twofold: as the very first examples of nationalist movements, and as the channels through which the solidarity of covenanted nations was carried and recharged.

What can we say about the characteristics of "covenantal nationalisms"? We need to remember that, despite sharing a common "core doctrine," nationalist ideologies and movements have been expressed in diverse forms in different historical periods and culture areas. We should not be surprised, then, if covenantal nationalisms were religious not only in form, in the generic sense in which all nationalism is constituted as a secular form of religion, a this-worldly religion of the people, but also in content, in the substantive sense of being imbued with a specific transcendental religion of salvation "from beyond," as the many kinds of Protestantism undoubtedly were. Here God, not the nation, was sovereign in the commonwealth, even if to an increasing extent. He worked through godly churches and elect nations. Moreover, it was the equality, not of citizens, but of believers, that was paramount. However, as we saw with Calvin's doctrine of "general election," it undoubtedly helped that the believers belonged to a single wider historic community – a city-state, a canton, a kingdom, or a republic – and that they could all read the Bible and Prayer Book in a single vernacular language and follow a single native liturgy, and so constitute, like ancient Israel, a single covenanted, albeit mixed, church. This meant that all who belonged to a particular ethnopolitical community were potential members of the elect, but only the godly among them were likely to be saved through the gift of grace. Only they would become the "righteous remnant" of Israel whom God, according to the ancient Prophets, would redeem and restore to the Promised Land. This, too, has its counterpart in later nationalisms: the leaders and cadres of nationalist movements have not infrequently considered themselves (or their idealized peasants) to be purer and more "authentic" than the mass of their ethnic townsfolk who are so often their main constituents.

In terms of social composition, covenantal nationalisms were not unlike their later secular counterparts. Here it is important to recall that nineteenth-century nationalisms were distinctly movements of minorities; outside Paris, the barricades in 1848, the "Spring of the Peoples," were in fact manned only by some hundreds of nationalist insurgents. Compare this to the armies of the zealous and godly in seventeenth-century Scotland, England, and the Netherlands, where the core at least fought for the elect nation out of ideological conviction. Moreover, the contrast that is sometimes drawn between premodern elite national sentiments and movements and modern mass nationalisms does not hold for covenantal nationalisms. While the leadership of the latter was undoubtedly middle class in nature, as in the later secular movements, covenantal nationalisms attracted adherents from all classes, except perhaps the very poor (who are also absent from later nationalisms). Some idea of the composition of Reformist movements can be obtained from Geoffrey Parker's investigation of the social background of convicted "heretics" in the Habsburg provinces of the southern Netherlands in the mid-sixteenth century, which found that as many as 50 percent were of lower-class origins. (49)

The political programmes and goals of covenantal nationalisms were likewise no less clearcut and visible than those of their more secular successors. We saw that these included freedom from external interference and defense of the commonwealth; creating a uniform society of the godly, based on a single code of moral discipline, including such things as sabbath observance and sumptuary laws; restoring a free and true church; cleansing the commonwealth of its enemies within; and encouraging strong government able and willing to prosecute warfare against the ungodly and indeed all those who threatened the commonwealth, economically as well as militarily, including other Protestant realms. In these ways, covenantal nationalists were able to galvanize peoples with the promise of national autonomy, unity, and identity as elect nations covenanted with God. It was exactly this *political* focus of covenantal nationalisms that made the Pentateuchal political model so relevant: the unfettered choice by the Almighty of His people, the new Israel, and their acceptance of Him as their God and themselves as His people by agreeing to obey His law and keep His commandments, as a political community of the faithful and as individual believers. Of course, these political goals were not set out in printed programmes or party manifestoes. They were circulated in tracts and pamphlets, and preached in the pulpit, but were no less potent or widely disseminated for that. In this sense, the programmes of covenantal nationalism represented an early form of popular politics in Europe, at a time when the legitimacy of rulers was coming under increasing scrutiny, and the right to rebel was widely discussed. The "interests of the Nation," in Cromwell's words, were beginning to take precedence over all other considerations except those of divine providence; and between these a growing harmony was increasingly perceived. In other words, we can see in this form of nationalism not only a precursor and harbinger of later secular nationalisms, but also a first stage and model for subsequent movements. For these reasons, not only was the analogy with Israel long-lived, indeed well into the eighteenth century in Protestant states like England, the Netherlands, and Sweden, but also, as we shall see, the covenantal model of ancient Israel, with its ideals of unity, mission, and sacred territory, was transmitted to later nationalist movements across Europe, alongside other cultural traditions. (50)

Meanwhile, these first great outbursts of religious nationalist fervor intensified the sense of national identity and greatly expanded the range of existing national sentiments among the self-designated populations, placing the ideal of the godly nation in the forefront of political perceptions and actions. And, even if the commonwealths which they brought into being foundered or disappeared after a short time, the sense of national election, the ideal of unity, and the attachment to territory which these movements had fostered had lasting effects for the chosen people they were designed to enhance, helping to endow them with a national self-confidence and a spirit of enterprise and innovation.

6

Republican Nations

In the afternoon of July 14, 1790, on the Champs de Mars in Paris, before a crowd of four hundred thousand, fifty thousand National Guards, the representatives of the Paris Commune, the delegates of the departments, and the members of the National Assembly, Talleyrand began the ceremony of Mass and benediction at the "Altar of the Fatherland." Raising his arms over the banners, he told his congregation, "Sing and weep tears of joy, for on this day France has been made anew." Then Lafayette, mounted on a white charger, rode through the ranks of the Guardsmen and asked permission of the king "to administer the oath to the assembled *fédérés*." The oath was relayed all across the field, and it was met by "a thunderous chorus of '*Je le jure*,'" followed by a volley of cannon. Then Louis XVI, using his new title of "King of the French," swore to "employ all the power delegated to me by the constitution to uphold the decrees of the National Assembly." (1)

Oath-Swearing in Western Europe

This was not the first time, Schama points out, that such an oath had been sworn. Already on February 4 that year, Louis had sworn to "defend and maintain constitutional liberty, whose principles the general will, in accord with my own, has sanctioned." Even earlier, in the preceding autumn, Lafayette, who had helped form the National Guards, had presided over similar oath-swearing ceremonies. One might even say that oaths were the immediate catalyst of revolutions. On June 21, 1789, shut out of the Estates General's regular meeting place in

Versailles due to its reconstruction, the Deputies of the Third Estate had turned aside to a nearby Tennis Court and sworn an oath "to God and the *Patrie* never to be separated until we have formed a solid and equitable Constitution as our constituents have asked us to." At this, the six hundred Deputies, as one body, stretched out their right arms taut, to swear the oath, in conscious imitation of the manner in which the Roman Horatii brothers had sworn on the sword held aloft by their father to conquer or die for their fatherland – a scene which was not in Livy's original story, but was invented by Jacques-Louis David for his celebrated painting of five years earlier, *The Oath of the Horatii.* It was this same Oath of the Tennis Court that David was later commissioned to paint, though he only managed to leave a record in a great unfinished cartoon a few years later. (2)

David's Roman model was only one of a line of such oaths. It had been preceded by a powerful rendering of the *Oath of the Rütli* painted in 1779–81 for Zürich's Town Hall. Here, in three Herculean figures, Heinrich Füssli has portrayed the first oath of Alliance of the Swiss *Eidgenossenschaft* in 1291. In his striking image, Füssli has the representatives of the three original forest cantons, Uri, Schwyz, and Unterwalden, swear an oath of liberty on a sword held aloft on the meadow of the Rütli beside the lake of Lucerne, across which they had rowed, as shown in Füssli's drawings. As we know from other sources, the representatives swore to form an Everlasting Alliance to resist Habsburg tyranny and restore their former rights by liberating their valleys of unjust judges and unfair taxes. In this image, the oath of defiance is sworn by three determined and muscular figures with outstretched arms, in the mannerist style adopted by Michelangelo whom Füssli had so admired during his long sojourn in Rome.

Yet, as Robert Rosenblum first demonstrated, this was but one of a series of "neo-classical" depictions of oath-swearing, going back through Antoine Beaufort's *Oath of Brutus* of 1771 to Gavin Hamilton's *Oath of Brutus* of 1764, probably the earliest of the series. In the latter, a vast, theatrical canvas, Brutus, who would later become the first consul of the Roman Republic, swears with his friends to avenge the suicide of Lucretia by driving out of the city the tyrant Tarquin, who had raped her. Lucretia herself is shown prominently on the left side of the painting, expiring after stabbing herself; to the right, the three friends swear the oath on Brutus' sword. The subject had been one treated by artists since the Renaissance. But, where before the main interest, both literary and artistic, had centered on the nobility of Lucretia's sacrifice, it now shifted to the political consequences of her act. This introduced the relatively novel theme of collective liberation from tyranny and accorded a central role to the ceremony of oath-swearing – a fact emphasized by the sheer scale of the canvas and the great size of Hamilton's protagonists, as well as their proximity to the spectator's space. (3)

What did this newfound passion for oaths and solemn swearing ceremonies signify? Could it not be said to embody the covenantal relationship discussed in the last chapter – in other words, a secularized version of what was originally a religious act? Oath-swearings and covenants were, after all, decidedly public institutions, and both served to bind together a large body of people, in a solemn act of sanctification witnessed by all. In the original covenant at Sinai, the people of Israel, on receiving the Ten Commandments from God through Moses, affirmed: "All the words which the Lord hath said will we do" (Exodus 24:3). Similarly, the king and the people during the French Revolution agreed to obey the laws and defend the liberty of the nation and the fatherland, subordinating their private interests to the general will.

But this is only part of the story. Certainly, the form of the oath ceremonies, at least in the early years of the Revolution, was religious in character, and it evoked reverence, if not awe. But the ceremony's content was no longer primarily religious, much less specifically Christian, and it was to become even less so as the Revolution proceeded and began to affect other parts of Europe. No longer God's will, but the law of the nation, no more a covenanted people, but autonomous and equal citizens, not the quest for holiness, but ideals of liberty and fraternity, had now become the lodestars of the Revolution's oaths, guiding the nation towards national regeneration and a new secular era. From these new ideals and realities flowed the destruction of all hierarchical forms and persons, the bitter anticlericalism of the later Revolution, the vivid displays of popular unity on the great *fêtes*, the orgy of violence against all who resisted, notably in the Vendée, and the missionary fervor which sought to bring to other peoples the blessings of patriotism and the Revolution. (4)

The Lineage of Patriotism

At the heart of this new ideology lay the Enlightenment conviction of the directive power of human reason and the ability of humanity to fashion society in accordance with its precepts. For Elie Kedourie, the key figure in the intellectual evolution of a secular, revolutionary nationalism was Immanuel Kant, who taught that human morality, not God's will, was the only valid source of political action, and that the good will is the free and autonomous will, free, that is, of the laws of God and Nature. Despite the example of political activism provided by the French Revolution, it was German intellectuals like Kant and Herder and their Romantic followers, Fichte, Schleiermacher, Schlegel, Arndt, Schlegel, Muller, and Jahn, who provided the systematic groundwork of a theory of national politics. In this theory, state and nation are fused in a satisfying whole and the individual only finds true freedom by being absorbed in a nation-state which embodies the Will of the culturally and linguistically purified people. It is this subjective Will that ultimately undermines the edifice of systematic enlightened reason, and determines for itself its life and destiny. (5)

Such an intellectual lineage would place the birth of nationalism in the German-speaking states after the defeat of Prussia at Jena in 1806. Its arrival was signaled by Fichte's *Addresses to the German Nation* of 1807–8, which for Kedourie represented the first fully elaborated text of a genuine and unadulterated nationalist doctrine. Yet, some thirty-five years earlier, a similar consuming ardor for the fatherland had been evinced by the Genevan Jean-Jacques Rousseau in his advice to the Poles following the first Partition of their country, entitled *Considérations sur le Gouvernement de Pologne*. Here, Rousseau anticipated Fichte's fervent belief in the molding power of secular national education to shape the character of the young: "It is education that must give souls a national formation, and direct their opinions and tastes in such a way that they will be patriotic by inclination, by passion, by necessity." Speaking of the love of the *patrie*, Rousseau brings together the characteristic themes and sentiments of the neo-classical revolution:

> This love is his whole existence; he sees nothing but the fatherland, he lives for it alone; when he is solitary, he is nothing; when he has ceased to have a fatherland, he no longer exists; and if he is not dead, he is worse than dead. National education is proper only to free men; it is they only who enjoy a collective existence and are truly bound by law. (6)

Freedom, law, equality, national education, citizenship, love of the *patrie*: these are the motifs that recur throughout the Revolution and indeed all the revolutions of the period; and all of them lead into the vision of fraternity, the male bonding of brothers animated by the same love and united by the same ideals, at once kinsmen and friends, like the Horatii. It was a vision inspired by a reading of classical antiquity, notably of Sparta and Republican Rome, that owed more to Plutarch than to Thucydides, and to Livy rather than Tacitus. In this idealized image of the ancient world, heroic deeds and a stern morality of frugality, chastity, and self-sacrifice provided *exempla virtutis* for societies whose middle classes felt increasing distaste for an enfeebled and arbitrary *ancien régime* devoted to the pleasures and trifles of the few in their secluded courts and palaces. An even greater revulsion was felt for the fanaticism and superstition, as they saw it, of a Church which, only a few generations ago, had sanctioned the most brutal, indeed bloody, of massacres in the Wars of Religion. Against court and Church, against all forms of hierarchy, the "neo-classical" revolution of the middle classes, forgetting the many historical divisions and conflicts of Rome, Athens, and the other ancient *poleis*, proclaimed the ideals and emulated the model of the ancient city-state with its compact citizen body, clear territorial limits, devotion to the law, and fervent patriotism. Here was a form of political solidarity that reason could sanction and morality inspire; and that solidarity could, in turn, through civic education and a public culture, create free and equal men, devoted to the *patrie* and its laws, participating in the commonwealth and acting in unison for the good of all. Was this not the purpose of all those patriotic rites and ceremonies that David choreographed for the Jacobins at the height of the Revolution, to the music of Gossec and the poetry of Chenier, culminating in the oath of citizenship sworn at the altar of the *patrie* and, above all, in Robespierre's Festival of the Supreme Being in June 1794? (7)

Though the legacy of classical antiquity was one that was recovered by eighteenth-century European intellectuals, as they openly averred, it was not without precedent. After all, as we have seen, by 1100 the forms of Roman political institutions had been revived, and adapted, by many of the Italian city-states, themselves often established on older Roman settlements or cities. By the early fifteenth century, the humanist intellectuals and statesmen of Florence had sought to recover and adapt the *virtù* of Roman patriotism as well as a secular and practical conception of history, and the republican model and ideals of Rome continued to attract powerful support, even when the republic itself had given way to the *signoria* of the Medici, much as it had in most other Italian city-states, except Venice. (8)

Italy was not alone in reviving the republican ethos. Echoes of Roman patriotism, or of its idealized image, could be heard in Swiss cantons, German cities, and Dutch provinces. Certainly, oath-swearing became integral to the formation of the Swiss *Eidgenossenschaft*. After the Swiss victories over the Habsburg armies at Sempach in 1386 and Näfels in 1388, the Confederation attracted the powerful city-states of Lucerne, Berne, and Zürich, and later Geneva, into its fold; and as it expanded, new, more inclusive oaths like the *Pfaffenbrief* (Priests' Charter) of 1370 and the *Sempacherbrief* (Charter of Sempach) of 1393 were sworn for mutual defense against Habsburg encroachments, and by the sixteenth century for the well-being of Helvetia. This tradition had its effects on both the Swiss chroniclers like Aegidius Tschudi and the Swiss Reformation, where humanist politicians and scholars like Johannes Stumpf and Heinrich Bullinger "endeavoured to define the Swiss Confederation as a separate cultural and political community within the *Reich*." Moreover, oaths and pacts tied in well with the ideal of the Covenant, to which the Swiss Reformers, as we saw, were particularly partial. The Dutch provinces also embraced "Roman" traditions. Though less dynamic and potent than the covenantal tradition, the myth of the ancient Batavian republic and the popular resistance and conspiracy of Claudius Civilis against Rome was influential for a time among some Dutch intellectuals and artists, and chimed well with the use of the term "nation" for the Dutch and with the spirit of the Dutch war of independence, symbolizing a nascent patriotic consciousness and sense of separate national identity. (9)

Nevertheless, when the French intellectuals and professionals looked back in order to recover and adapt to their own ends the tradition of civic republicanism, they found it necessary to go back to its sources in classical antiquity and reforge them anew. Rediscovery and adaptation of traditions are perhaps the least potent of the ways in which the past is related to the present, and for this very reason the process of recovery is often strenuous, emphatic, and shrill. Perhaps, too, because the republican and civic legacy of classical antiquity was not "carried" by a single powerful and enduring institution like the Church, but was revived fitfully by cities, city-states, and cantons seeking legitimacy and meaning in what was at the time known and retailed of ancient Greece and Rome, the republican and civic tradition did not re-emerge fully until the late seventeenth and eighteenth centuries. More important, its revival was long delayed by the fact that religious dogma and hierarchical rule combined to exclude what were perceived as secular traditions and institutions. It was only when the modern, professional, and scientific state had begun to be freed from the dominance of personal rule and hierarchical forms that a secularizing tradition like civic republicanism could begin to emerge. Even then, the first examples of republican political forms outside the city-states, in the Netherlands and in the England of the Commonwealth, were born into and through religious institutions and Puritan zeal in covenanted nations. But it was not until traditional forms of religion had begun to diminish in their appeal and hold that a new national republicanism could begin to flourish. In this respect, eighteenth-century England stands out as the most "advanced" secular state; even the public sermons of senior clergy attest to the decline of biblical ideas of nationhood and the model of ancient Israel after mid-century, and the rise of secular, classical, and patriotic conceptions. (10)

The idea that a secular republican nationalism can emerge only when *public* religious sentiments and ideals have declined is one of the central themes of David Bell's analysis of the "cult of the nation" in eighteenth-century France. Terms like *nation* and *patrie*, he argues, gained currency in eighteenth-century France, because of fundamental transformations in the ways in which Frenchmen began to think of their relationships both to God and to the material world. It was not that they ceased to believe in God, even if church attendance did diminish to some extent; rather, God became increasingly distant, leaving the world to itself, or rather to a humanity now enabled and ready to reconstruct it according to human needs and interests. As a result, traditional religion became increasingly privatized. In other words, the vacated space was occupied by new concepts of society, civilization, and nation, and new ways of thinking about and organizing the physical and political world, freed of religious determinations, at least among the elites. As an early example of the new concepts and methods, Bell gives us Rousseau's account of the work of the ancient lawgivers, Lycurgus, Numa Pompilius, and Moses. In the latter case, not only does Rousseau subvert the sacred history of the Jews and replace it with a secular, political history, he also proposes one of the first instances of the idea of social construction, in this case, of "nation-building," with Moses praised because he formed and executed "the astonishing enterprise of shaping into a national Body a swarm of unhappy fugitives . . . Moses dared turn this wandering and servile band into a political Body, a free people." (11)

There was another more specific reason in the French context for the increasing privatization of religion among the elites, namely, the painful memory of the horrific massacres of the Wars of Religion between Catholics and Protestants in late sixteenth-century France. These memories were still fresh in the eighteenth century, and among professionals and intellectuals especially, they caused a growing revulsion against religious fanaticism. Already in the sixteenth century, appeals to the shared *patrie* and to the common interest of all Frenchmen were often heard, but to little avail. These appeals had been supplanted after 1600 by a new emphasis on dynasty and the monarchical state. But, given the dubious role played by the state in the Wars of Religion, and its visible decline through the eighteenth century, men and women turned increasingly to the neutral, and, according to Bell, more hopeful, concepts of nation, society, civilization, public, and *patrie* through which to understand and rebuild France. (12)

For all that, Enlightenment secularism was only one of the factors that brought the concept of the nation to the fore. Despite the intellectuals' antagonism to the *ancien régime*, the effects of growing state power and centralization for the idea of a national community cannot be gainsaid. Though several regions retained their separate cultural identities, the cultural and political dominance of Paris was daily more apparent. So was the sense of France as a single territorial community. One sees this in the eighteenth-century maps of France, and such paintings as Claude-Joseph Vernet's early romantic series of seaport views. This sense of growing identity was reinforced by the rivalry with Britain, especially during the Seven Years' War and the American War of Independence, which France helped to subsidize. Not least was the palpable need among the elites to recover the country's leadership, political and cultural, which it had possessed in the preceding *Grand Siècle* and which was felt to be ebbing away under an effete and arbitrary regime.

Finally, we should not overlook the importance of the republican models and covenantal ethos offered by the Dutch Republic and, albeit briefly, by the English Commonwealth, and later, by its Glorious Revolution. This is not just a question of the influence exerted by England and its liberties, in particular over individual French intellectuals. It was also a matter of the new style of politics introduced by covenantal nationalism, the idea that a body of men could enter into a compact with God and king of their own free will, and dispense with intermediate bodies; and that this body in its assemblies could make and unmake laws, and express the general will of the political community within a given territory. Here lay a powerful new impetus to the formation of an autonomous and unified French nation, answerable only to its members. From this, we can see that the concept of the civic-republican nation grew, not only out of the tradition of classical patriotism from ancient Greece and Rome to medieval Italy and the northern free communes and cantons, but also from the preceding historical form of the national community, which was based more on biblical than on classical beliefs and narratives, even if in later stages those same beliefs were to be denied and, in some cases, jettisoned.

Republican Nationalism

Of course, these developments – state centralization, privatization of religion, and the influence of the covenantal type of nation – did not flourish or come together immediately. As a result, it was only in the later eighteenth century that we can begin to discern the beginnings of an ideology of the civic-republican nation *per se*. But it is a type of nationalist ideology that, given the centrality of the French and American Revolutions for Western history, has provided the benchmark for all subsequent forms of nationalist ideologies, even those that set themselves up in conscious opposition both to the West and to its varieties of nationalism.

The ideology in question is republican in form and civic in content. It emerged from the specific social and cultural milieu of late eighteenth-century England and France, as the leading powers and cultural models of the period. Basically, as we saw in chapter 1, the ideology posits a civic-territorial model, in which the nation is regarded as a territorially bounded and compact community, with a single code of laws and uniform legal institutions, mass participation in political life, a mass public culture, collective autonomy and statehood, membership in an international comity of nations, and with the ideology of nationalism as its legitimation, if not its creative inspiration. This is a conception that reflects not only the Enlightenment vision of rational optimism but also its idealized image of classical patriotism and exemplary virtue. It is also an ideal that seeks political community and solidarity through the active participation of citizens, obedience to the laws, and the cultivation of civic virtue – something that requires the dissemination of a distinctive public culture, which in turn can best be achieved through mass public standardized education and the emulation of past heroic *exempla*. Hence citizenship, law, and secular education have become the hallmarks of the nation seen as a political community of patriots. (13)

Civic patriotism is sometimes held to be quite other than and even opposed to nationalism. From very different traditions and starting-points, Maurizio Viroli and Walker Connor argue that the term patriotism should only be applied to sentiments and loyalties that take as their object the state or *respublica* and its territory, whereas nationalism's object of devotion is the nation as an ethnocultural community. In contrast, patriotism is part of the tradition of the city-state from antiquity to Rousseau's Geneva, and it is not to be confused with the ethnic nationalism of the Romantics and their followers. For example, the eighteenth century witnessed the proliferation of all kinds of "patriotic societies" for the improvement of morals, health, agriculture, and the like. These fraternal middle-class associations for specific collective ends were, it is sometimes argued, quite different in form and content from later nationalist societies whose aims were largely philological, historical, and folkloristic, though in several cases there was some overlap. Thus, in Denmark, the many patriotic societies that sprang up in the course of the eighteenth century were devoted to national "improvement" in such practical realms as agriculture, health, and commerce, as opposed to the nineteenth-century nationalist movement that aimed to regenerate the nation's cultural and social fabric; though one might equally argue that this represented but a first stage in the development of a sense of national identity, even if it was to take a later historicist movement of national*ism* to bring this process to fruition. (14)

There is, undoubtedly, an important and useful distinction to be made between the concepts of state and nation. As we saw at the outset, the concept of state refers to a set of autonomous institutions in a given territory, while the nation denotes a type of cultural and historical community. It is also true that for centuries, the term "patriotism" has referred to an attachment to either one's birthplace – be it district, region, or land – or to one's city-state, as in medieval Italy; and, more recently, it has come to denote loyalty to the territorial state as such. On the other hand, in these latter cases, the state and its political community may become coextensive with the cultural community of the nation, and in practice it is difficult to distinguish the two kinds of loyalty, with many members, mainly of the dominant *ethnie*, having little regard to the analytic distinction between a state and its political community and the nation as an ethnocultural community. This was very much the case in France, where over time the state and the nation, as well as the political community and the ethnocultural community, coalesced to become two sides of the same coin – though this was increasingly at the cost of the smaller ethnic communities and nations like the Bretons and Alsatians within *la grande nation* of France, or of the Catalans and Basques in Spain. (15)

The distinction becomes even more confused by the tendency not just to distinguish but to oppose an "ethnic" to a "civic" conception of the nation. In the former, the nation is viewed as an extended kinship group, bound by genealogical ties and sharing a common ancestral culture. In the latter, the nation is regarded as a political community of citizens who live under the same government and laws in a given territory, and share common values and ideals – the kind of definition given in the *Encyclopédie*. France is often regarded as the prototype of the civic nation as a political community. But, in fact, in France the two kinds of collective attachment, the political and the cultural-historical, were combined, and by the eighteenth century were directed against the aristocratic and monarchical state; and myths of Gallic ancestry helped to ground the *patrie* in a single ethnic nation. Moreover, the growing drive for cultural homogenization and the new emphasis on Parisian-French linguistic uniformity during the Revolution, designed to undermine regional dialects and customs, anchored the civic *patrie* and built the French nation on the foundations of a single, politically unified *ethnie*. That there was a degree of cultural and social engineering involved did not detract from this unique fusion of civic-republican and ethnonational identities and communities. (16)

Even the distinction between city-state patriotism and ethnocultural nationalism drawn by Viroli is not as clearcut as he suggests. As we saw in chapter 4, Venice and Florence were often regarded, both within and outside Italy, as nations; even ancient Athens, as Edwin Cohen argued, was thought by Aristotle to constitute a nation on account of its size and scale, as well as its myths of origin. Partly this has to do with a factor that features in Viroli's account: the strong emphasis on history and on heroic forebears, and their sacrifice, in the self-images of the citizens of city-states. This is also a familiar feature of most nationalisms, and it is a prominent characteristic of Ernest Renan's classic definition of the nation. (17)

In a republican nationalism, then, the political and the cultural nation are fused in the service of a territorial community of citizens obeying the same laws and sharing the same values and ideals of virtue and love of the *patrie*. In the worldview of republican nationalists, the earth is divided into nations, each with its own character, history, and destiny, each dwelling in its historic homeland and striving for unity and full autonomy as a political community of equal citizens. The nation and its laws constitute the sole source of political power, and there is no existence outside of the nation. True freedom can only be achieved through belonging to and participation in the life of the nation and through a secular education which will inculcate a fervent love of the fatherland, its history, symbols, values, and ideals. The will of the nation is the highest court of appeal and the fount of all goodness. This means that the form of its government, if it is to embody and express the sovereignty of the people, of the whole community of citizens, must be republican and ultimately democratic.

A Secular Religion?

Republican nationalism offered, then, a purely secular account of citizenship and political solidarity. Its insistence on grounding the community of the nation in human interests and needs alone, as opposed to divine law or the laws of nature, underpinned its civic and republican ideals. Perhaps even more important, it affirmed the necessity of revolution through collective autoemancipation and the capacity of human beings everywhere to organize a rational and more perfect type of society. From these premises, it followed that the members of each and every society could and should reconstitute it on the basis of the novel secular principles of liberty, popular sovereignty, and patriotism. In practice, this meant that all peoples could and should overthrow their tyrants and *anciens régimes*, sweep away ignorance and clerical superstition, educate their youth in the virtues of fraternity and patriotism, galvanize their citizens into active political participation, and imbue them with the desire to renew their community and defend it against external foes and enemies within.

Here, then, was an ideology of the nation in action, if not at arms, one founded, as I said, on purely secular principles of human rationality, will, and solidarity. Yet, though the doctrine might be secular, the practice of this ideology bore a close resemblance to the religions it was supposed to supplant. It was not simply that these secular principles evoked a "religious" devotion and awe, or that in the early days, as we have seen, a secular ideology was decked out in borrowed religious garb. It went much deeper than that. In seeking to replace traditional Christianity as the basis of community, republican nationalists embraced a deity every bit as exclusive and demanding as the God whom they sought to dethrone. In turning the nation itself into the sole object of worship and veneration, republican nationalism created a new secular religion, based on the sacred communion of the people and replete with its own symbols of honor and devotion – emblems, flags, coins, calendars, anthems, parades, oaths, lawcodes, ceremonies of remembrance and celebration, national academies, national museums and libraries, and all the paraphernalia of institutions and classifications that united the citizens and separated them from outsiders. As the Petition of Agitators put it in 1792: "The nation is the sole divinity whom it is permitted to worship." (18)

Undergirding this religion of secular collective action were certain fundamental assumptions about the type of community that could act as the object of its labors. First of all, following Rousseau's dictum that every people must have a distinctive character, it was assumed that the sovereignty of the people could only be predicated of *a* people, that is, a particular and distinctive human community, one of the primary divisions of humanity. Of course, every people had to assume sovereignty and become the sole source of law and citizenship, but a people was formed into a separate historic division of humanity by the cultivation of peculiar customs, mores, and habits, and by the heroic self-sacrifice of successive generations of its members. Together, these expressed the "genius" of a people, an idea that went back at least to Lord Shaftesbury and Bolingbroke, and was developed by Montesquieu as the spirit (*esprit*) of the nation. The missionary spirit of the French *patriotes* after 1792, while it insisted on replicating the form of its revolution with its concepts of popular sovereignty and citizenship in the lands and among the peoples the revolutionary armies occupied, nevertheless accepted the differences between peoples and nations, and their distinctive characters, mores, customs, and histories. All they desired was to endow these "subject peoples" with the liberty and sovereignty that had been denied them by kings, priests, and nobles. (19)

The distinctive character of peoples and nations was reinforced by differences in their languages and cultures. The emphasis on language is not just a product of German Romanticism, despite the influence of Herder in Eastern Europe and the Balkans. Ever since the first translations of the Bible, augmented in the sixteenth century by mass print circulation, language had become a political issue, if only indirectly at first. Certainly, by the seventeenth century, vernacular Bibles and prayer books served to impress and seal the distinctive characters of nations, notably in Protestant states. The change to the vernacular in religious texts was supplemented by the rise of a more secular literary canon of indigenous poets, dramatists, historians, and philosophers. The growth of a native literature, and a public able to consume its products, was part of a wider appreciation of the distinctive national traditions, artifacts, memories, values, and institutions, in short, the particular culture, of each nation. Language had already surfaced as a factor in the divided northern provinces of the Netherlands, with its distinction between eastern and western Dutch, but it posed a particular problem for the Jacobins who sought to create a united France out of the medley of its provinces – *la République une et indivisible* within its "natural borders." Hence the report on the dialects of France by the Abbé Grégoire, dialects that had to be eradicated because they upheld the local customs, mores, and institutions of France's various provinces, and thereby prevented the linguistic and cultural unification of the republic. In other words, given the assumption of a world of separate nations and national states, it quickly became apparent that national unity in a republic was dependent on cultural unification and linguistic homogenization. (20)

That republican nationalism increasingly sought to preclude the presence of "nations within nations" was vividly illustrated by the revolutionary and Napoleonic treatment of the Jews in France. The Jews were seen as a foreign, and debased, ethnic community; so, if they were to be accorded the privileges and benefits of French "civilization," it was clear that they would have to be emancipated not just from their traditional disabilities, but from their "narrow" and restrictive ethnic identity. To become citizens of the republic, the Jews would have to sever their "religion" from their "ethnic identity" with which it had always been bound up, as the religion of the children of Israel (or Jacob), and henceforth practice it solely as individuals in the private domain. They would have to exchange their largely autonomous, if unequal and disadvantaged, existence as a separate Jewish community for public equality as *individuals* and citizens within the French national state, and thereby become French nationals of the "Israelite" persuasion. Moreover, the history that they, and after them many a colonial people, would have to learn and embrace was not the sacred history of their people from Abraham to Rashi and Maimonides, but French history from Vercingetorix – or perhaps Clovis – to Napoleon. In time, it was hoped, their grandchildren would even identify themselves as descendants of the Gauls, exchanging their traditional ethnic identity for the new secular national identity. More recent conflicts in respect of Muslim immigrants only serve to confirm not just the overt French commitment to secularism, but also the implicit ethnocultural basis of its civic-republican nationalism. (21)

This suggests that republican nationalism, at least at its inception, assumed not just a cultural unity but an ethnic basis for the nation that it sought to liberate from tyranny and superstition. This was as true in the American as in the French case: blacks, slave or free, were assumed to constitute a separate ethnic, in this case racial, category, and it took centuries of conflict and protest to accept them as full Americans. Besides, even among the whites, the Anglo-Saxon ethnic basis and domination of the emerging American nation were widely accepted. These examples reveal the importance of the ethnic element in republican nationalism, thereby undermining the fashionable polarity of (though not the distinction between) "civic" and "ethnic" nationalisms. (22)

Two further features of republican nationalism illuminate its character as an "inner-worldly" or "secular religion." The first is the devotion of its adherents to the homeland as a historic territory, the land of "our ancestors" and our birth. As we saw, homeland sentiments have a long history, going back to the ancient Egyptian *Tale of Sinuhe*, the Psalms, especially Psalm 137, and the paeans to Hellas' beauty of the choruses in the tragedies of Sophocles and Euripides. Recognition of the distinctive features of urban and rural landscapes appears again in the Italian Renaissance, and above all in Flemish and Dutch paintings, where it begins to assume a national character. In eighteenth-century

British, French, and Swiss painting and poetry, too, the national character of their respective landscapes begins to be emphasized, for example, by Haller in his Alpine poetry and by English poets like Gray and Thomson, and the early British watercolorists – Cozens, Girtin, and Sandby. Romanticism undoubtedly made such attitudes and sentiments popular and widespread at the turn of the century, sharpening the national focus and idealizing the peasantry and their rural way of life. (23)

Nevertheless, the accompanying drive for national unity also contributed to the cult of the homeland. On the one hand, it tended to bring together within the republic often disparate regions, through both the administration of officials and the participation of the members of all the provinces in the army, the schools, the public festivals, and the politics of the center. On the other hand, it established the symbolism of, for example, *la France* and its concepts of the "natural frontiers" of the nation, thereby recognizing the political significance of mountains, rivers, coasts, and the like in determining the boundaries and the very nature of the nation. Given the fluidity of such conceptions, not to mention the ever-changing political circumstances, it is hardly surprising that the drive for national unity introduced further pretexts, and catalysts, for border conflicts and wars, as in the case of Alsace-Lorraine or Trieste and Fiume. Nevertheless, the ready acceptance of such conflicts by so many people attests to the almost sacred quality of the nationalist conception of the homeland and its frontiers – a theme introduced by republican nationalists committed to sensible and rational ideas of the national community and its place in a world of homologous nations. (24)

The sacred quality of the homeland was particularly evident in its association with the heroism of the fallen: *la terre et les morts.* Though themes of communal sacrifice are not altogether new, until the Reformation, heroic sacrifice was seen largely in terms of individual crusading kings and knights, or of martyred saints, with cases of communal sacrifice in Scotland, Switzerland, and Spain constituting the exception. Ideas of love of and sacrifice for the *patrie* began to creep into French poetry and prose in the fifteenth century, and were taken up in England and the Netherlands, particularly in the latter's seventeenth-century cult of William the Silent. By the eighteenth century, the cult of heroic emulation began to link the national community to the canon of great men, notably medieval warriors and patriots like Du Guesclin, Bayard, Tell, and Alfred, which it supplemented with contemporary heroes like General Wolfe. But it was republican nationalism that was to develop this interpretation and greatly extend its popular significance. From mid-century, French philosophers, publicists, and critics called on leaders and people alike to emulate the courage and patriotism of ancient heroes like Leonidas, Socrates, Scaevola, and Scipio, and cited above all their acts of civic virtue and self-sacrifice. The Revolution added its quota of contemporary martyrs – men like Le Peletier and Marat – and developed quasi-religious ceremonies, symbols, and cults in their honor, which the *patriotes* used to inculcate in the populace the austere morality required of citizens in the reborn national community. The cult of the war experience and of national sacrifice, both of individuals and of masses, became the lifeblood of the republican nation, through which particular communities and their civil religions could be continually reinvigorated, turning defeat and setback into victory and triumph. (25)

The cult of the Glorious Dead was not, of course, confined to republics or civic nationalisms. In the wake of the carnage of the Great War, many Britons felt the need for a permanent memorial to the fallen, and they ensured that the Cenotaph designed by Lutyens and erected for the parade of 1919 would remain as an everlasting tribute to the memory of the fallen. In this way, through the annual ceremony of Remembrance Day, the popular character of the nations of Britain would find symbolic significance and reverent expression. Yet, in this respect, Britain followed where France and others had led, after the later democratization of its erstwhile hierarchical and covenantal nation. It was the civic-republican variety of nationalism that had helped to create the symbols and ceremonies of commemoration for the fallen patriots of a republican nation, and it pioneered the expression of its popular and secular character, thereby creating a new form of "inner-worldly" religion suited to the sacred community of citizens, one that was capable of being exported to other would-be republican nations. (26)

Popular Election, Secular Mission

Republican nationalism presents something of a paradox. On the one hand, the content of its doctrine is radically secular. The stress is on the needs of citizens, obedience to the law, and the cultivation of virtue and patriotism. On the other hand, the practice of its ideology is fervently religious. Its type of public culture, its devotion to the homeland, and its cult of the fallen present an image of sacred communion enacted by its citizens in public rites and ceremonies, as well as through laws, customs, symbols, and institutions. Similarly, for republican nationalism, the "nation" (as opposed to "its" state) is seen as a secular community with distinctive mores and customs, vernacular language and culture, an ancestral homeland, and a history and public ritual of heroic self-sacrifice. But these very attributes also help to turn it into a religious category, a sacred communion of the people, and hence an object of religious devotion and public worship.

This shift was powerfully encouraged by the long and influential tradition of ethnic election. We saw that already in the seventeenth century, radical Protestantism had transferred the quality of chosenness from the monarch and his kingdom to the community of the faithful and the elect nation. Now, the ideal of popular sovereignty became fused with that of ethnic election: the republican nation consisted of all its members, irrespective of rank or wealth, and as a result republican nationalism sought the elevation of both the ordinary people or "common folk" and a particular people, a distinctive sacred community – a dual character well illustrated by Grundtvig's conception of the folk character of the Danish people in the nineteenth century, or the Slavophile ideal of the sacred communion of the Russian people. This also helps to account for the self-reflexive character of republican nationalism, its insistence on collective self-worship as an exclusive, and often superior, community assured of its unique character and qualities. (27)

The exemplary character of the republican nation was revealed and reinforced by its unique role and mission, which usually complemented its myth-memories of golden ages. Its mission might be to shine as a beacon of civilization or a repository of culture, to constitute an example of military prowess or provide a model of social integration or industrial progress. Whatever its field of distinction, each nation could justify, at least in its own eyes, its special place in the moral framework of the planet through a myth of its unique character and role in history, like the French revolutionary myth of a nation of liberty and fraternity bringing to others the blessings of a new order. Even more important, its members could find comfort and pride in the peculiar mission of the nation, and be assured of its collective destiny, achieving a measure of immortality through the knowledge that posterity would continue to fulfill the nation's distinctive role as it "progressed" through time into an unknown future. In all times, good or bad, the essential worth of the nation would be revealed in and through its God-given or history-ordained mission. (28)

From this, it is not difficult to see why the republican nation should become an object of devotion, or why its public ceremonies should assume a sacred and reverential character as secular "acts of worship," so evident in the great *fêtes* of the French Revolution or the early German student celebrations. But as new nations were created in the nineteenth and twentieth centuries, their leaders and ideologues felt the need to establish similar public rituals and instill in their members sentiments of religious devotion and exaltation analogous to those of the traditional religions. Through political symbols, choreographed mass ceremonies, heroic statuary, and sites of celebration and remembrance, they sought to create a sense of collective history and destiny of a nation at once eternal and developing through time to fulfill its historic mission. This was very much the case in nineteenth-century Germany whose festivals and monuments were documented by George Mosse; but we find similar rituals and commemorations in late nineteenth-century France, Italy, Britain, and the United States, among others. To this end, architects, artists, musicians, and poets were encouraged to create vivid images and monuments of the nation that would evoke its grandeur and its omnipresent and beneficent reality, making specific and palpable that which was necessarily general and abstract. In this too, nationalism aped traditional religions. Just as the latter had revealed the godhead through divine laws and icons, so for nationalists the nation could be apprehended in the decrees of the sovereign people and through the imagery of its artists and writers. And just as traditional faiths had incorporated the individual soul into the community of the faithful, so the secular religion of nationalism sought to absorb the individual into the sacred communion of citizens and its civic historical culture. (29)

Republican Nationalism Ascendant

Nowhere is this close connection between the elevation of the sovereign people and the nation's secular mission more clearly illustrated than in modern France. Of course, the idea that the French were a "chosen people" was a common motif in the Middle Ages and beyond. What was new was the transference of this conviction from the kingdom of France to the French people, the fraternal citizens of the republic. While in former ages the French people had been an elect nation, but only insofar as they formed the body of the French kingdom and the subjects of the "most Christian king," during the Revolution the people and the nation as an idea became not only separated from, but superior to, the king and the kingdom, and, after 1792, the sole bearers of "election" in the modern, secular form of national will, liberty, and virtue. This was not a sudden reversal. Already, in the time of Louis XIV, the idea of France as a nation of civilization and grandeur was combined with the cult of the Sun-King, setting the standards of taste and culture for other absolutist states in Europe. During the eighteenth century, the idea of the nation as a "public" and a "society" had gained ground, freed from its links with deity and monarch alike. But, despite this conceptual preparation, the content and scope of the republican nationalist ideology of national will and popular liberty was novel, for it envisaged the nation as the sole and original source of all law and sovereignty; in the words of the Abbé Siéyès, writing in early 1789:

> The Nation exists before all things and is the origin of all. Its will is always legal, it is the law itself . . . Nations on earth must be conceived as individuals outside the social bond, or as is said, in the state of nature. The exercise of their will is free and independent of all civil forms. Existing only in the natural order, their will, to have its full effect, only needs to possess the *natural* characteristics of a will. In whatever manner a nation wills, it suffices that it does will; all forms are valid and its will is always the supreme law. (30)

For the Jacobins, in particular, the ideals of liberty, virtue, and the *patrie* were regarded as sacred. But they were not alone. For many, the nation was part of the natural order and the ground of social life and politics, the secular counterpart of the deity, with the Revolution enabling men to recognize and worship on the altar of this *ersatz* god. The Marquis de Condorcet noted at the time the religious quality of the Revolution:

> this Revolution of ours is a religion, and Robespierre is leading a sect therein. He is a priest at the head of his worshippers. (31)

Hence, the need to drive out rival religions, and crush any signs of a revitalized Catholicism, notably in the protracted revolt of the Vendée. But, for the same reason, by early 1794 Robespierre had begun to restrain the frenzied campaign of de-Christianization on the part of his more extreme followers, and to try to stabilize the Revolution by founding a secular religion of the all-seeing Supreme Being, celebrated in a carefully choreographed popular festival in June 1794. (32)

Over the next century, the secular religion of French republican nationalism, though often challenged by Catholic conservatism, was repeatedly strengthened, first by the policies and institutions of Napoleon, and thereafter by the determined secular campaign of the Third Republic, notably in the fields of mass education, monumental statuary, and public ritual. In this period, as Eric Hobsbawm so amply documented, the ideal of a secular French nation of all its citizens was propagated through the flag, the adoption of the *Marseillaise* as the anthem, the establishment of the Pantheon, and the choice of Bastille Day as the national holiday. Despite severe conflicts between conservative monarchists and Catholics and the radical secular republicans, especially during the Dreyfus Affair and in the mid-twentieth century, the dominant form of nationalism in France during the modern period has remained radically secular and republican. Even today, the pursuit of these ideals by the political elite can be seen in their hostile attitude to the public display of Muslim and other religious practices, notably in schools. Jacobin ideals of secularism, liberty, and the *patrie* continue to find powerful political, social, and symbolic expression, as the purely secular ceremonies of Bastille Day remind us. (33)

All over nineteenth-century Europe, France's example and with it the secular religion of republican nationalism have helped to transform a medley of absolutist states and petty principalities into outwardly similar sovereign national republics based on principles of law, citizenship, and secular education. Napoleon's success was, in part, due to the appeal of these revolutionary republican principles, and the ensuing grant of secular constitutions based on citizenship, civil liberty, and the rule of law, notably in the German states, the Low Countries, and in Switzerland. In the latter, the Helvetic Society was formed in 1762, and under the influence of Johann Jakob Bodmer and his pupils, Albrecht von Haller and Johann Jakob Breitinger, its members increasingly linked the ideals of the Enlightenment and progress to the character and destiny of the Swiss *Eidgenossenschaft.*

Hence the imposition by revolutionary France of the Helvetic Republic in 1798, though it marked a significant social transformation, when the old oligarchies of Berne, Zürich, and other cities gave way to radical middle-class patriots, could be seen as the logical culmination of Switzerland's long history of resistance to tyranny and belief in liberty. Partly as a result of the international climate after Napoleon's fall, and also because it lacked sufficient popular support, the Helvetic Republic soon gave way to conservative regimes; but "the fusion of democratic constitutionalism and popular nationalism" from the 1830s ultimately led, after the brief 1847 civil war between Protestant and Catholic cantons, to the victory of the radical republicans and the adoption of the 1848 federal Constitution for Switzerland. (34)

In much the same way, the majority of the Greek intelligentsia, as well as many merchants and professionals, followed Iosippos Moisiodax and Adamantios Korais in desiring a secular national republic for a regenerated Greece, worthy of its ancient progenitors, which was identified largely with ancient Athens and its democracy. Hence the desire for a purified Greek language stripped of foreign accretions, and a return to secular education in the ancient classics, so as to fit modern Greeks for political participation in a democratic republic and restore Greece to its leading cultural position. It was a hope that seemed capable of being fulfilled through citizenship of the small Hellenic state created in 1832 by the Great Powers, despite its formal status as a constitutional kingdom, because its elite was committed to Enlightenment ideals of reason, liberty, the rule of law, and a programme of secular Greek education. (35)

Nor was republican influence confined to Europe. A century later, in neighboring Turkey, the republican spirit reappeared in the stridently secular constitution and policies propounded by Mustafa Kemal Atatürk in the 1920s. Apart from abolishing both the Sultanate and Caliphate, Atatürk's government pushed through a programme of modernization largely identified with Western civilization, of which republican France was held to be the leading exemplar. The regime's chief ideologue, Ziya Gökalp, was greatly influenced by Comtean positivism and its radical secularism. Education was seen as the key to both citizenship and a compact national society, able to compete on terms of equality with the leading Western powers. Republican principles were particularly strong among the professionalized military, who have remained the guardians of a radical secular nationalism and statism to this day, remaining suspicious of any Islamist leanings among political parties. They have closely followed the French example, despite the quite different social and cultural setting, placing the state above society and its religious and ethnic divisions; and in this, they have proved largely successful to date, perhaps because of the absence of a revolutionary tradition, but also because of conducive international constraints. (36)

Finally, French influence, and its secular republican model in particular, has been pervasive in much of French-speaking sub-Saharan Africa. No doubt this was greatly encouraged by French colonialism and its elite cultural traditions. But, during the era of elite nationalist movements striving for independence, both the rhetoric of men like Sekou Touré and Leopold Senghor and the slogans and goals of political movements in the French colonies were imbued with Rousseauan and Jacobin ideals of social contract, liberty, democracy, equality, and citizenship. Again, these were linked to a programme of education (though usually only for an elite), an education that was secular and humanistic, despite the strong influence of Christian missions in this field. Above all, the need to ground the "nation-to-be" in the ex-colonial territory and overcome deep ethnic divisions in the new states made secular republican nationalism the only viable and realistic ideological basis for the new African nations, and the civic-republican nation the only inclusive and legitimate type of modern political community. Despite the attractions of race consciousness and pan-Africanism (and, in some of the French territories, of the ideology of Négritude), the forms of national solidarity and the dominant political ideals of the new sub-Saharan African states were derived mainly from the traditions of Rousseau and the French Revolution as these were mediated by the Third Republic (or, in the British colonies, from Locke and Mill) – and modified at times by African symbols, rituals, and beliefs. (37)

Conclusion

As a model of modern political community, the civic-republican nation has penetrated most areas of the globe, and its secular form of nationalism has become almost canonical – both for national communities and their states and for many theorists of nations and nationalism. For the participants, this is due not just to the power and relevance of its ideas and practices for modern societies, but to its strong religious quality and emotional appeal. As I pointed out in chapter 4, the civic-republican legacy of classical antiquity combined secular with religious dimensions in the ancient *polis*: a compact made by and for human beings, but one guarded and sanctified by the gods and celebrated in civic myths, rituals, and festivals – a duality also visible in its medieval Italian and northern counterparts. The ancient tradition was revived, more or less consciously, by the *philosophes* in search of models of non-hierarchical community and secular solidarity. They and their followers in France and other states embraced a secular religion of human progress, liberty, virtue, and the exercise of reason, a religion whose natural political expression was the free republic of equal citizens bound by common ideals and traditions of loyalty to the sovereign nation. This in turn required the creation by the members of a common and distinctive national culture, and the institution of a "civil religion" of patriotism consisting of shared beliefs and practices, with shared political symbols, memories, myths, and values, expressed in monumental statuary, literature, patriotic music, and above all in public festivals and ceremonies. In this strong political, cultural, and institutional expression lay the key to the wide appeal and durability of the republican nation and of its secular and territorial nationalism. (38)

A second reason for its global success was the ease of its diffusion to all kinds of societies by a secularizing intelligentsia. Many theorists have noted the leading role of intellectuals and professionals in the diffusion of secular nationalism and its idea of the republican nation, if only because it provided a congenial arena for their aspirations and talents for which traditional societies had neither interest nor use. But it was the actual process of "ideologizing" the secular republican nation, giving recognizable shape to its characteristic ideals of autonomy, unity, and identity and forging a ready-made transferable blueprint, that provided the key to the transforming role of both global nationalism and its chief bearers, the intelligentsia, in modernizing societies. In the process, the ideology of national*ism* became disembedded from particular historical forms of the national community, including ultimately the republican nation itself. (39)

For all that, we need to remember that this republican ideology was only one variety of modern nationalism, and provided only one kind of national model; and, for all its success, it was not without its problems and limitations. It was here that earlier covenantal nationalisms might provide an alternative. Even the unelaborated ideology of the hierarchical nation could perhaps be adapted for political communities in the modern world. Therein lay grounds for difference and conflict, and it is to these modern alternatives that I turn in the final chapter.

7

Alternative Destinies

When the Great Powers carved out a small Hellenic kingdom from the Ottoman empire on the Greek mainland in 1832, they endowed it with a Bavarian king and his German advisers, and expected it to follow the Western model, that is, the peculiar fusion of state and nation assumed to be characteristic of civilized societies. Nor were they at first disappointed. The new state was given a constitution, civil liberties, and a parliament, as well as the other basic institutions of state, including the subordination of the Orthodox Church, now separated from the Patriarchate in Constantinople. Citizenship, secular education, and the rule of law were, at least in theory, the key features of what was in effect a republican nation. Moreover, the underlying ideology and programme of the state was a form of republican nationalism, which was supposed to translate into practical policies the Enlightenment vision of the leaders of the Greek intelligentsia from Rhigas Velestinlis to Adamantios Korais – a vision that was itself, in the eyes of Greek intellectuals, derived from the heroic achievements of their ancestors in ancient Athens. We see this vision clearly expressed both in Rhigas' map of Greece and in the Constitution of 1797 which he drew up for his proposed Republic of Hellas, in which he declared the equality of all citizens:

> the sovereign people are all the people of this state without distinction of religion or dialect, Greeks, Bulgarians, Albanians, Vlachs, Armenians, Turks, and every other race. (1)

But, from the first, not everyone shared this vision. While no doubt the modern Greek state, backed by the Great Powers, was able to provide a political framework and set of institutions for the newly created Greek nation, its elites were unable to infuse the majority of the Greek-speaking population with a Hellenic spirit and an Enlightenment vision. The latter did not share the republican nationalist ideology of the professional and commercial elites, nor did they subscribe to their dogmatic secularism, much less to their passion for classical education. This was not just a question of class and social interest, nor even a lack of literacy and education, important though these were. Nor was it simply ignorance of the glorious classical heritage or a failure to appreciate the benefits of Western civilization. The fact was that the peasants, shepherds, and klephts of Morea and Rumeli who had to be aroused to fight the Ottomans and thereafter to provide the bulk of the new state's citizens were inspired by alternative ideals and visions, insofar as their interests and identities were not purely local. It was as Greek Orthodox Christians that they rose up against the Muslim Ottoman oppressor, and as Greek speakers of the Orthodox rite that they had to be mobilized and incorporated into a Greek kingdom that was thereby propelled to expand in order to do so. So, from the first, the Hellenic vision of the intelligentsia and business classes found itself challenged by the rival ideals of the very people of the nation in whose name the new national state and its ideology had been established. (2)

The alternative ideal espoused by the non-elites was based on the myth of Orthodox Greek election, a variant of the common motif of a chosen people. Of course, Orthodox Christianity was a universal faith, and its community and kingdom were ultimately not of this world. Nevertheless, as we have seen, in its human and worldly form, the Orthodox Church saw itself as the only genuine Christian faith and therefore the true successor of ancient Israel, the original chosen people who had been forsaken by God when it had rejected Christ. However, this universal religion was increasingly combined with a Greek cultural particularism, encouraged by the fact that the language of the New Testament was Greek, and by the Greek language of Orthodox rites and liturgy and the Grecophone clergy of the Church. This process was already underway during the last centuries of the Byzantine empire, when the Hellenic revival among the Byzantine elites, coupled with fierce hostility by the monks to the Latin Church, and the loss of outlying non-Greek territories, had given a stronger Greek cultural inflection to the empire and Church. After the catastrophe of

1453, the Greek Orthodox *millet-i-Rum*, which the Ottoman rulers had designated and placed under the ecclesiastical and civil administration of the Patriarch in Constantinople, became imbued with a sense of Christian Orthodox difference and identity, but as *Romaioi* (Eastern Romans), in opposition to both the ancient Hellenes and the Latin Franks. Their identity was nurtured by shared memories of the glorious Byzantine past, when God's chosen people had lived in his kingdom under His Vice-gerent on earth, the Byzantine emperor. It was also continually renewed by an apocalyptic tradition of prophecy which envisaged the resurrection of the last Byzantine emperor, Constantine XI, and the restoration of his empire after the term of God's punishment of His people for their sins had been fulfilled and the infidels had been driven from the sacred City. (3)

This is a vision which, in stark opposition to the Hellenic republican ideal, combined a covenantal tradition with a strong hierarchical conception of the Greek Orthodox community. On the face of it, this alternative destiny mapped out for the Greek community, having little or no purchase on the Western modernity espoused by the Greek-speaking elites, stood little chance of influencing, let alone shaping, the destiny of the newly created Greek kingdom. After all, the Western powers had insisted on a strong European influence in the shape of the regency, including the separation of the Greek Orthodox Church in mainland Greece from the Patriarchate in Ottoman-controlled Constantinople, the dissolution of many of its monasteries, and the subordination of its hierarchy to the Greek state. Yet, it would be a mistake to think that the Church thereby ceased to exert any influence. Like the Gallican Church in France, the Church increasingly became a national Greek institution, and was ultimately recognized as such by a Patriarchate that had eventually come to accept "phyletism," the division of the universal Church into ethnic and national churches such as were (or had already been) established in such emergent states of the Balkans as Serbia and Bulgaria. (4)

In Greece, not only did the Church maintain its religious monopoly in what was a confessionally almost homogeneous population. Its "Byzantine" ideal, if not its hierarchical underpinnings, became from 1844, after Kollettis' speech in the National Assembly, more attuned to the language and aims of Greek politics in the form of the *Megale Idea*, the irredentist ideology of recovering the lands and populations of the Greek Orthodox scattered across the Aegean, northern Greece, and present-day western Turkey. In the event, the small kingdom carved out of part of mainland Greece by the Great Powers was to expand to include the Dodecanese Islands, Thessaly, Epirus, Crete, Thrace, and other historic areas where the majority of the inhabitants were Greek speakers of the Greek Orthodox rite. In other words, in place of the purely secular ideology of the territorial citizen nation, religious and ethnolinguistic criteria came to define the Greek nation and its citizens – criteria which led, almost inevitably, to a reinterpretation of Greek history and to a radical political movement and programme.

The political programme is well known: the *Megale Idea* which issued in the disastrous attempt of 1922 to recover from an almost extinct Ottoman empire the Greek-speaking and Orthodox populations of Anatolia and the territories which they inhabited, and which in the eyes of Greek ethnonationalists comprised the descendants and lands of the early Ionian colonies of Asia Minor. But equally important was the historical reinterpretation. This did not entail a simple rejection of the Hellenic vision. Rather, it attempted to incorporate classical antiquity, along with the Byzantine empire, in a single coherent narrative of "the Greek nation" from the Mycenaeans to modern Greece. It fell to the folklorist Spiridon Zambelios, who in 1852 published his collection of folksongs with a lengthy introduction, and the historian Konstantinos Paparrigopoulos, in his five-volume *History of the Greek Nation* (1860–77), to propose an interpretation which centered on the Greek nation as the prime collective actor in all three main periods of a single narrative of Greek history, ancient, medieval, and modern. Using personal expressions such as "our medieval Empire" and "our medieval forefathers," Paparrigopoulos in particular was able to reincorporate the Byzantine legacy and its glorious heritage and promise into his vision of the Greek nation and its millennial destiny. He did this by giving new political meanings to long-established Orthodox rituals and liturgy, and the associated shared memories of Christian emperors and the sacred City – whose recovery, many came to feel, would usher in, if not the restoration of the Orthodox Byzantine empire, at least the resurrection of Greece to its former cultural and political eminence. In practice, this type of reinterpretation attempted to realize the old Christian ideal of an Orthodox *Oikumene*, but shorn of its non-Greek (Serb, Albanian, Bulgarian, etc.) communities and lands, within the context of an expanded modern Greek kingdom which sought the ingathering of all the "unredeemed" Greek-speaking, Orthodox populations, and the territories of their residence. (5)

Cleavage and Reinterpretation

The Greek case provides us with a concise illustration of a number of general issues in the shaping of modern nations.

The first is that the republican nation and its nationalism, for all its aptness for westernization and modernization, did not sweep away other historical forms of community. On the contrary, civic-republican nationalism was repeatedly challenged and forced to accommodate other, earlier historical conceptions and traditions. Even in its "homeland," France, it has been forced to fight to retain its authority and to stamp its characteristic form on the whole nation, not only in 1848, 1871, and during the Dreyfus Affair, but well into the twentieth century, from the Vichy government to Le Pen's movement. Both within and between nations, covenantal and hierarchical forms of national identity have frequently reappeared in complex permutations, in opposition to or in conjunction with republican forms. (6)

In the Greek case, an earlier hierarchical but universalist conception of empire and Orthodoxy, with at its core a covenantal element of apostolic fellowship, was challenged and initially replaced by a particularist territorial and republican conception of a specifically Greek nation. But the attractions of the vision of the Orthodox *Oikumene* centered on Constantinople continued to present a resonant alternative destiny for an expanding Greek nation; and it was not long before the complex religious and ethnolinguistic mosaic of the Balkans encouraged this alternative vision to be translated into a political movement and public policy. In the process, the Byzantine heritage was reinterpreted and annexed to an overarching conception of the millennial Greek nation, so that, like the golden age of classical Athens, that of imperial Byzantium and its Orthodox faith became products of the creative genius of a retrojected conception of the Greek nation. (7)

Second, these earlier conceptions were very often entrenched in those strata least exposed to Western ideas and social change. Hence, ideological conflict within a nation or national state was often accompanied by social cleavage, sometimes localized and fragmented, at other times political and explosive in character. But, whereas this division was often manifest in mass apathy or opposition to the republican ideal, it was accompanied by open conflicts within the more westernized intelligentsia, as those espousing the cause of the republican nation were attacked by other intellectuals wedded to more hierarchical or covenantal ideals of the nation. Apart from the Greek intelligentsia, perhaps the best known of these public splits were the long-running conflicts between conservatives and radical republicans in nineteenth-century France, and the vehement verbal battles between Slavophiles and westernizers in nineteenth-century Russia in the same period. Outside Europe, too, we can chart such conflicts among the intelligenstias in early twentieth-century Egypt where the Pharaonic movement challenged the supremacy of an Islamic Arab identity; and in India, where Hindu revivalists have from the time of the Arya Samaj to the BJP proclaimed for India an alternative destiny to that charted by the dominant republican and social nationalism of the Congress Party. (8)

Third, these ideological conflicts, where they did not issue in full-scale revolution, could often be at least partially resolved through a process of generational selection and reinterpretation. In each generation, opposed conceptions of national identity were successively modified, with received national traditions, myths, memories, and values periodically subjected to intense scrutiny and more or less radical prunings and reinterpretations whose aim was to combine elements from the different conceptions into a larger, more coherent whole. Something of this synthesis was attempted in nineteenth-century Greece, to the extent that Hellenic republicanism was combined with ethnoreligious criteria derived from a more "Byzantinist" ideal of the nation, notably in the ideological schema offered by the historian Konstantinos Paparrigopoulos. One might claim that, in Egypt, too, while the Pharaonic conception has been rejected, some of its premisses – the emphasis on a specific territory and environment, and the singling out of an ancient nation separate from other Arabs – have been incorporated into the dominant nationalist outlook of the ruling elites.

Fourth, these mechanisms of social cleavage, ideological conflict, and generational selection and reinterpretation help to explain both the impetus to social change and its relative containment within the social and cultural parameters of the national state. In this respect, it is not enough to invoke external pressures, the fact that, once in being, the modern national state is *ipso facto* part and parcel of the "inter-national" system of national states which necessarily preserves its form, as was undoubtedly the case with the Greek kingdom. In this case, opposed internal cultural factors emanating from shared Greek and Orthodox cultural traditions have been equally decisive; and these served to limit the range and degree of change in the forms and conceptions of the Greek nation.

Finally, for the most part, as I hope to show, these shared traditions are interrelated insofar as they all stem from cognate cultural legacies reaching back ultimately to antiquity and undergirded by a long-standing belief in common ethnicity and an ethnic model of social organization. Not only do republican, covenantal, and hierarchical forms of the nation overlap at any given point in time. They are often closely interwoven, the more so when they pertain to more or less unified ethnic communities; and while the proportions of each may vary, and be varied, in a given instance and during a particular period, these forms rarely disappear beneath the official veneer of political rhetoric. Thus the changing configurations of modern national identities can be seen to be, for the most part, so many variations on the three great cultural traditions and their permutations.

In this respect, modern Greece is exemplary. Its dominant republican form has had to compromise with the alternative destiny mapped by intellectuals who have drawn on the very different but cognate cultural traditions of the Orthodox Church and its Byzantine heritage. This was made easier by the fact that, in retrospect, it was not difficult to claim a long-standing, indeed millennial, Greek ethnocultural heritage founded on the durability of forms of the Greek language and especially on the widespread Greek belief in modern Greek descent from their ancient Greek forebears. That conversion to Orthodox Christianity had created for many later Greeks a deep social and cultural rupture with classical antiquity was not seen by nineteenth-century intellectuals and politicians as sufficient ground to undermine the compromise with Byzantinism which encouraged the pursuit of the *Megale Idea* by republican nationalists wedded to the Hellenic project. (9)

In terms of ideological conflict and reinterpretation, nineteenth-century Switzerland provides an interesting parallel to Greece. In the old chronicles of its foundation, the origins of the Swiss *Eidgenossenschaft* were ascribed to a peasant uprising led by Wilhelm Tell against Habsburg oppressors and their castles in autumn 1307. This myth of rebellion and liberation was the received tradition found in the

White Book of Sarnen of 1471 and in Aegidius Tschudi's influential *Chronicon Helveticum* of 1526; and it was also the tale accepted, and used, by the peasants in their uprising in 1653 (the Peasants' War) against the urban oligarchies. Even Johannes von Muller, in his *History of the Swiss Confederation* of 1786 – and therefore written after Johann Gleser's discovery of the original *Bundesbrief* of 1291 – kept to the popular tradition of Tschudi and the White Book of Sarnen. However, the discovery of the original *Bundesbrief* at Schwyz, which documented the pact between the three forest cantons of Schwyz, Uri, and Unterwalden, traditionally agreed on the Rütli meadow on Lake Lucerne, suggested a very different interpretation of the social and political origins of the Swiss Confederation. Rather than a mass peasant uprising, it pointed to the need of the leading families of the inner forest cantons to preserve their ancient rights on which their Habsburg feudal overlords were encroaching, at a time when the St. Gotthard crossing over the Alps had been opened to lucrative commercial traffic. This pact, the first of many between these and neighboring cantons, made no mention of Wilhelm Tell or mass uprisings and burnings of feudal castles. Instead, it insisted on the sole prerogative of the cantons, and the native-born, to sit in judgment on their fellow-members, and stressed the absolute need for cooperation between the cantons, including military defense, to preserve their ancient freedoms. This was a theme that recurred in several medieval societies; for example, the Scots barons swore a not dissimilar pact in the Declaration of Arbroath of 1320. (10)

Of course, the different strands of "Swiss origins" were not so far apart in time, place, and general motive that they could not be reconciled in a more "inclusive" account. Friedrich Schiller, for example, in his drama *Wilhelm Tell* (1805), was able to include elements of both myths of Swiss origins and point the way to a Swiss destiny founded on freedom and peasant virtue. While the Oath of the Rütli between Stauffacher and his associates was accorded marginal chronological priority, it was accompanied in the play by Tell's refusal to acknowledge the Habsburg governor, Gessler, and the shooting of the apple, and was followed swiftly by the slaying of Gessler and the peasant movement against feudal oppressors – a reading that was apparently confirmed by the proximity of the crucial victory of the cantons over the Habsburg cavalry at Morgarten (1315), as well as by the later victories at Sempach (1386) and Näfels (1388). By the time of the six hundredth anniversary celebrations in 1891, this combination of traditions could become the official version and be celebrated, under the direction of the federal government, over two days in early August in both Schwyz and on the Rütli meadow on the lake of Lucerne.

Once again, this example illustrates both the multistranded traditions and memories of the "national past" and the ways in which such ideological and social conflicts could be contained. Of course, this was not a smooth process of evolutionary change. Indeed, the conflicts of value and national outlook which were so pervasive in the nineteenth and early twentieth centuries persist even today. In modern Switzerland, the rural inner cantons in the mountain valleys (most of them also Catholic), with their more conservative ethos, remain wary of the secular modernizing capitalism of the towns and cities, notably of Zürich and Berne, which from the time of the Helvetic Republic of 1798, and then again the Federal Republic of 1848, have increasingly dominated Swiss politics and urban society. These alternative destinies of intensified civic-republican nationalism and a more canton-based "covenantal" type of nationalism surfaced in the debates triggered by the seven hundredth anniversary of the Swiss foundation document, as well as in their responses to the pressures of globalization and immigration. (11)

Modern Hierarchical Nations

It might be thought that if even the rural Swiss cantons show no hankering after traditional hierarchies, that there is no room in the modern world for the ancient legacy of hierarchy. Yet, while it is true that, with very few exceptions, the concept of a "hierarchical nation" such as we saw in medieval Europe has had its day, conservative traditions and even elements of hierarchical community persist, often in counterpoint to the dominant republican nationalism of modern national states.

In the nineteenth century, a number of national communities were constituted as republics with constitutional monarchs, and a few major states persisted or were reformed as hierarchical national states, notably Germany and Japan. The German case is complex, involving permutations from all three traditions of community in the last two centuries. But in Japan we encounter a predominant hierarchical tradition, first in the Tokugawa Shogunate which by its exclusionary measures gave Japanese feudal society an increasingly national character, some of it borrowed from Western examples, with the elaboration of myths of national origin and election which echoed those of Europe, and then again in the Meiji Restoration of 1868, after the penetration of American power. In the latter process, the revolt of some of the samurai clans against the Shogun and the restoration and transfer to Edo (Tokyo) of the Meiji emperor whose court had continued through all these centuries in the ancient capital, Kyoto, was in essence a conservative revolution which used neo-traditional forms to legitimate and sanctify the desire of these elites to achieve parity between Japan and the West through a programme of rapid modernization. Crucial to the success of this programme was the conjunction of popular religion, mass education, and emperor worship. If Japanese society was to embark on deep reforms which would enable it to survive and compete with an intrusive West, its members had to be made conscious of their commonality and intimate communion as a "family nation," which up to that time existed only in outline, as it were, in the minds of a few intellectuals and statesmen harking back to ancient texts. To this end, the Meiji elites aimed to enhance the Shinto family rituals and the patriotic Shinto cult of the war dead, especially in the revived Yasukuni shrine; and they also sought to link them with both the popular religion of the rural masses and the worship of the emperor as father and protector of the "family-nation." It was to the modernization of the emperor's "family-nation" that the new system of mass compulsory education, outlined in the celebrated Imperial Rescript on Education of 1890, was directed, in the expectation that it would provide the motor of Japanese social and economic development. (12)

In this way, Japanese forms of hierarchy were reattached to Western ideas of the nation, to produce a late development of the "hierarchical nation," in a form that appeared to owe more to indigenous traditions than to legacies and models emanating from the West, although it was not uninfluenced by Western forms of modern community. How far the romantic nationalism of the 1930s that immediately preceded the fascist regime was indebted to the German Romantics and to what extent it influenced the fascists is unclear. But, in the subsequent regime, the emphasis on imperial power and national kinship under the emperor was undoubtedly intensified through the long war of conquest and defense in Asia, and the official propaganda accompanying it. The subsequent Japanese debacle and unparalleled suffering of the Japanese people appeared for a time to encompass the demise of the hierarchical principle itself and with it to undermine Japanese national cohesion, but the American decision to retain the emperor and his family and subject Japan to foreign occupation helped to revive national bonds around the idea of collective victimhood in the "Pacific War." The restoration of independent Japanese institutions and politics revealed how much of the former conservative and deferential social forms had been preserved, as well as the continuing centrality of the imperial family to the concept of Japanese nationhood. (13)

The other great example of hierarchical forms embedded in evolving national institutions exemplifies a very different pattern of cultural relations. In England, hierarchy has been blended with a strong covenantal nationalism stemming from the brief, but violent, interlude of a Puritan Commonwealth. Though swiftly abolished, its religious and cultural legacy for the development of an English, and later Anglo-British, national identity has been immense. As we saw in chapter 5, the type of hierarchical *ethnie* pioneered by the Anglo-Saxon kings and developed by the Normans and later, after several vicissitudes, entrenched by the Tudor monarchs into a sense of territorialized national identity with common laws and customs and a distinctive public culture was, for a short but turbulent period, broken by the irruption of covenantal forms of national identity and community under the Puritans. For Cromwell, as for Milton, England was an elect nation of God, God's first-born, a worthy successor to ancient Israel, to be realized in the new Commonwealth which abolished monarchy, the House of Lords, and the Anglican Church. With the failure of Army rule these hierarchical forms of public culture were restored after 1660, but they were situated in a new ideological context of political liberty and a new religious pattern of national election – of the English as an elect nation of civil liberty and progress – a concept that helped to fuel the ideals of the Glorious Revolution of 1688, as well as the largely Protestant Anglo-British nation of the eighteenth-century Union, and to some extent the social and Christian movements of the Victorian era. (14)

Nor have these hierarchical and conservative forms completely faded even in a climate of post-imperial decline and incipient republicanism. Though the monarchy has fallen into popular disfavor from time to time, it has succeeded to a considerable extent in reinventing its style, and in moments of crisis like the Second World War has provided a center of gravity for an anxious national community. Its sheer longevity, its centrality to national public culture, its colorful ceremonies, and its progressive demystification by media glare, not to mention the lack of mass support for any alternative, continue to contribute to its enduring appeal. Unlike the Anglican Church, the monarchy, despite being separated from the vast majority of the British by wealth and tradition, has largely succeeded in upholding the sense of national uniqueness, in perceived contrast to the republics of the European continent – a contrast which is, if anything, reinforced by popular devotion to Parliament and the long-established parliamentary tradition, as well as to the common law. All these institutions are seen as part of, and evidence for, the difference, indeed the uniqueness, of Britain, but more especially of England, in relation to the states of the European Community – a difference that one can trace back to the separation from Rome under Henry VIII, and which was crystallized under Elizabeth and especially by Puritan national covenantalism; a difference that embeds hierarchical concepts and forms within a wider Anglo-British covenantal tradition to this day. (15)

Modern Covenantal Nations

By a similar token, one might ask: where are the covenantal nations today? Did they not disappear with the demise of Ulster and apartheid South Africa?

Certainly, both these societies appeared to reflect a stage of early modernization and industrialization, in which separation of labor forces along racial or ethnoreligious lines was not uncommon. In both, a dominant minority community separated from the majority to found their own states which were at once hierarchical in the wider context and covenantal within each community. In the case of Ulster, the partition of the six counties in 1921 placed a minority of Catholics within a Unionist Ulster, even as the Protestant Unionists formed a minority in the island of Ireland. A strong covenantal impulse stemming from the original Protestant settlers was later institutionalized in the Orange Order and the annual marches commemorating the Protestant victory at the battle of the Boyne in 1690. In the case of South Africa, the flight of many Afrikaners from a British-controlled Cape Colony in the 1830s came to be seen as a latterday Exodus from an oppressive Pharaoh in search of promised lands on the veldt. By the late nineteenth century, an Afrikaans language revival was accompanied by a growing cult, notably in Paul Kruger's Transvaal republic, of the Great Trek and the miraculous victory of a Boer army over Dingaane's Zulus at the battle of Blood River in 1838. By 1938, the cult was re-established by Dr. Malan's Nationalist Party in the Ossawatrek centenary celebrations and in the frieze recording the heroes of the Great Trek and their exploits in the imposing *Voortrekker* monument outside Pretoria, as well as in subsequent commemorations under the Nationalist apartheid regime. (16)

These, then, were examples of latterday Protestant covenantal nations which combined their original biblical impulse to separation with domination over people of different religious persuasion or ethnic origins. In the case of the United States, that same biblical impulse was also originally interwoven with clear hierarchical elements, in the pre-existing strong regional cultures of the colonies. But, in the course of the struggle against Britain, while retaining their state rights, the colonies succeeded in uniting around a shared foundation myth, set out in the Declaration of Independence and the Constitution, texts which combined both covenantal and civic-republican elements. On the one hand, the various white Anglo-Saxon Protestant states increasingly marginalized, where they did not exterminate, the Native peoples, while at the same time both dominating and exploiting (especially in the slave-owning Southern plantations) the black populations forcibly brought to North America, and subsequently segregating them from the dominant white areas and resources. On the other hand, the American Revolution and Republic was presented in Roman garb as a civic and republican nation of free and equal (white) men, and its Founding Fathers undoubtedly drew a great deal of their inspiration from classical precedents as well as the ideals of the Enlightenment. (17)

At the same time, the original biblical Protestant vision of the more Puritan settlers experienced periodic renewals, and still commands a large following in various parts of the United States. This has sometimes led to pressures for isolationism from the wider world, and a concentration on the uniqueness of the American experience and its vast landscapes, and alternately to evangelical crusades on behalf of liberty as the leader of the free world, first in relation to Soviet communism and latterly to various forms of violent extremism. Nevertheless, the covenantal spirit which rejected traditional forms of hierarchy and opened the way for the adoption of republican civil and political liberties has helped to shape an open, pluralist, and enthusiastic nation committed to the rule of law and democracy, one which oscillates between a more separatist stance of purity reminiscent of the ancient Israelite covenant and a more expansionist and missionary confrontation with the "profane" world. (18)

A not dissimilar combination of covenantal vision, republican forms, and ethnic hierarchy can be found in modern Israel. While Israel is seen in some Western intellectual circles as a colonial settler society, its original impulse and guiding vision was both practical and biblical: the separation of the homeless, persecuted Jews from their host societies and their restoration to their ancient homeland, in accordance with the prophetic promise. Hence, unlike the Afrikaners who, for example, kept their Cape Colony slaves, the early Zionist pioneers sought to evacuate an inhospitable Europe and create a new and separate society based on self-reliance and the dignity of manual labor, and freed of the degradation to which they and their forebears had been subjected. (19)

Nevertheless, from quite early on, the perceived need to employ cheaper Arab labor and, after the creation of the state of Israel, the longer-term social disadvantages of the Arab minority within Israel, as well as of the Oriental Jews, introduced unsought ethnic inequalities. However, these were balanced by a strong civic-republican framework and a commitment to democracy, civil liberties, and free speech, as well as the rule of law inherited from the British Mandate. So that, while Israel at its inception might fairly be described as a covenantal nation, seeking to create a unique egalitarian pioneering society, its process of "normalization" as both state and national society has increasingly placed the emphasis on its civic-republican tradition, tempered by ethnic hierarchies which are in great part the result of hostile external pressures, but which are also encouraged by a persisting ethnoreligious ideal of national election. (20)

Modern Republican Nations

Though of equal antiquity to the other cultural traditions, the ideal of the civic-republican community did not become widespread until the full advent of modernity and secularism. Till that moment, it was overshadowed and encompassed by grandiose hierarchical structures against which the adherents of republican ideals struggled and eventually broke free. The fervor of the republican nation owed much to the severity of its initial rupture with traditional hierarchies, whether indigenous or colonial.

In retrospect, though not the first, the most influential of these convulsions appeared in France during the Revolution which, even more than in America, entrenched the civic and secular ideals of the republican nation. From the Middle Ages, the kingdom of France had embodied the quintessential model of a sacred hierarchical community under its "most Christian king." This model achieved an unparalleled clarity through the kingdom's compact territory – the so-called hexagon – in the early modern period, and even some degree of uniformity among the urban publics as a result of the growing penetration of centralized royal administration and Parisian language and culture, despite the persistence of regionalism and rural local cultures and dialects. But, from the late seventeenth century, a succession of modernizing intellectuals, inspired by the liberal patriotism of England's revolution and by the political solidarities of ancient city-states, began to articulate a novel secularizing sense of French national identity. This new concept of the republican nation was carried by a growing revolutionary middle-class movement espousing the ideals of "popular sovereignty" and the "will of the nation," in order to delegitimize and overthrow the monarchical, Catholic hierarchy of the *ancien régime*. During the course of the Revolution, between 1789 and 1794, a form of popular covenantalism momentarily surfaced, replete with mass oath-swearing, rituals, festivals, martyrdoms, and a new calendar. In these ceremonies, popular representatives embraced the symbolism and choreography of a salvation drama of the nation in mass displays of secular religious devotion to the *patrie* whose forms and trappings became increasingly secular, Roman, and republican. (21)

If the succeeding Napoleonic regime sought a new uniform order based on civic-republican ideals, its demise allowed the forces of Catholic and monarchical reaction the chance to refashion France as a hierarchical neo-conservative kingdom, in the manner advocated by Bonald. But the attempt failed, and from then on right up to the Vichy regime, French politics alternated, sometimes violently, between an increasingly radical secular republicanism and a powerful Catholic and monarchical military conservatism. These alternative destinies of *la France* were vividly enacted in the Assembly, in the courts, and on the streets during the Dreyfus Affair (1894–9), which preceded the disestablishment of the Catholic Church in 1905. But the republican victory was only temporary. The duality and cleavage demonstrated throughout the development of French national identity in the nineteenth and early twentieth centuries can be witnessed in its characteristic monuments, statuary, and architecture, and in the debates over admission to and use of the Pantheon. Equally symptomatic of this cleavage was the growing cult of St. Joan, who was canonized in 1920, and became an icon of Catholic integral nationalism, while simultaneously being regarded on the Left as a popular heroine of French liberty and resistance. In the twentieth century, France's alternative destinies once again manifested themselves in the conflict between strong, authoritarian, and charismatic leaders like Pétain and de Gaulle, who seemed to embody the bond between the French soil and the nation's heroic dead and who acted as "fathers of the nation," and popular movements of liberty, egalitarianism, and revolt like the Maquis, which faced the tyranny of German occupation, or the students' revolt of 1968, which was directed against the bureaucratic order of the capitalist state. Nevertheless, these conflicts, however violent, have been contained within the powerful forms of the French republican nation, committed to the civic values and ideals of an overriding secular French nationalism, which notwithstanding is grounded on a powerful sense of a common ethnocultural identity. (22)

The convulsions that brought the modern German republic into being were equally drawn out and, if anything, even more violent. We saw in chapter 4 that, already by the later Middle Ages, the German educated classes regarded the Holy Roman Empire as primarily an empire of the Germans and that an incipient sense of national identity, fostered by external stereotypes and the recovery of Tacitus' *Germania*, and by the spread of German language and literature, manifested itself among the humanist intelligentsia of the Renaissance. Yet, this elite sense of a wider German cultural and political identity failed to survive the carnage of the Thirty Years' War and the division of German-speaking lands outside Austria into a few great and many small absolutist states. By the eighteenth century, the fragmentation of hierarchy, together with the pervasive influence of French culture, appeared to put an end to any dreams of a German-speaking state or nation on the current English or French model, except perhaps in a few obscure regional circles.

However, the example of the French Revolution and the shock of the defeat at Jena encouraged civic reforms in Prussia and national resistance in the name of Germany on the part of intellectuals and students increasingly influenced by Romantic cults of heroism, which culminated in the exploits and myth-memories of the Volunteer Corps in the victory over Napoleon at Leipzig in 1813. This was followed by some striking, if rather limited, covenantal displays of German brotherhood at the Wartburg Castle in 1817 and at Hambach in 1832, during a general period of hierarchical reaction in Europe. Had this movement of covenantal reform been able to overcome the deep divisions among the delegates at the Frankfurt Parliament over the definition of German territories and German identity, the revolutionary year of 1848 might have witnessed the birth of a republican and liberal German nation. As it was, the old hierarchical states were able to regroup and the way was open to Prussian consolidation of its hold over the northern German-speaking territories and ultimately to a Prussian-dominated German *Reich.* (23)

On the surface, monarchical hierarchy with its illiberal *Kleindeutsch* nationalism appeared to triumph. But the failure of its official Sedan Day celebrations to capture the popular imagination and the continual undercurrents of popular movements harking back to the liberal constitutions of the period of the French Revolution, as well as the growth of the socialist movement, revealed the persistence of alternative destinies for a German republican nationalism. Again, this could be seen in the monuments paid for by public subscription, notably that to Hermann the Cheruscan in the Teutoberg forest, in the rise of various cults of Gothic medievalism and German "genius," particularly of Luther and Dürer, in the many *Volkisch* novels of this period, in Wagner's communal festival of the arts at Bayreuth conjuring ancient Germanic and Icelandic mythology, and subsequently in the often mystical racism of the fringe *volkisch* circles and their militant political counterpart, the Pan-German League. (24)

If defeat in the Great War and Versailles reparations forced a republic onto a weary and starving nation, Weimar was soon swept away by a determined movement that wedded covenantal elements to a racial and military hierarchy of unprecedented proportions and explosive violence. If Himmler's "union of German Germanic tribes" encapsulated the essence of Hitler's racial vision, it was nevertheless encased within a military command structure headed by the Führer, which incorporated the several competing hierarchies of state, party, army, and SS. Nazism presented a dual image: on the one hand, vast processions, marching songs, swastika flags, banners, and lighting effects, in carefully choreographed mass ceremonies in which "ethnic" Germans renewed their compact to obey the Führer and die for the Fatherland in fraternal unison, in what amounted to a secular parody of religious covenant; on the other hand, an imperial racialized state run by an inflated centralized bureaucracy and an increasingly powerful SS elite which sought to counter the deep divisions of class, confession, and region. (25)

One might have thought that total defeat would have shattered this fusion of political hierarchy and ideological covenantalism, but in East Germany both were renewed, albeit for diametrically opposed ends. This became apparent in the later phases of the communist regime of the German Democratic Republic with its attempts to harness for its own Marxist ends carefully chosen popular episodes and heroes from German history as *exempla virtutis* in order to bolster its legitimacy and bonding with "the people." However, in the West, hierarchy and covenant found no place in the *Bundesrepublik*. Not only in form, but also in spirit, the quest for economic renewal and political democracy entailed a rejection of charismatic populism and imperial hierarchy in favor of economic rationalism and a civic-republican nation, within the European union of nations. Indeed, the ideal of European integration appeared to offer the West German elite the prospect of liberation from the burdens and demons of the recent past in a well-ordered civic state. Nevertheless, the eagerness with which these same leaders sought political union with East Germany, upon the demise of its communist republic in 1990, revealed the persistence and strength of long-standing German ethnic bonds, and suggested that the ideal of submerging past particularisms in a purely constitutional state may not have been as secure as had been hoped by those like Jürgen Habermas who preached the virtue of a purely "constitutional patriotism." (26)

Similar reflections may be pertinent in the case of contemporary Russia. Here, too, we encounter a civic-republican nation in the making, albeit with many more problems and uncertainties. In the Russian case, we witness a similar trajectory from imperial hierarchy to republican nationalism, with only a brief moment of covenantal fraternity in the early 1920s. As we saw in chapter 4, the Muscovite state had developed as a patrimonial hierarchy, with a strongly interdependent state and Church under the tsar as sacred ruler and father of his people. But the Great Schism, following the modernizing Church reforms of the Patriarch Nikon in the 1660s, had created fervent resistance in the various martyr communities and covenantal sects of Old Believers, some of which survived well into the nineteenth century and emphasized the growing divide between a westernizing court and bureaucratic state and an Orthodox ethnic Russian society, especially in the countryside. (27)

By the late nineteenth century, tsarist social reforms and modernization "from above" had undermined the hierarchical ideal and created the conditions for populist and Marxist groups to preach the brotherhood of the masses and the equality of subject nations in the tsarist "prison of the peoples." But their message could only be translated into action after the disasters of the Great War had destroyed the traditional hierarchies, along with tsarism. With rival radical movements vying for power, it fell to the better-organized Bolsheviks, who emerged victorious from the Civil War, to guide the revolutionary movement. Proclaiming land to the peasants and the rule of worker soviets, Lenin's revolution elevated "the people" and ostensibly envisaged the birth of a new covenantal nation of the fraternal masses, only to have it succumb swiftly to an even more rigid and despotic secular-historical version of hierarchy under the Central Committee of the Communist Party, its Politburo, and ultimately its General Secretary. A new secular civic religion of multinational proletarian rule was manufactured to galvanize the energies of the peoples and to camouflage the interests of an all-powerful party and state. However, in the Great Patriotic War, Stalin found it necessary to harness the spirit of Russian ethnic nationalism with its ancient Russian heroes like Alexander Nevsky, and in 1941 he was even prepared *in extremis* to use the rituals and icons of the battered Orthodox Church to unify and mobilize Russians in the face of Nazi invasion. Despite the constant official criticism of Great Russian chauvinism, there is little doubt that a Russian state nationalism was an intrinsic component, albeit unofficial, of the subsequent ideologies and policies of the Soviet leadership. (28)

With the fall of Soviet communism, the leaders have turned their backs on both traditional hierarchies and fraternal ideals, in order to construct a more civic form of republican state and a more specifically

Russian nation. This has meant drawing on the secularism of the preceding regime, accentuating its national undertones, and reviving its command structure and state control, while rejecting its socialist ideology. In a few decades, then, Russian society has moved from a traditional, if modernizing, hierarchy through a revolutionary moment of popular covenantal solidarity to, first, a new communist form of republican society and economy directed by an all-powerful centralized bureaucratic state and party, and most recently to a more civic and less ideological but more overtly Russian, and statist, republican nation.

The Triumph of the Republican Nation?

These are not the only examples of a trajectory in which hierarchical and often imperial nations are more or less rapidly and violently transformed into civic-republican nations. Nor are they confined to Europe and the West. Modern Turkey provides a particularly interesting instance of this transformation. The long decline of Ottoman imperial power and the accompanying loss of its territories ended in two sudden ruptures of Ottoman continuity, the first in the revolt of the officers of the Committee of Union and Progress (CUP) in 1908, the second and more radical revolution after the defeat of the Greek invasion of 1922 and the establishment of the Turkish Republic by Mustafa Kemal Atatürk in 1923, when both the Sultanate and Caliphate were abolished. Both of these ruptures were inspired by the new vision of Turks as a separate ethnic nation. For the CUP officers, they constituted the dominant nation of a multinational Ottoman empire, but an empire conceived along increasingly nationalist lines. For Kemal and his followers, on the other hand, it was more a question of a Turkish republican nation separated not just from its former subjects but also from other Turkic-speaking nations outside the former empire. The Kemalist ideology was firmly territorial and westernizing. With its chief ideologue, Ziya Gökalp, looking to republican France as his model, Kemalism embraced a civic, modernizing conception of the nation as a community of order and progress, through which it was hoped Turkey would achieve parity with the West by joining the comity of "civilized" nations. This has remained its overriding aim to this day. Its stalled application to join the European Union provides merely the most recent evidence of an ideological republicanism, in which the statist secular and territorial nationalism of much of the military and political elite is counterposed to both the modernist political Islamism of the present ruling party and the Islamic faith of the rural majority. Yet, in both cases, the taken-for-granted assumption of a distinctive Turkish ethnonational community provides the arena and grounding for these alternative destinies. (29)

Similar convulsions and transformations have occurred in many of the states formerly ruled by imperial bureaucracies and feudal magnates from China and India to Egypt and Ethiopia. In the great majority of cases, revolution, social and national, threw up charismatic leaders and a mass following in an upsurge of covenantal brotherhood. But this moment quickly subsided, to be followed by the more or less painful emergence of a new civic order in the republican national state. Alternatively, foreign conquest and colonial rule, notably in Africa, introduced the forms of civic and territorial republicanism, as well as the national model, which the nationalist "founding fathers" adapted to indigenous mores and traditions. We see this particularly clearly in the first generation of leaders in West Africa, who sought to retain their colonial borders against the threat of ethnic fragmentation, but who often represented particular, usually dominant, *ethnies*, even as they aspired to build a united civic-republican nation. In either case, by whatever route it was reached, the end-point appears to be the same. (30)

This raises the question of the inevitability of a secular progression to the civic-republican nation. I have cited some counter-cases – Japan, Britain, to a lesser extent, the United States, and Israel. But might these "deviant" cases be more apparent than real? Might they not go the same way as the Afrikaners and the Protestants in Northern Ireland? After all, Israeli society has largely left behind its messianic pioneering ethos, except among the vocal Orthodox minority, and the Christian revival movement in the United States is continually challenged by the liberal intelligentsia and the East Coast political establishment. As for Japan and Britain, insistent political modernization of mores and institutions is gradually diminishing the political role of their traditional hierarchies, from the family to the monarchy.

Yet, civic republicanism remains only one of the many kinds of nationalist destiny. From time to time, further convulsions initiate novel national forms and destinies. Modern Iran is only the most obvious of such cases. Here, after the collapse of the Qajjar dynasty in the Constitutional revolution of 1905, power was seized by the Pahlavi dynasty, with Reza the self-proclaimed Shah. Again in 1953, the bid to create a secular republic under Dr. Mossadeq was crushed by the Great Powers, and power was handed to the Shah's son. He embarked on a programme of rapid modernization and an "Aryan" nationalism that harked back to the pre-Islamic Achaemenid past, using tight state and police control to secure his goals, but this only succeeded in alienating both the bazaar merchants and the clerics. On the Shah's fall in 1979, Iran did not return to the path of Mossadeq. Instead, it fell increasingly under the control of Ayatollah Khomeini and his fellow clerics in a revolution that reinstated a guiding Islamic Sharia and Shiite hierarchy within the relatively new framework of the republican nation and its nationalism. (31)

The Iranian example may be the best known, but it was not the only case of a modern hierarchical nation. In the 1950s, the prime minister of Burma, U Nu, attempted to combine Buddhism with socialism, using the ancient hierarchical ideals of savior rulers to represent the people. In Thailand, modern political government is combined with wide popular respect for sacred kingship, which combines long-standing traditions of personal rule with Buddhist ideals. And in Saudi Arabia, in the heart of Islam, the House of Saud renewed itself and its patrimonial political rule through the zealous promotion of a puritanical Wahabi Islam, echoing the original covenantal mission of the Prophet. (32)

But, beyond these singular examples, we find hierarchical and covenantal elements often intertwined with republican nationalism to this day. This is true not only in Britain and Japan, Israel and the United States, but it can also be seen in national states ranging from Ireland and Poland to Serbia, Greece, and Mexico, where the Church retains a strong following. Here, the covenantal ideals of ethnic election and mission continue to animate segments of their population, and thereby to offer alternatives to the secular national destinies charted by liberal and socialist elites, or to infuse into the latter some part of the covenantal alternative.

Conclusion

In the light of these considerations, any attempt to predict the shape of modern nations would be both premature and unwise, and would run the risk of mistaking the outward forms of political rule for the much more variable social and cultural contents. All that can be said with any degree of certainty is that a sense of shared ethnic identity remains a powerful and resilient component in even the most civic and republican of national communities, and that from antiquity to the contemporary era ethnic ties, sentiments, and models have continually made their influence felt, even in periods where imperial, feudal, and city-state forms of politics and society have predominated. (33)

In this short survey, I have sought to show that a different approach to the dominant modernist paradigm reveals the persistence, not only of ethnic identities and models, but also of those social and symbolic processes that encourage the formation of nations. These can be traced even in the ancient world, although only in a very few cases did they combine to create the conditions for human communities to approximate to the ideal type of the nation, rather than other kinds of cultural and/or political collective identity and community.

It was really only in the later medieval epoch that, with the fragmentation of the unity of Christendom, these conditions were created anew in Europe, and that a national type of identity began to be linked to monarchical states, creating among the elites what I have termed "hierarchical nations." On the other hand, we cannot speak of national*ism* as an ideology or movement during this period. That had to wait for the seventeenth century when, after the radicalization of the Reformation, a "covenantal" nationalism drawing its inspiration from the biblical narratives of ancient Israel, especially in the Pentateuch, emerged in a few states like England, Scotland, and the Netherlands. Though apocalyptic and European in outlook, this radical Protestant form of nationalism began to see divine providence in godly churches and elect nations, and to draw the logical political conclusions. In many ways, it provides the focal point of a sociological history of the formation of nations and nationalism, in the sense that radical covenantal Protestantism constituted the means to a "breakthrough" to modern nations and nationalism. Without its inspiration and achievements, it is doubtful whether nations as we have come to know them would have been forged, or whether nationalism would have become so dynamic and powerful an ideological movement. To that extent, the modernist dating, and understanding, of nationalism needs to be revised.

On the other hand, the rise of radical civic-republican nationalism, notably in France, and the inauguration of the first secularizing nation and state, confirms the modernist thesis of the "modern nation," so long as it is understood as only one, however influential, among the different forms of the nation. Here, nationalist ideology comes into its own, though never entirely separate from other ideologies like liberalism and socialism. On the other hand, the civic-republican type of nation was repeatedly challenged by other kinds of national identities based on the alternative traditions of hierarchy and covenant, with which it soon found it was necessary to seek some accommodation. This suggests that we cannot separate the issue of periodization and dating of the concept of the nation from broader questions of the historical forms of individual nations, nor from the fundamental cultural traditions in which they have been embedded and which to this day give rise to alternative national destinies.

Conclusion

The point of departure of this enquiry was the problem of periodization of nations: the epoch or epochs in which the historical communities we call nations emerged and flourished. It soon became apparent that different kinds of nation or national community emerged in different periods. So the problem became one of accounting for the relationship between the periods of their emergence and their varied cultural forms: between what we might term the "dating" and the "shaping" of nations.

Such a formulation presupposed the continuing utility of terms like "nation" and "national identity" as categories of analysis alongside other categories of collective cultural identity. For purposes of clarity and demarcation, defining the concept of the nation in ideal-typical terms constituted a necessary first step. This in turn allowed us to identify various forms of the nation as a historical community held to possess a cultural and/or political identity. Accordingly, I defined the category of the nation as a named and self-defining human community, whose members cultivate shared myths, memories, symbols, values, and traditions, reside in and identify with a historic homeland, create and disseminate a distinctive public culture, and observe shared customs and common laws. In this context, it was important to separate the category of "nation" from that of "national*ism*" defined as an ideological movement for attaining and maintaining autonomy, unity, and identity for a human population some of whose members deem it to constitute an actual or potential nation. For, while some of its elements appeared well before the conventional late eighteenth-century dating, the theory and ideology of nationalism are relatively modern. On the other hand, though the majority of present-day nations emerged in the last two centuries, both the concept of the nation and some well-known examples of national communities and national sentiments long predated the advent of modernity.

By adopting an approach that emphasizes the significance of ethnic ties and ethnic symbols, myths, memories, and traditions, we can chart the processes and cultural resources that encourage the formation and persistence of nations, as well as tracing their different historical forms. As a result, it becomes possible to highlight the periods and locations in which nations and national identities became salient and widespread, not only in terms of such processes as self-definition, symbol cultivation, territorialization, public culture, and the like, but also through the presence and use of various cultural resources – myths of ethnic election, memories of the golden age, ideals of sacrifice, and the sanctification of homelands.

In the ancient world of classical antiquity and the Near East, ethnic ties and identities were prevalent, alongside attachments to city-states, tribes, and, to a lesser extent, empires – notably in ancient Greece and Persia. On the other hand, the processes that conduce to the rise of nations (let alone nationalism) were generally absent. Notwithstanding, there were a few exceptions: ancient Egypt, early Christian Armenia, and especially Judah just before and after the exile in Babylon. In the two latter cases, the creation of different symbolic and cultural resources helped to ensure the survival, albeit in altered forms, of the normative community after the exile of many of its members from their homelands.

Perhaps even more significant for the subsequent shaping of nations have been the legacies bequeathed to later periods by the ancient world. Here I singled out three main cultural traditions of public culture: those of hierarchy, covenant, and commonwealth or civic republic. The first was, of course, dominant and widespread throughout the ancient Near East and the Mediterranean from Old Kingdom Egypt and the Akkadian empire of Sargon to the Hellenistic kingdoms and the Roman empire. It provided a model of sanctified inequality and sacred rule, and when conjoined to a dominant *ethnie* and to the memory of the Davidic kings of Israel and Judah, an ideal of sacred kingship, as in medieval France – a legacy that, mediated through imperial Rome, was drawn upon time and again throughout the Middle Ages from Pepin and Charlemagne to Charles V and Henry VIII.

Equally important in the long term were the other two cultural traditions. The covenantal ideal of ancient Israel was purveyed, first through the Hebrew Bible and the Septuagint, and then by the Church in the Greek Orthodox East and the Latin Catholic West, particularly the beliefs in ethnic election and unity and in divine mission. Similarly, the civic model of the republic or commonwealth took as its inspiration the patriotism and citizen solidarity of the Greek *polis*, notably ancient Athens, and the heroic simplicity and self-sacrifice found in an idealized Republican Rome. Revived in the medieval Italian city-republics, it was taken up by many of the free communes of medieval Germany, Switzerland, and Flanders.

However, for the most part, much of the European land mass as well as the Near East was the domain of successive empires. Here, the basic processes of formation of nations were not developed, and hierarchy was seldom linked to an isolated or dominant ethnic community. Where, after the fragmentation of European Christendom and the rise of centralizing states, it did come to be conjoined with a dominant *ethnie*, as in the states of Muscovy, Spain, France, England, Denmark, and Sweden, it helped to provide the underpinning for a hierarchical type of nation, in which, despite the fact that the sentiments of the mass of the population went largely unrecorded, a powerful and often exclusive sense of national identity nevertheless manifested itself among rulers and elites. Such national sentiments were in turn encouraged by, as they helped to stimulate, commercial competition and warfare between rival European states, which in turn mobilized armies, instilled in them the virtue of solidarity and the need for defense of "their" national territories, and provided them with myths of battle and heroic deeds. In this sense, we may speak of *hierarchical nations* in the later Middle Ages, in which a predominantly "crown-centered patriotism" began to percolate down to the urban middle classes, providing a fulcrum for powerful national sentiments within the framework of an increasingly bounded and centralized national territory, standardized legal order, and distinctive public culture.

It was the Reformation that provided the "breakthrough" to both popular nations and the first kind of national*ism*. Its return to the Old Testament in the radical Reformist versions, notably Calvinism, reintroduced the covenantal model, so long a theological concept, into the political mainstream. In late sixteenth- and seventeenth-century Scotland, England, and Holland, as well as in many of the American colonies and Swiss cities, the covenantal ideal and the Exodus narrative, vividly conveyed in the vernacular Bible, came to provide the dynamic for radical change in the quest for individual salvation and collective election – including the election of nations. In many ways, this period is pivotal for the rise of both nations and nationalisms. Building on pre-existing national sentiments among the elites, *covenantal nations and nationalisms* were able to offer broader and more dynamic conceptions of the nation and its ideals – even creating republican commonwealths – and thereby to mobilize large numbers of people for political programmes and military action.

At first sight, the modern secular *civic-republican nation* appears to mark a rupture with any earlier historical form of the nation, just as its nationalism seems so different in tone and style from earlier covenantal nationalism. This parallels the way in which the republican patriotism of classical antiquity introduced a quite different cultural tradition, collective sentiment, and model of community from those round about. But in fact the modern republican forms and ideologies of the nation build on the examples, and use many of the symbols, values, and traditions, of earlier covenantal nations and nationalisms. In this sense, modern nationalisms, starting with the French Revolution, are best viewed as forms of a secular religion of the people, alongside or in opposition to traditional religions. What gives them their radical character is their disavowal of hierarchy and a concomitant revolutionary programme against the *ancien régime* in which sacred monarchy played so large a part. But, as the fashion for oath-swearing ceremonies and sacred compacts demonstrated, no such antagonism existed towards covenantal nations and nationalisms. In fact, many elements which were ultimately derived from the Old Testament Covenant remained embedded in several European and Western nationalisms. Even some of the traditions of hierarchical nations like monarchy have been retained, if in attenuated form, and, along with covenantal traditions, they pose continuing challenges to the global progress of the republican nation. Similarly, myths and memories of hierarchical or covenantal "golden ages" may inspire alternative destinies among wide sections of the community. Hence, the often multistranded character of many nations which can be read as so many palimpsests of different collective pasts and cultural traditions.

What lessons may we draw from this account of nations and nationalisms for the contemporary world? The first is the continuing power of ethnic community and identity to form one of the enduring bases for social and political solidarity throughout history right up to the present day. Even now, there is no sign of that waning of ethnic ties predicted by so many liberal observers. If anything, globalizing pressures have, through large-scale migration and mass communications, revitalized ethnic ties and sentiments across the globe.

The second is the multifaceted nature of most nations and nationalisms, the often layered character of their cultural traditions, the result of gradual evolution or of drastic change and revolution. This in turn testifies to the continuing importance of different cultural traditions, especially those of covenant and republic, endowing national communities with a richness and diversity that is often at odds with nationalist attempts to create uniform cultures and citizens. But such diversity does not diminish the distinctive nature of a nation's core public culture or the uniqueness of its mythic and symbolic repository, as the three major cultural traditions transform its ethnopolitical core in different permutations and sequences.

A third lesson is the longevity of nations and the durability of national conceptions. Even if we can find only a few examples of nations in the ancient world, the idea of the nation, so clearly expressed in the Hebrew Bible, has been part of the political vocabulary of European elites for over a millennium, and much earlier in the Near East. The reality may have been ethnocultural (or imperial or urban), but the aspiration was often national. What tended to be lacking, even among ethnic communities, were some or all of those processes and resources that encourage the formation of nations – territorialization of memories and attachments, development and dissemination of a distinctive public culture, and observance of standardized laws and shared customs, as well as traditions of the golden age or mission and sacrifice. But that did not diminish the appeal of the model of the nation, as it was exemplified and purveyed in the Hebrew Bible through Christian traditions, across many centuries of turmoil and change. In other words, the national idea and model long antedate the French Revolution, and possess a durability that must warn us against too premature a verdict on its early demise.

Finally and perhaps crucially, the fact that nationalism as ideology and movement emerged in the wake of the Reformation as part of, and as stimulus for, a wider popular revolution against entrenched authority of priest and king should alert us to its central and continuing role in the modern world. While expressions of nationalism and national identity have waxed and waned with world wars and other major events, the core of nationalist ideology has remained intact, since its first irruption into politics in seventeenth-century Western Europe. Since then, it has reinforced older national conceptions and sentiments, and provided a blueprint for ethnic communities to transform themselves into political nations. Disembedded from its early historical habitats, nationalism has become available for purposes of popular mobilization and legitimization in every continent, and is likely to continue to do so as long as the need for cultural identity is fused with the quest for popular sovereignty.

Notes

Introduction: The Theoretical Debate

1 See Connor (1990). For further discussion, and empirical examples, see the essays in *Geopolitics* (2002); and A. D. Smith: "Dating the Nation," in Conversi (2002, 53–71).
2 See Connor (1994, chs. 4, 8); and for a thorough analysis of this issue through the main rival paradigms of nations and nationalism, see Ichijo and Uzelac (2005).
3 For an extended examination of the varieties of "modernism," see A. D. Smith (1998, Part I).
4 See Gellner (1983, chs. 2–3).
5 See Hobsbawm (1990, ch. 2); Breuilly (1993).
6 See Kedourie (1960), and for nationalism's diffusion outside Europe, Kedourie (1971, Introduction); cf. Gellner (1964, ch. 7).
7 See B. Anderson (1991, chs. 1–3); and cf. A. D. Smith (1991b).
8 See Hastings (1997), and the assessments of his thesis in *Nations and Nationalism* (2003).
9 See, *inter alia*, Wormald (1984); Reynolds (1984, ch. 7); and Gillingham (1992).
10 See W. Connor: "The Timelessness of Nations," and A. D. Smith: "History and National Destiny: Responses and Clarifications," in Guibernau and Hutchinson (2004, 35–47, 195–209).
11 Hastings (1997, 26). For the ancient Israelites, see Grosby (2002); for the medieval Swiss, see Im Hof (1991, ch. 1).
12 On the small scale and size of nationalist movements in nineteenth-century Europe, see Argyle (1976).
13 Hobsbawm (1990, 75); Breuilly (1996, 151, 154).
14 Llobera (1994, 87–8); see also Reynolds (1983) and (1984, ch. 8).
15 See Armstrong (1982); also Armstrong (1995).

16 See B. Anderson (1991, ch. 1).
17 Shils (1957); Geertz (1973). See Eller and Coughlan (1993) for a critique of "primordialism."
18 For this defense, see Grosby (1994, 1995).
19 See van den Berghe (1995) and (2005).
20 See Horowitz (2002).
21 Grosby (2002, 120).

1 The Concept and Its Varieties

1 No modernist spells out this conception in its "pure" form. I have constructed the ideal type of the modern nation from the various conceptions proposed by Deutsch (1966), Nairn (1977), Gellner (1983), Giddens (1984), Hobsbawm (1990), and Mann (1993).
2 On the other hand, outside Europe, in Latin America, and large parts of Africa, where a bourgeoisie was much less in evidence, civic-territorial and republican conceptions of the nation prevailed, with Rousseau's ideals providing the chief inspiration in French West Africa and Mill's writings for British West Africa. On which, see Geiss (1974) and Hodgkin (1964). On the "stoic" phase of the Enlightenment, see Leith (1965).
3 On the ancient Greek usages, see Geary (2001, ch. 2) and Tonkin et al. (1989, Introduction). For the history of the term "*natio*," see Greenfeld (1992, ch. 1) and Zernatto (1944). On the distinction between "ethnographic" and "political" usages of nation, see the powerful argument in Breuilly (2005a) – though premodern usages often had political dimensions.
4 The mass character of the modern nation is emphasized by Deutsch (1966), Gellner (1983), and Mann (1993), and may be compared with E. H. Carr's (1945) typology, and progression, from monarchical to democratic-Jacobin to social mass nations and nationalism.
5 For a highly critical analysis of the core doctrine of nationalism, see Freeden (1998); cf. Miller (1993) and A. D. Smith (1983, ch. 7) for somewhat more sympathetic accounts. More recently, see Hearn (2006, ch. 1).
6 On the language of nations at the Council of Constance, see Loomis (1939) and Toftgaard (2005), which appear to contest the view of John Breuilly (2005b, 81) that at the Church Councils the term "nation" had no ethnic or linguistic connotations. For references to earlier usages, see the essays in Scales and Zimmer (2005), notably those by Reynolds and Scales; also Scales (2000). Reynolds, indeed, argues for the common assumption of "nations" in medieval Europe, albeit as a conception quite different from that of the modern nation.

7 See Plamenatz (1976), Seton-Watson (1977), and Ignatieff (1993). For the uses of this distinction, see Breton (1988) and, on a more philosophical level, Miller (1995). For a critique of "civic" nationalism, see Yack (1999).

8 For this analysis of the Arab national identities, see Suleiman (2003). Other works which link a sense of common ethnicity to modern nations include Hutchinson (1987) on Ireland (and more generally, Hutchinson 2000), Hosking (1993) on ethnic Russianness, and Panossian (2002) on Armenian nationalism. For the historiographical debates, see A. D. Smith (2000a).

9 Other terms like "social class" also possess different uses and meanings; see Ossowski (1962). In fact, cultural and political identities are usually combined in different ways and to varying degrees; and it is difficult, perhaps even futile, to seek to disentangle them and place them in some kind of causal-historical sequence, as Weber (1968) attempted with his suggestion that political action tends to forge ethnic community.

10 On the other hand, perennialists who tended to see nations everywhere generally operate with an analytic category which was defined too imprecisely to discriminate the national from other kinds of community and identity. In this respect, the "neo-perennialist" historians are more circumspect, usually confining themselves to making a case for a few well-chosen examples like England.

11 A purely inductive method of defining the concept of the nation in terms of the ideas of self-styled nationalists – apart from posing the problem of having to define the term "nationalism" in the same manner – relies too much on the variability and self-categorization of its subjects. Hence, in contrast to the method I adopted in A. D. Smith (1983, ch. 7), a large element of stipulation is required for constructing the ideal type and to provide a benchmark for subsequent analysis.

12 For a discussion of competing definitions of the concept of the nation, see Connor (1994, ch. 4) and Uzelac (2002). See also Dieckhoff and Jaffrelot (2005, Introduction and section I) and A. D. Smith (2001, ch. 1). For a critique of the latter, see Guibernau (2004).

13 For Armstrong (1982), these social processes and symbolic resources span much of the medieval epoch in both Christian Europe and the Islamic Middle East. For the links between ethnicity and religion, see Fishman (1980).

14 See Routledge (2003) for his critique of modernist uses of the premodern past as a mirror of the present. The idea of continuity of nations and national sentiment has been most clearly argued for England and its neighbors by Hastings (1997); see also Gillingham (1992) and Lydon (1995). On Slavophilism, see Thaden (1964); and for the Gaelic revival in Ireland, see Lyons (1979) and Hutchinson (1987).

15 For this approach, see Armstrong (1982) and Grosby (2006). Though close at times, this view is to be distinguished from that of both the cultural and the biological "primordialists," on which see Horowitz (2002).

16 For the rediscovery of the past in the "national awakening," particularly in Eastern Europe, see Pearson (1993), Agnew (1993), and Hroch (1985). For a vivid example in Hungary, see Hofer (1980); and for Greece, Herzfeld (1982). On the role of the intellectuals, see, *inter alia*, Breuilly (1993, 46–51), Pinard and Hamilton (1984), and Zubaida (1978). For premodern revivals, see A. D. Smith (1986, chs. 3, 8).

17 Hastings (1997, 186) on the Christian adoption of the polity of the Old Testament. On the European uses of the idea of holy lands in states like England, France, Spain, Bohemia, and Muscovy, see Housley (2000).

18 On the reception of the classical tradition in Europe, see Bolgar (1954); also for the rediscovery of Greek intellectual achievements, Campbell and Sherrard (1968, ch. 1).

19 See Brubaker (1996, ch. 1); cf. A. D. Smith (1998, 77–8).

20 For this tendency to accept national assumptions as ingrained and "enhabited," see Billig (1995).

21 On "situational ethnicity," see especially Okamura (1981), and Wilmsen and McAllister (1995), and for the pervasive quality of national identity, see Connor (1994, esp. ch. 8).

22 See Scheuch (1966) on the methodological problems of analyzing political culture.

23 M. Weber (1948, 176). For an assessment of the political version of modernism in the work of Giddens, Mann, and Breuilly, in particular, see A. D. Smith (1998, ch. 4).

24 See Breuilly (1993; 2005a); Mann (1993, ch. 7; 1995).

25 See Hutchinson (2005, chs. 2–3); for the nations without states, see Guibernau (1999).

26 For general surveys of the growth of the "national state" in Western Europe, see Tilly (1975), Ranum (1975), and A. Marx (2003).

27 See Guibernau (1999); and for Scotland, Ichijo (2004).

2 Ethnic and Religious Roots

1 There is a vast literature on the concepts of ethnic identity and ethnicity. I have found particularly illuminating Sugar (1980), Horowitz (1985), and Eriksen (1993), as well as Barth's (1969) path-breaking analysis. See also Wilmsen and McAllister (1995). For elite competition for cultural and symbolic resources, see Brass (1985, 1991). On ethnicity and war, see A. D. Smith (1981).

2 On the conviction of ancestral ties, see Connor (1994, ch. 8). For critiques of the concept of ethnicity, see Hobsbawm (1990, 63–7) and Poole (1999).

3 For these distinctions, see Handelman (1977) and Eriksen (1993). On the concept of *ethnie*, see A. D. Smith (1986, chs. 2–5; 1991a, chs. 2–3).

4 This paragraph is based on A. D. Smith (2001, ch. 1). See also Hutchinson (2000).

5 On the thesis of an ancient Athenian "nation" (as opposed to *polis*), see E. Cohen (2000). For the ambiguous legacy of city-state patriotism for nationalism, see Minogue (1976) and Viroli (1995) – indeed, Viroli sharply opposes such patriotism to an ethnocultural nationalism (on which, see chapter 6 below). For arguments about "civic" nationalism, see Miller (1995).

6 For the Phoenicians, see Moscati (1973); and on the collective designation of the ancient Hellenes, see E. Hall (1992). For medieval English denigration of the Irish, see Lydon (1995). More generally on English attitudes, see the interesting account in R. Davies (2000); and for modern immigrants and their reception in Southern Europe, see the perceptive analysis in Triandafyllidou (2001, chs. 3–4).

7 For the designations of *France* and *français*, see Beaune (1991); and on those of the *Teutonici* and *deutsch*, see Scales (2000), whose survey of medieval historians reveals wide differences in the dating of nations both among themselves and even more between medieval and modern historians.

8 For an often controversial "constructivist" argument about the Roman ethnic designation of "barbarian" tribes, when in reality we are dealing with fluid political alignments of leaders and their followers, see Geary (2001, chs. 3–4). A not dissimilar example of ethnic classification by outsiders in sub-Saharan Africa, in this case by British colonialists, is described in Young (1985).

9 On Latin literature in this early period, see Wilkinson (1976, ch. 2), and for the elaboration of cultural identities and myths of descent in early Republican Rome, see the fascinating accounts in Gruen (1994) and Fraschetti (2005). Connor's thesis about the centrality of myths of ancestry is lucidly set out in Connor (1994, ch. 8).

10 For a succinct survey and discussion of British reactions to black and Muslim immigrants, see Kumar (2003, ch. 8).

11 On the territorialization of attachments and memories, see A. D. Smith (1999a, ch. 5). The discourse of "home" and "abroad" is analyzed by Billig (1995).

12 For Horace's eulogies of the Sabine hills, see Highet (1959). The late medieval ideal of the Garden of France is described in Beaune (1991,

296), and the impact of the sea and plain on seventeenth-century Holland is vividly evoked by Schama (1987, ch. 1). For the effect of the Alpine landscape on Swiss identity, see Zimmer (1998).

13 On the pre-Romantic cult of Nature, see Charlton (1984). Schama (1995, 479–93) also describes the growing association of the pure Alpine landscapes with virtue and liberty, both generally and for Swiss national identity, especially in Albrecht von Haller's eulogy, *Die Alpen* (1732). For the transformation of Russian attitudes to their landscapes and the Romantic appreciation of vast spaces, see the suggestive account in Ely (2002).

14 For the New Year festivals in ancient Mesopotamia, see Frankfort (1948); and for the Panathenaic festival in Athens, see Andrewes (1971, 246, 263). The rituals of kingship in France are discussed by Le Goff (1998) and in sixteenth-century Russia by Crummey (1987, esp. 134–7). Hastings' thesis about the early development of literary culture in medieval England is critically assessed in Kumar (2003, ch. 3); see also the essays on medieval English literature and national identity, in Lavezzo (2004).

15 For the ancient Persian laws, see Wiesehofer (2004, Part I); and for the various definitions of Jewishness in the Second Temple period, see S. Cohen (1998), Schwartz (2004), and chapter 3 below.

16 Of the modernists, Giddens (1984) and Breuilly (1993) are the strongest exponents of the association between legal standardization in a community, citizenship, and the modern state. The role of lawmaking by the religious institutions of diaspora Armenians and Jews is discussed by Armstrong (1982, ch. 7).

17 For the use of cultural resources by intellectuals, see especially Kedourie (1971, Introduction) and Hobsbawm and Ranger (1983, Introduction and ch. 7); and especially Brass (1991, ch. 2).

18 On which, see O'Brien (1988a) and, for the French Revolution, O'Brien (1988b). The "sacred" dimensions of nations and nationalism are discussed in A. D. Smith (2000b).

19 On Egyptian myths and religion generally, see David (1982), and for their Creation myths, Oakes and Gahlin (2005, 300–7); for the Japanese myths, see Blacker (1984).

20 For political myth generally, see Tudor (1972) and Armstrong (1982, chs. 4–5). The Romulus myth is analyzed by Fraschetti (2005); and the myths of Athens' origins in E. Cohen (2000, ch. 4) and, in Greek art, Robertson (1987, 175–6). Tiridates' conversion in Armenia is discussed in Redgate (2000, ch. 6); for Clovis' conversion, see E. James (1988, ch. 4); and for the tales of Vladimir's conversion, see Milner-Gulland (1999, 91–6). The rediscovery of the Swiss foundation myth is analyzed

by Kreis (1991) in its nineteenth-century setting, and for the Scots Declaration of Arbroath in 1320, see Duncan (1970) and Cowan (2003).

21 See Connor (1994, ch. 8) and Horowitz (1985, chs. 1–2).

22 See especially Novak (1995) and Nicholson (1988) for the biblical Covenant with ancient Israel. Its implications for later Jews, as well as other *ethnies*, are discussed in A. D. Smith (2003, chs. 3–4). See also the special issue of *Nations and Nationalism* (1999).

23 For discussion of covenantal myths of election, see O'Brien (1988a); also the essays in Hutchinson and Lehmann (1994). For a rich and incisive account of the workings and consequences of living according to the biblical Covenant among Afrikaners, Ulster-Scots, and Zionist Jews in Israel, see Akenson (1992).

24 Medieval Christian *antemurale* myths of missionary election, especially in the European shatter zones, are discussed in Armstrong (1982, ch. 3). See also Housley (2000) and *Nations and Nationalism* (1999), especially the essays by Hastings and Templin; and A. D. Smith (1986, ch. 3; 2003, chs. 4, 6; 1999b) for this and the following paragraph.

25 See Grosby (1991, 240; also in Grosby 2002, 36); also, more generally, Grosby (1995; 2006). On the connections between geography and nations, see Hooson (1994).

26 On sacred territories, generally, see Hastings (2003); on the vision of Poland as a sacred territory, see Kristof (1994).

27 For Ashur-bani-pal's library of Babylonian texts, as well as his nostalgia for earlier Mesopotamian culture, see Roux (1964, chs. 20–1); also Oppenheim (1977). Early Roman literature and piety are discussed in Wilkinson (1976, ch. 2). On Ethiopia, D. Levine (1974, ch. 7) describes the medieval "Solomonic" dynasty's attempt to revive the culture of the ancient kingdom of Aksum. For an analysis of "golden ages" and their uses, see A. D. Smith (1997).

28 On the Greek nationalist Hellenic vision, see the perceptive analysis in Kitromilides (1979). The Egyptian Pharaonicist movement is discussed with rich detail by Gershoni and Jankowski (1987, chs. 7–8). For other "golden age" myths, see the essays in Hosking and Schöpflin (1997), especially by N. Davies and Wilson.

29 The ideal of martyrdom in early Christian Armenia is discussed in the introduction to Elishe's *History* by Thomson (1982); see also the perceptive account in Nersessian (2001, ch. 2). For the Dutch sense of national suffering, see Schama (1987, chs. 1–2). Sacrifice for the glory of the ancient *polis* is praised in Simonides' epitaphs to the Spartans at Thermopylae and at Plataea, and above all in Pericles' Funeral Oration to the Athenian dead of the first year of the Peloponnesian War; on which see E. Cohen (2000, ch. 4).

30 On the Pantheon and its uses, see Ozouf (1998). The cult of the war experience and the focus of the civic religion of nationalism on mass sacrifice and the war dead are superbly analyzed by Mosse (1990), and for Germany, Mosse (1975, esp. ch. 3); see also the moving account in J. Winter (1995, ch. 4).

31 On the essential "goodness" of nations, see Anderson (1999).

3 Community in Antiquity

1 For surveys of the ethnic communities of the ancient Near East, see Wiseman (1973) and, for the Hellenistic period, Mendels (1992). I have discussed some of the issues raised in this chapter in A. D. Smith (2004, ch. 5).

2 Gellner (1983); also Hobsbawm (1990, esp. ch. 2); and for a clear rejection of any premodern nations or nationalism, see Breuilly (1993; 2005a).

3 Cited in S. T. Smith (2003, 137, and see *passim*), a careful and thought-provoking archaeological exploration of Egyptian relations with Nubia. See S. Jones (1997) for her cultural approach to the archaeology of ethnicity; also Welsby and Anderson (2004, ch. 5).

4 The Pharaohs of the New Kingdom, of course, acquired an empire in the mid-second millennium BC, but, as with other later empires, this did not prevent them from categorizing as "foreign" and denigrating the populations that they subjugated, while at the same time assimilating these same individuals, including the Nubians, some of whom came to serve in the Egyptian police force, and even as soldiers on becoming free citizens; on which see S. T. Smith (2003) and Hayes (1973).

5 Reade (1984, 23); and for the propaganda of Assyrian art, Reade (1979). On the Nimrud ivories, see Mallowan (1978).

6 Liverani (1979, 305; italics in original).

7 For the relations between Assyrians and other conquered peoples in this period, see Tadmor (1997) and Liverani (1979); and more generally, Larsen (1979b) and the essays in Larsen (1979a, Part IV). The Assyrian ideology of kingship and hierarchy can be clearly seen in their reliefs and statuary, especially those of their kings; on which, see I. Winter (1997). For this and several of the subsequent references on ancient Mesopotamia, I am indebted to Professor Mark Geller.

8 Nylander (1979, 374–5). See also Wiesehofer (2004, 26).

9 Herodotus: *Histories* I, 125, cited in Wiesehofer (2004, 35).

10 See Barth (1969, Introduction). On the relations between Achaemenid Persians and their subject peoples, see Wiesehofer (2004, chs. 2–3); Cook

(1983, chs. 7–8); and with regard to Persian–Jewish relations, Widengren (1973).

11 For Sumerian responses to these incursions and a vivid lament for the "land of Sumer," see Pongratz-Leisten (1997). For Sumerian religion, see Jacobsen (1976); and for the revival under the Third Dynasty of Ur, see Roux (1964, ch. 10).

12 Millard (1973, 38); and generally on the Phoenicians, Moscati (1973).

13 Ap-Thomas (1973, 262). One needs to recall that most Phoenician literature is not extant. On the lack of any political unity among the Phoenicians to match their shared cultural practices, see Routledge (2003).

14 On early Greek genealogies and the rules of royal succession, see the detailed analysis of Finkelberg (2005, chs. 2–3). The uses of ethnic origins by "Ionian" Athens and "Dorian" Sparta in their arguments before and during the Peloponnesian War are assessed by Alty (1982).

15 On the rise of pan-Hellenic sentiments and stereotypes of Greek freedom and Persian servility, see E. Hall (1992); also Bacon (1961). For a perceptive analysis of the internal "aggregative" manner of constructing a Greek identity in the archaic age, see J. Hall (1997).

16 Herodotus: *Histories*, VIII, 144.2, cited in J. Hall (1997, 44).

17 On pan-Hellenism and its limits, see Finley (1986, ch. 7) and the essays in Fondation Hardt (1962).

18 For the thesis of an Athenian "nation," see the stimulating analysis of E. Cohen (2000), though the extent to which its culture was really distinctive in the wider Greek ethnocultural community can be questioned. However, see the recent forceful argument in favor of an Athenian nationhood that contributed to, and drew strength from, a wider pan-Hellenic sense of national identity, in Roshwald (2006, 22–30). For the Athenian myth of "Ionian" descent, see J. Hall (1997, ch. 3).

19 For these Sumerian complaints from the "Marriage of Martu," see Liverani (1973, 106). The most detailed cultural analysis of the construction of the "Amurru" and their god by the Sumerians is Beaulieu (2002).

20 See Malamat (1973) for an overview of the various Aramean tribal confederations.

21 The Sefire stele with its references to "all-Aram" is well analyzed by Grosby (2002, chs. 5–6); see also Zadok (1991).

22 Tadmor (1991). For the thesis that "all-Aram" in Syria designated an incipient nationality, see Grosby (2002, chs. 5–6). On the possibility of an Assyrian "national state," see below and n. 34.

23 See Grosby (2002, 123–5) for this characterization of Edom and its territory; also Bartlett (1973).

24 See Noth (1960) for the idea of an Israelite amphictyony. Israelite myths of descent are discussed in Cazelles (1979). For a recent balanced assessment of the vexed problem of Israelite origins, see Frendo (2004).

25 For this assessment, see Eissfeldt (1975, 551–2). More recent research focuses on the peasant or nomad origins of Israel, on which see Ahlstrom (1986, chs. 2–3) and Dever (2003). On the centrality of Ephraim and Joshua, see Cazelles (1979, 280–3), and for the ancient Near Eastern social milieu, see Zeitlin (1984).

26 Hosea (13:10–11) for a prophetic rebuke; but cf. the strong counter-arguments in Talmon (1986, Part I). Skepticism towards the existence, let alone significance, of the United Monarchy can be found in Ahlström (1986, ch. 7) and, of course, in the writings of "revisionists" like P. Davies (1992) and Finkelstein and Silberman (2001). But see the vigorous critique in Dever (2004).

27 For the shift from an oral to a textual culture among the elites in eighth- and seventh-century Judah, see the excellent analysis in Schniedewind (2005, ch. 5). For the editing of the Pentateuch, see Friedman (1997); also Emerton (2004), and other essays in Day (2004). On the Covenant ideal, see the detailed analysis in Nicholson (1988).

28 See Grosby (2002, 94–7). For the view that most of the geographical locations in the Pentateuch are best placed in the period of king Josiah, see Finkelstein and Silberman (2001, chs. 10–11), a view firmly rejected by William Dever (2003).

29 Ackroyd (1979, 339). See also Ahlström (1986, ch. 7).

30 For the political symbols of Jewish "nationalism," see Mendels (1992) who distinguishes them from modern national symbols. The extent, manner, and scope of Jewish adoption of surrounding Hellenistic material and literary culture are carefully assessed by L. Levine (1998). For the ideological system of most Palestinian Jews in the late Second Temple period, see the thought-provoking analysis in Schwartz (2004). See also Roshwald (2006, ch. 1) and Goodblatt (2006).

31 On the Greeks, see J. Hall (1997) and, for the Mycenaean and Homeric epochs, Finkelberg (2005); also Finley (1986, ch. 7). For the Israelites, see especially the essays in Day (2004); also Schniedewind (2005).

32 See Kumar (2006) for a comparison of the French and British imperial nations and their respective nationalisms.

33 See Oppenheim (1977, III); also Brinkman (1979); and for the monumental art of Assyrian monarchy, see Reade (1979); and I. Winter (1997).

34 For his thesis, see Parpola (2004); but cf. Machinist (1997) and Liverani (1979).

35 For this nostalgia of legitimation, see Wiesehofer (2004).

36 The *Tale of Sinuhe* cited in Grosby (2002, 31–2) and Pritchard (1975, 5–11); and Trigger et al. (1983, 316–17), where the mixture of Egyptian cultural superiority and assimilation of foreigners is underlined for the Late Period and under Persian rule, especially through the detailed testimonies of Herodotus.

37 Kemp (1983, 71–3). Routledge (2003) argues for the mobility of individuals into the elites, whereas Beyer (1959) stresses the social and educational divide between noble and priestly families and the rest of the population in the ancient world.

38 Book of Numbers (34). On the territorial dimension of Judaism, see W. D. Davies (1982). On the sanctification of the Promised Land, see Zeitlin (1984, 171).

39 See Ackroyd (1979). For Josiah's reforms, see Schniedewind (2005, ch. 6); and Friedman (1997, ch. 5). More generally, see Roshwald (2006, 14–22).

40 For the Zealots, see Brandon (1967, ch. 2); but cf. the critique in Zeitlin (1988, chs. 2, 10). For the Roman–Jewish wars, see M. Aberbach (1966) and Mendels (1992). For a profound exploration of the various ways of defining Jewishness in this period, see S. Cohen (1998).

4 Hierarchical Nations

1 The ancient Near Eastern origin of medieval Islamic and Christian concepts of administration is signaled in Armstrong (1982, ch. 5). For Egyptian concepts, see Trigger et al. (1983), and for Mesopotamian ideas, see Frankfort (1948).

2 For the Assyrian combination of hierarchy and ethnicity, see the references to Liverani (1979) and Parpola (2004) in chapter 3 above. For the question of the continuity between ancient and modern Assyrians, see Odisho (2001).

3 The Armenian version of covenantal public culture through its Holy Apostolic Church is discussed by Garsoian (1999, ch. 12) and Nersessian (2001). For early Armenia in general, see Redgate (2000) and for the early Armenian Christian concept and history of martyrdom, in the wars against Sasanian Iran, see Thomson (1982).

4 The biblical Covenant is examined in Novak (1995) and A. D. Smith (2003, ch. 3); and by Walzer (1984) for its inspiration for the English and American Revolutions. See also Roshwald (2006, ch. 4).

5 The Ethiopian "Solomonic" dynasty and the myth of the transfer of the Ark of the Covenant from Jerusalem to Aksum in the *Kebra-Negast* (Book

of Kings) are described and analyzed in D. Levine (1974, ch. 7) and Ullendorff (1988). See also Henze (2000, 56–72).

6 On the Greek *polis*, see Andrewes (1971) and A. H. Jones (1978); on Greek festivals and civic religion, see Cartledge (1987).

7 See Ogilvie (1976) for the early history of Rome; also Fraschetti (2005). For Rome's expansion within Italy, see Grimal (1968, 84–123). Its encounter with Magna Graecia and the impact of Greek culture on Roman identity are analyzed by Gruen (1994).

8 For the Augustan poets, see Wilkinson (1976, ch. 5) and Highet (1959). The same republican nostalgia can be found in the *Histories*, the *Annals*, and the *Germania* of Tacitus, on which see Martin (1989).

9 For the Italian communes and their revival of Roman political forms, see Waley (1969) and Martines (2002).

10 On the Men of the Great Synagogue and the Pharisees in the Persian and then the Ptolemaic province of Yahud (Judea), see L. Finkelstein (1989), and for the Hasmonean revolt and kingdom, see Goldstein (1989). For a penetrating analysis of the belief system of the majority of Jews in Palestine in the Second Temple period, see Schwartz (2004, 49–74).

11 Hastings (1997, 186) also claimed that Christianity, in including the Old Testament in its scriptures, took over the almost monolithic image of the nation contained therein, especially as the New Testament lacked a political model. One should add that in its early days, Christianity appeared to appreciate the covenantal ideal of the nation, whereas later, when it became the official religion of the Roman empire, it looked to the more hierarchical model offered by the Old Testament's ideal of sacred kingship.

12 On these early Swiss intercantonal oaths, see Im Hof (1991, ch. 1) and Zimmer (2003, ch. 1).

13 Wiesehofer (2004, 165); and ibid., 171, for Shapur's inscription.

14 On Chosroes' reforms, see Frye (1966, 259, 261). For the cycles of legends, see *Cambridge History of Iran* (1983, Vol. 3, Part 1, 359ff.) and Wiesehofer (2004, 224–5).

15 For Kartir's reforms, see Wiesehofer (2004, 200); and for later developments in medieval Iran, see Frye (1978).

16 For the self-definition of the Byzantines, see Mango (1980, 6, 27–31, 218–20); also Hupchik (2002, 26–8).

17 Vasiliev (1958, 562). For the possibility of a "precocious nationalism" in late Byzantium, after the restoration of the empire under the Palaeologi in 1261, see Armstrong (1982, 178–81, 216–17). But this is generally rejected by historians of Greece such as Kitromilides (1989) and Roudometof (1998).

18 For the quotation from the Russian Primary Chronicle, see Milner-Gulland (1999, 149). The growing Byzantine tendencies of the Muscovite autocracy, especially under Ivan III, are described in Crummey (1987, 132–4); see also Franklin (2002). For Ivan IV's autocracy, see Pavlov and Perrie (2003).

19 See Crummey (1987, 137–9). For Philotheus of Pskov's letter, see Zernov (1978, 49); but cf. the skeptical comments of Franklin (2002, esp. at 191–2).

20 For the two myths, tsarist and ethnic Russian, see Cherniavsky (1975) and Hosking (1997, 47–56).

21 On early Russian myths and legends, see Hubbs (1993); also Franklin (2002). The later rise of Russian ethnoscapes and national identity is discussed by Ely (2002).

22 On the opposition between westernizing tsarist court culture and popular ethnic Russian culture, see Hosking (1993).

23 See Geary (2001). While Geary's "constructivist" interpretation fits well the fluid conditions of the late Roman empire and its aftermath, he seems to take far too seriously the tendency of some nationalisms to seek the origins of "their" nations in this period and the succeeding "Dark Ages," and thereby passes over later periods from the tenth century, in which it is possible to begin to discern the outlines of national division, if not national identity, in medieval Western Europe – of knowing, in Walker Connor's words, not who we are, but who we are not. Geary also underplays the persistence and near ubiquity of the "ethnic lens" in so many periods and areas, and of more specific ethnic models of social organization, from the Old Testament and Herodotus to postcolonialism and postcommunism.

24 See Reynolds (1984, 250–1; 1983); cf. the more traditional interpretation of Seton-Watson (1977, 15).

25 See Reynolds (2005); cf. the modernist stance of Breuilly (2005b).

26 See Hastings (1997, ch. 2); also Wormald (2005).

27 Kumar (2003, 42–3, 47–8); cf. the contributions by Susan Reynolds, Robert Colls, and Anthony D. Smith in the debate with Krishan Kumar, published in *Nations and Nationalism* (2007).

28 See Wormald (2005, esp. 117–18) and Foot (2005). For some objections, see Breuilly (2005b, esp. 73–4) and Kumar (2003, 41–8). See also the essays in Smyth (2002a), especially Smyth (2002b) and Reuter (2002). For the Anglo-Saxon migration, identity, and literature, see Howe (1989).

29 See Kumar (2003, 49–53); Gillingham (1995); and for medieval Anglo-Irish relations, see Lydon (1995). For Anglo-Saxon and Norman ethnic myths, see MacDougall (1982) and Mason (1983).

30 R. Davies (2000, 106); see also Gillingham (1992) and Frame (2005).
31 See Knapp (2004, 144–5); see also Galloway (2004, 41–95).
32 Kumar (2003, 58); and see Clanchy (1998, 173–5) and Keeney (1972). For Shakespeare's biblically inspired portrait of Henry V, see S. Marx (2000, ch. 3).
33 See Housley (2000, 237, 238–9).
34 See Beaune (1985, 287) and Strayer (1971, chs. 17–18).
35 For the text of the eighth-century prologue to the Salic Law, see E. James (1988, 236). See also Citron (1989, 114–17).
36 For this development, see Strayer (1971, chs. 17–18); also Beaune (1991, 173).
37 Strayer (1971, 302).
38 On de Sauqueville, see Beaune (1991, 176); on Nogaret, see Strayer (1971, 309, 311). For the quotation from the papal bull, *Rex Glorie*, in *Registrum Clementis Papae V*, Rome 1885–92, no. 7501, see Strayer (1971, 312–13).
39 Beaune (1991, 192), to whose magisterial analysis this and the following paragraphs are heavily indebted. For Chastellain, see also Beaune (1991, 180).
40 See Beaune (1991, 285) for this analysis and for the quotations from the chancellor of France (ibid., 296), *Doctrinal de Noblesse* (ibid., 305), and for the prayer for Jean de Bueil (ibid., 308). See also the brief comments in Potter (2003, 3–5).
41 On the royal public culture, see Le Goff (1998).
42 Cowan (2003, 42). I am indebted to Dr. Atsuko Ichijo for this reference.
43 Webster (1997, 85–9). On the Declaration of Arbroath, see Duncan (1970).
44 Webster (1997, 89). See, on this, Ichijo (2002). This is especially true of William Wallace's uprising and campaign. For the rise of national identity in medieval Wales, see Richter (2002).
45 Cowan (2003, 57–8).
46 Kumar (2003, 80–1). The fact that many Scots were Anglicized hardly invalidates their national sentiment. So were the elites in Latin America, America, much of Africa, and India. This does not deter us from designating these secession or resistance movements as cases of nationalism.
47 Webster (1997, ch. 5; 1998). An interesting comparison can be made with early Armenian historiography, which also delineated a sense of Armenian national identity, albeit here tied to and interpreted through the lens of the Old Testament and Apostolic Christianity; on which see Garsoian (1999, ch. 12) and Atiyah (1968).

5 Covenantal Nations

1 See Kedourie (1960, chs. 2–3); Gellner (1964, ch. 7); Hobsbawm (1990, 10).
2 Gellner (1983, 91, n. 1); Hobsbawm (1990, 75).
3 Scales (2005, 172); and idem (2000). For a slightly later period, see Poliakov (1975, 77–8).
4 Housley (2000, 240); see also Zacek (1969, 171–4). But while the Czech language flourished, and anti-German sentiment was prevalent, burgeoning national sentiment was insufficient to bind the nobles to the artisans, or reconcile the Utraquist and Taborite wings of Hussitism in what was basically a religious revolution.
5 See N. Davies (1979, Vol. I. ch. 6); Petrovich (1980). Knoll (1993) argues for a widespread elite sense of Polish national identity in the fifteenth century.
6 See Llobera (1994, 79–80) and Linehan (1982).
7 See Housley (2000) and Llobera (1994), to whose account I am indebted. But cf. A. Marx (2003) for the view that Spain's "exclusionary nationalism" of the sixteenth century created a relatively homogeneous nation.
8 Stergios (2006) concentrates mainly on the fifteenth and sixteenth centuries. For an earlier period, and an equally negative view of any Italian national sentiment, see Hankey (2002).
9 Llobera (1994, 68–70) and Toftgaard (2005, 62–5, 176).
10 Toftgaard (2005, 96). I am grateful to Dr. Toftgaard for allowing me to quote from his PhD thesis, which compares language and national identity in medieval and Renaissance Italy and France.
11 Toftgaard (2005, 23, 140–3, 278–80); cf. Hankey (2002). For later nationalist use of these "cultural materials," see Doumanis (2001, ch. 1).
12 See Beaune (1991, esp. 296) and Toftgaard (2005, 180–200). See also Llobera (1994, 55–6).
13 Toftgaard (2005, 65–72, 210–38); Rickard (1974, 87–94).
14 Llobera (1994, 39), citing Kohn's early article on seventeenth-century English nationalism (Kohn 1940, 70).
15 Greenfeld (1992, ch. 1); and for his critique of Greenfeld's thesis of an English sixteenth-century nationalism, see Kumar (2003, 90–103). Interestingly, Kumar is much more favorably disposed to Kohn's arguments of a seventeenth-century English nationalism.
16 Marcu (1976); but cf. Breuilly (1993, Introduction).
17 Both quotations in Mundy and Woody (1961, 344), cited in Toftgaard (2005, 60–1); see also Loomis (1939), who claims that the term "*natio*" signified both a territorial and a linguistic and descent community, and that churches were becoming increasingly "national" in this period.

18 On this fragmentation, see Keen (1973, ch. 19) and Perkins (2005).
19 See A. Marx (2003); also on war and national states in early modern Europe, Howard (1976) and Tilly (1975, Introduction, and essay by Finer).
20 See Llobera (1994, 78–80); also Linehan (1982). For medieval persecutions of heretics, lepers, and Jews, see Moore (1987).
21 A. Marx (2003, 6); also Tilly (1975, Introduction). For an extended critique of Marx's account, see A. D. Smith (2005).
22 Kedourie (1971, Introduction); cf. A. D. Smith (1979, ch. 2). For the Christian "vernacular thesis," see Hastings (1997).
23 For the Reformation as a general European movement, see the magisterial account of MacCulloch (2004). For Reformation culture, see Rublack (2005); see also the older historical account of Green (1964). For the influence of the Hebrew Bible on English literature and the national self-image of the English, see D. Aberbach (2005).
24 Schama (1987, 94–5, italics in original), still the most vivid and comprehensive account of Dutch seventeenth-century culture.
25 Walzer (1984) reveals the dual promise of the Almighty, the unconditional liberation of the children of Israel from Egypt, and the conditional attainment of the Promised Land only to those who receive and practice God's Torah – as well as its subsequent uses and inspiration in the English and American Revolutions.
26 Nicholson (1988) discusses the various Covenant texts in the Pentateuch, while Novak (1995) and Sacks (2002) range more widely, to look at the rabbinic and ethical aspects.
27 MacCulloch (2004, 106–115; and on the Covenant, 178–9); Green (1964, ch. 10).
28 MacCulloch (2004, 178–9, 243–4).
29 Williamson (1979, 4).
30 Cited in Mackie (1976, 206); see also Williamson (1979, ch. 3).
31 Cited in Mackie (1976, 212–13); see also Kidd (1993, 23–4).
32 Cited in Williamson (1979, 5); for the quote from the anonymous English pamphlet of 1554, see Loades (1982, 304).
33 MacCulloch (2004, 285); and Haller (1963). Loades (1992, 313) also stresses the English aspects of what became, with its successive expanded editions, an apology for English martyrs, and claims the importance for Foxe of England as an *elect* nation.
34 For these and other quotes on English election, see Hill (1994, 267); see also D. Aberbach (2005).
35 Fletcher (1982, 315–16).
36 Cited in Greenfeld (1992, 75). For the quote from Cromwell's address to Parliament, see Kohn (1944, 176); and for the Bible carried by Cromwell's soldiers into battle, see Calamy imprimatur [1643] (1997).

37 John Milton: *Areopagitica* iv, 339–40, cited in Greenfeld (1992, 76).
38 John Milton: *Prose Works*, London, Bell, 1884–9, iii, 315, cited in Kohn (1944, 171). Kumar (2003, 103–15) disputes the degree of national*ism* (as opposed to national sentiment) in Puritans like Milton, Cromwell, Baxter, and William Clarke; they were, primarily, ardent pan-European Puritans, waging war against the anti-Christ. Yet, he also concedes the national, if not national*ist*, tenor of many of their speeches and writings.
39 For the *biddagsbrieven*, see Gorski (2000, 1441–2).
40 See Gorski (2000, 1442). This is one piece of evidence in his case for an "anti-modernist" redating of the onset of nationalism, well over a century before the French Revolution. Yet, the theoretical part of his article appears to advance a "post-modernist" approach, at odds with the historical evidence he produces.
41 Joost von Vondel: *Passcha*, 58, cited in Schama (1987, 113).
42 Schama (1987, 106–17) gives a vivid account of the context of the biblical art of the period. See also Westermann (2004, ch. 5) for the art of Dutch political identity.
43 The *Gedenck-Clanck* prayer is cited in Schama (1987, 98).
44 For the Calvinist programme, see MacCulloch (2004, 367–78) and Gorski (2000, 1446–7).
45 On the Ulster-Scots, see Akenson (1992); for the Afrikaners, see Cauthen (1997, 107–31); on Hungary, see Graeme Murdock: "Magyar Judah: Constructing a New Canaan in Eastern Europe," in Swanson (2000, 263–74). For a brief overview of the first American Protestant colonies, see, *inter alia*, MacCulloch (2004, 533–45). On the French Wars of Religion, see Briggs (1998, 10–32); also MacCulloch (2004, 306–9, 337–40, 471–5).
46 For Denmark and the Reformation, see Jesperson (2004, ch. 5); on Sweden in this period, see Scott (1977, 124–30, 153–6).
47 Jesperson (2004, ch. 2); see also Ostergård (1996); Strath (1994).
48 For a classic account of this struggle, see Parker (1985); also MacCulloch (2004, 367–78).
49 Parker (1985, 57–63).
50 Ihalainen (2005).

6 Republican Nations

1 See Schama (1989, 507–11); also Cobban (1963, Vol. 1, Part 2).
2 Schama (1989, 389). On the *Horatii* of David, see, *inter alia*, Brookner (1980, ch. 5); also Rosenblum (1967, ch. 2).

3 Rosenblum (1961); on Füssli, see Antal (1956, 71–4). For other depictions of the Rütli Oath, see Jacob Kreis: "Schweiz: Nationalpedagogik in Wort und Bild," in Flacke (1998, 446–75, esp. 457–60). And for other oath-swearings from classical antiquity, including those by Beaufort (1771) and Caraffe (1794), see Detroit (1974).

4 O'Brien (1988b); H. M. Jones (1974, chs. 10–11); Cobban (1963, Vol. 1, Part 2).

5 See Kedourie (1960, chs. 2–3); and on Herder, Berlin (1976), and more generally, on Romanticism, Berlin (1999).

6 J.-J. Rousseau: *Considérations sur le Gouvernement de Pologne*, 1772, translated in Watkins (1953, 178); see also J.-J. Rousseau: *Du Contrat Social*, IV, viii, also in Watkins (1953, 147–8).

7 For the revolutionary *fêtes*, see Kennedy (1989, 300–8); and Herbert (1972). For the debt to city-state patriotism, see Minogue (1976); and for the many calls by cultural critics and writers on the arts to return to a heroic antiquity, see Leith (1965) and Rosenblum (1967).

8 See Martines (2002, ch. 11); and on Florence, see Brucker's assessment of Hans Baron's thesis on the humanist turn in Florentine politics, in Brucker (1969, 230–40).

9 Zimmer (2003, 19, note 10). For the Swiss Reformers, see MacCulloch (2004, 174–9). On the uses of the Batavian myth of Dutch origins, see Gorski (2000), and for its influence on Dutch artists, notably in Rembrandt's painting of *The Conspiracy of Claudius Civilis* for the Amsterdam Town Hall, see Westermann (2004, 99–101) and Rosenberg (1968, 287–92).

10 Ihalainen (2005, esp. ch. 2) exhaustively documents the importance of the analogy with ancient Israel in official sermons and rhetoric in Sweden, Holland, and England in the late seventeenth and eighteenth centuries, as well as its partial and uneven decline in the mid-eighteenth century, in favor of models of classical patriotism, especially in England. On the rise of the "scientific state," see A. D. Smith (1983, ch. 10). On the transmission of the classical heritage, see Bolgar (1954).

11 See Bell (2001, 39), citing J.-J. Rousseau: *Considérations sur le Gouvernement de Pologne*, 1772, and in Watkins (1953, 163).

12 See Bell (2001, ch. 1), a thought-provoking analysis, though it was only an elite that was able to give voice to these new ideas. On the Wars of Religion, and the contemporary reactions, see MacCulloch (2004, 469–74). For the place of the Catholic and other religions before and during the Revolution, see Aston (2000).

13 Mass education is emphasized by Gellner (1973; 1983) in his own theory of nationalism. On the French republican case, see Prost (2002, ch. 3).

14 See Viroli (1995); Connor (1994, esp. chs. 4, 8; 2004); and Hroch (1985) on the three-stage transition to ethnic nationalism. On the eighteenth-century Danish patriotic societies, see Engelhardt (2007).

15 See the debate referred to in the Introduction between Walker Connor and Anthony D. Smith, in Guibernau and Hutchinson (2004). For nations without states, whose members may feel dual allegiances, see Guibernau (1999); and for the Basques and Catalans, see Conversi (1997).

16 On the debate between the "Franks" and the "Gauls," see Pomian (1997) and Poliakov (1975, ch. 1). On the language policies of the Jacobins, see Lartichaux (1977).

17 Renan (1882), translated in Bhabha (1990); on medieval Italian city-states and identities, see Hankey (2002). On ancient Athens, see E. Cohen (2000).

18 Cited in Bell (2001, 38). For the sacred symbolism of nationalist movements, see Breuilly (1993, 64–8), Kedourie (1971, Introduction), and A. D. Smith (2000b; 2003, ch. 2). Roshwald (2006, ch. 4) sees in the revolutionary legacy a much contested covenantal tradition.

19 See O'Brien (1988b) on the export of revolutionary French nationalism. On ideas of national "genius" and "character," see Perkins (1999) and Kemilainen (1964).

20 On the canon of great men in France and the French language, see Bell (2001, chs. 4, 6); and on the English eighteenth-century national literary revival, see Newman (1987). The general trends in the growth of a national reading public are illuminated by Anderson (1991, chs. 2–3, 5); and for the role of language in national identity, see Edwards (1985, ch. 2), and, in France, Lartichaux (1977).

21 On French Jewry in the Revolution and under Napoleon, see Benbassa (1999, chs. 6–7) and Vital (1990, ch. 1).

22 See, on the white Anglo-Saxon basis of the American nation, Kaufmann (2002) and Huntington (2004); and on WASP dominance and decline, Kaufmann (2004b). For ethnic change in the United States, see Gans (1979). For ethnic dimensions of "civic" nationalisms, see Yack (1999).

23 The pre-Romantic idealization of Nature is well analyzed by Charlton (1984). On landscape and memory, see the fascinating volume by Schama (1995); and on landscape and national identity in Switzerland and Canada, see the excellent analysis of Kaufmann and Zimmer (1998).

24 On the sanctification of territory and the ensuing conflicts, see A. D. Smith (1999b). For some case studies of the links between territory and national identity, see Hooson (1994).

25 For the commemoration of the dead in general, see the seminal work of Mosse (1990; 1994) and the essays in Gillis (1994). For the canon

of fallen heroes, especially in France, see Bell (2001, ch. 4) and Detroit (1974).

26 The cult of the Glorious Dead is discussed in J. Winter (1995, ch. 4) and A. D. Smith (2003, ch. 9); and especially by Mosse (1990) and Prost (1998; 2002, ch. 1).

27 For the reflexive character of nationalism, see Breuilly (1993, 64–8). By the time of Grundtvig's educational movement, Denmark was ceasing to be an absolute monarchy and was assuming a civic character, though not republican in form; on which, see Jesperson (2004, ch. 5). For the Slavophile conception, see Hosking (1997, 271–5).

28 On this conception of the nation and its character, see Anderson (1991; 1999). For such golden ages and missions, see A. D. Smith (1997; 2003, chs. 5, 7).

29 On German festivals and monuments, see Mosse (1975, ch. 3). On statuary and celebrations in England, Germany, and the United States, see Hobsbawm (1983, ch. 7). The cult of the fallen soldier and its role in American national identity is discussed by Grant (2005); and on national monuments generally, see Michalski (1998).

30 Cited in Cobban (1963, Vol. 1, 165, italics in original).

31 Cited in Scurr (2006, 214).

32 For a description of this festival, see Schama (1989, 831–6). On the Revolution and religion, see Aston (2000, Part 3).

33 Republicanism in France and its symbols are discussed in Prost (2002), Pilbeam (1995, ch. 1), Gildea (1994), and compared with England and Norway by Elgenius (2005).

34 Cited in Roudometof (2001, 63).

35 See Kitromilides (1989) for the novelty of the idea of a Greek nation; for the Greek Orthodox Church, see Frazee (1969).

36 On Atatürk's programme, see Poulton (1997) and Lewis (1968, ch. 10); see also the "ethnosymbolic" interpretation of Turkish nationalism by Canefe (2005) and a more "post-modern" interpretation of the Turkish republican view of history in Cinar (2005).

37 See Hodgkin (1964) for Rousseau's influence; also Geiss (1974).

38 See Viroli (1995); Herbert (1972, 39).

39 On this, see Chatterjee (1986).

7 Alternative Destinies

1 Cited in Roudometof (2001, 63). For classic accounts of the Greek War of Independence and modern Greece, see Dakin (1972) and Campbell and Sherrard (1968). For ideological aspects of republicanism and

nationalism, see Kitromilides (1979; 2006), though whether a distinction can be usefully drawn between republican patriotism and nationalism is questionable.

2 On this cleavage and trajectory, see Roudometof (1998) and Campbell and Sherrard (1968, ch. 1).

3 For the apocalyptic tradition and its influence on Greek nationalism, see Hatzopoulos (2005). For the role of Orthodoxy, see Roudometof (2001, 52–6); and for the growth of a possible Hellenic consciousness among the late Byzantine elites, see Armstrong (1982, 178–81).

4 On Orthodoxy and "phyletism" in the context of a new Greek national state, see Kitromilides (1989); on the position of the Orthodox Church in Greece, see Frazee (1969).

5 On Spiridon Zambelios and Konstantinos Paparrigopoulos, see Roudometof (2001, 108–10), and for the links with Greek Orthodox traditions in the latter, despite the novelty of his conception, see Kitromilides (1998). For the *Megale Idea* and its consequences, see Koliopoulos and Veremis (2004, chs. 12, 14).

6 See especially Pilbeam (1995); also Prost (2002).

7 See Gallant (2001, ch. 4), and Koliopoulos and Veremis (2004, 228–35).

8 For the ideology of the Slavophiles, see Thaden (1964); for the Pharaonic movement in early twentieth-century Egypt, see Gershoni and Jankowski (1987, chs. 7–8); and for French nineteenth-century conflicts, see Gildea (1994) and Pilbeam (1995, esp. chs. 5–6, 10). The rise, nature, and ideals of Hindu nationalism in India are analyzed in Bhatt (2001) and the major study of Jaffrelot (1996) of the politics of Hindu nationalism.

9 For the modern "myth" of Greek descent from the ancient Greeks, see Just (1989); and for the Greek need to articulate a national "mission," in the face of Jacob Fallmerayer's "Slavic" interpretation of modern Greek descent, published in 1830, see Roudometof (2001, 106–7).

10 For a résumé of recent research on Swiss origins and historical development, see Zimmer (2003, ch. 1); and for the early oaths, see Im Hof (1991, ch. 1). The conflicting currents of Swiss historiography of the late nineteenth century are discussed in Zimmer (2000).

11 For the 1891 celebrations, see Kreis (1991). On modern Switzerland and its overlapping identities, see Steinberg (1976).

12 For the development of modern Japan from the Tokugawa period, and its myths of origin, see Lehmann (1982, esp. 133–5), and Oguma (2002); on the cult of the war dead at the Yasukuni shrine, see Harootunian (1999).

13 For the Romantic movement in Japan, see Doak (1997). Modern theories of Japan's origins and presumed homogeneity are critically analyzed

by Oguma (2002). For a thoughtful study of postwar Japanese "victimhood," see Shiiyama (2005).

14 On the Protestant culture and mission of eighteenth- and early nineteenth-century England and Britain, see especially Clark (2000); and Colley (1992, ch. 1).

15 For the British Protestant tradition, see Clark (2000); for English (rather than British) cultural and political exceptionalism, see A. D. Smith (2006).

16 For Ulster and South Africa, see Akenson (1992); and on Afrikaner celebrations, see Templin (1999) and Thompson (1985).

17 The processes involved in the growth of an American nation are charted in Kaufmann (2002); for the American conviction of Protestant destiny and national election, see Tuveson (1968), Huntington (2004, chs. 3–5), and Roshwald (2006, ch. 4).

18 On this missionary stance, see Cauthen (2004). The covenantal spirit in American visions of its unique wilderness nature and in American landscape painting by artists like Cole, Church, and Bierstadt is described and beautifully illustrated in the pioneering history and catalogue by Wilton and Barringer (2002).

19 On early Zionist ideologies, see the excellent study of Shimoni (1995); and for its religious dimensions, see Mendes-Flohr (1994), and especially Luz (1988).

20 For the ethnonationalist underpinnings of Zionist socialism, see Sternhell (1999). Shafir (1989) analyzes the vexed issue of the use by early Zionists of Arab labor.

21 On the "hexagon" of France, see E. Weber (1991, ch. 3). The new concepts of nation, public, and society are discussed in Bell (2001, ch. 1). For the oaths and ceremonies of the Revolution, see chapter 6 above, notes 1 and 2.

22 For the controversies about admission to the Pantheon, see Ozouf (1998). The cult of St. Joan in late nineteenth-century France is discussed in Gildea (1994, 154–65), and her images in Warner (1983). For a vivid analysis of the unique festival of *La Pucelle* in Orléans, see Prost (2002, ch. 7).

23 On the rise of a German national identity in the late eighteenth and nineteenth centuries, see H. James (2000) and Blackbourn (2003). See also Kohn (1967, Part 2).

24 The *volkisch* literary movement is discussed by Mosse (1964). For German public monuments, see Mosse (1975); and for the nineteenth-century cult of Dürer, see Kuhlemann (2002). Wagner's theories are located in their German Romantic philosophical setting in the controversial analysis of Rose (1996).

25 See Bracher (1973); on the Hitler myth, see Kershaw (1989). For Nazism as a secular religion, see Burleigh (2001). On the relationship of Nazism to nationalism, see A. D. Smith (1979, ch. 3).

26 On East Germany, see Staab (1998). For some problems of modern German national identity, see Fulbrook (1997).

27 On the Great Schism and the Old Believers, see Hosking (1997, 64–74).

28 For the history of the Soviet Union, see Hosking (1985). For monuments and rituals of the Great Patriotic War, see Merridale (2001). The image of Stalin, compared to that of Ivan the Terrible, is analyzed by Perrie (1998); and for Russian nationalism under postwar Soviet communism, see Dunlop (1985).

29 On the Turkish revolution, see Poulton (1997); and for the Turkification of the Ottoman empire after 1914, see Ulker (2005). The alternative destinies, and golden ages, of secular Turkish and Islamic-Ottoman Turkish ethnohistories are interestingly analyzed by Cinar (2005, ch. 4).

30 For European influence on West Africa in particular, see July (1967) and Geiss (1974).

31 On some religious and cultural causes of the Iranian Revolution, see Keddie (1981).

32 On the Buddhist background of Burmese socialism, see Sarkisyanz (1964); for Thailand and its traditions, see Winichakul (1996); on Saudi Arabia and Wahabism, see Piscatori (1989).

33 On dominant *ethnies*, see Kaufmann (2004a).

References

Aberbach, David (2005): "Nationalism and the Hebrew Bible," *Nations and Nationalism* 11, 2, 223–42.

Aberbach, Moses (1966): *The Roman–Jewish War (66–70 AD)*, London: The Jewish Quarterly/Golub Press.

Ackroyd, Peter (1979): "The History of Israel in the Exilic and Post-Exilic Periods," in G. W. Anderson (1979, 320–50).

Agnew, Hugh (1993): "The Emergence of Czech National Consciousness: A Conceptual Approach," *Ethnic Groups* 10, 1–3, 175–86.

Agulhön, Maurice and Bonte, Pierre (1992): *Marianne: Les Visages de la République*, Paris: Gallimard.

Ahlstrom, Gosta (1986): *Who Were the Israelites?*, Winona Lake, IN: Eisenbrauns.

Akenson, Donald (1992): *God's Peoples: Covenant and Land in South Africa, Israel and Ulster*, Ithaca, NY: Cornell University Press.

Alty, J. H. (1982): "Dorians and Ionians," *Journal of Hellenic Studies* 102, 1–14.

Anderson, Benedict (1991): *Imagined Communities: Reflections on the Origins and Spread of Nationalism*, London: Verso.

Anderson, Benedict (1999): "The Goodness of Nations," in van der Veer and Lehmann (1999, 197–203).

Anderson, G. W. (ed.) (1979): *Tradition and Interpretation*, Oxford: Clarendon Press.

Andrewes, Antony (1971): *Greek Society*, Harmondsworth: Pelican.

Antal, Frederick (1956): *Fuseli Studies*, London: Routledge and Kegan Paul.

Ap-Thomas, D. R. (1973): "The Phoenicians," in Wiseman (1973, 259–86).

Argyle, W. J. (1976): "Size and Scale as Factors in the Development of Nationalism," in A. D. Smith (1976, 31–53).

Armstrong, John (1982): *Nations before Nationalism*, Chapel Hill: University of North Carolina Press.

Armstrong, John (1995): "Towards a Theory of Nationalism: Consensus and Dissensus," in Periwal (1995, 34–43).

Aston, Nigel (2000): *Religion and Revolution in France, 1780–1804*, Basingstoke: Macmillan.

Atiyah, A. S. (1968): *A History of Eastern Christianity*, London: Methuen.

Bacon, H. (1961): *Barbarians in Greek Tragedy*, New Haven: Yale University Press.

Barth, Fredrik (ed.) (1969): *Ethnic Groups and Boundaries*, Boston: Little, Brown.

Bartlett, J. R. (1973): "The Moabites and Edomites," in Wiseman (1973, 229–58).

Beaulieu, Paul-Alain (2002): "The God Amurru as Emblem of Ethnic and Cultural Identity," *Proceedings of the 48th Rencontre Assyriologique Internationale on Ethnicity in Ancient Mesopotamia*, Leiden, 1–16.

Beaune, Colette (1985): *Naissance de la Nation France*, Paris: Editions Gallimard.

Beaune, Colette (1991): *The Birth of an Ideology: Myths and Symbols of the Nation in Late Medieval France*, trans. Susan Ross Huston from *Naissance de la Nation France* (1985), ed. Fredric L. Cheyette, Berkeley and Los Angeles: University of California Press.

Bell, David (2001): *The Cult of the Nation in France, 1680–1800*, Cambridge, MA: Harvard University Press.

Benbassa, Esther (1999): *The Jews of France: A History from Antiquity to the Present*, trans. M. B. DeBevoise, Princeton, NJ: Princeton University Press.

Berlin, Isaiah (1976): *Vico and Herder*, London: Hogarth Press.

Berlin, Isaiah (1999): *The Roots of Romanticism*, ed. Henry Hardy, London: Chatto and Windus.

Beyer, W. C. (1959): "The Civil Service in the Ancient World," *Public Administration Review* 19, 243–9.

Bhabha, Homi (ed.) (1990): *Nation and Narration*, London and New York: Routledge.

Bhatt, Chetan (2001): *Hindu Nationalism: Origins, Ideologies and Modern Myths*, Oxford and New York: Berg.

Billig, Michael (1995): *Banal Nationalism*, London: Sage.

Blackbourn, David (2003): *History of Germany, 1780–1918: The Long Nineteenth Century*, 2nd edition, Oxford: Blackwell.

Blacker, Carmen (1984): "Two Shinto Myths: The Golden Age and the Chosen People," in Sue Henny and Jean-Pierre Lehmann (eds.), *Themes and Theories in Modern Japanese History*, London: Athlone Press.

Bolgar, R. R. (1954): *The Classical Heritage and its Beneficiaries*, Cambridge: Cambridge University Press.

Bracher, Karl D. (1973): *The German Dictatorship: The Origins, Structure and Effects of National Socialism*, Harmondsworth: Penguin.
Brandon, S. G. F. (1967): *Jesus and the Zealots*, Manchester: Manchester University Press.
Brass, Paul (ed.) (1985): *Ethnic Groups and the State*, London: Croom Helm.
Brass, Paul (1991): *Ethnicity and Nationalism*, London: Sage.
Breton, Raymond (1988): "From Ethnic to Civic Nationalism: English Canada and Quebec," *Ethnic and Racial Studies* 11, 1, 85–102.
Breuilly, John (1993): *Nationalism and the State*, 2nd edition, Manchester: Manchester University Press.
Breuilly, John (1996): "Approaches to Nationalism," in Gopal Balakrishnan (ed.), *Mapping the Nation*, London and New York: Verso, 146–74.
Breuilly, John (2005a): "Dating the Nation: How Old is an Old Nation?," in Ichijo and Uzelac (2005, 15–39).
Breuilly, John (2005b): "Changes in the Political Uses of the Nation: Continuity or Discontinuity?," in Scales and Zimmer (2005, 67–101).
Briggs, Robin (1998): *Early Modern France, 1560–1715*, Oxford: Oxford University Press.
Brinkman, J. A. (1979): "Babylonia under the Assyrian Empire, 745–627 BC," in Larsen (1979a, 223–50).
Brookner, Anita (1980): *Jacques-Louis David*, London: Chatto and Windus.
Brubaker, Rogers (1996): *Nationalism Reframed: Nationhood and the National Question in the New Europe*, Cambridge: Cambridge University Press.
Brucker, Gene (1969): *Renaissance Florence*, New York: John Wiley.
Burleigh, Michael (2001): *The Third Reich: A New History*, Basingstoke and Oxford: Pan Macmillan.
Calamy, Edmund (1997) [1643]: *Cromwell's Soldier's Bible* (Reprint in Facsimile), Whitstable, Walsall, and Winchester: Pryor Publications.
Cambridge Ancient History (1973): Vol. 2, Part 1, *The Middle East and the Aegean Region, 1800–1380 BC*, Cambridge: Cambridge University Press.
Cambridge Ancient History (1975): Vol. 2, Part 2, *The Middle East and the Aegean Region, 1380–1000 BC*, Cambridge: Cambridge University Press.
Cambridge History of Iran (1983): Vol. 3, Parts 1 and 2, *The Seleucid, Parthian and Sassanian Periods*, ed. E. Yarshater, Cambridge: Cambridge University Press.
Cambridge History of Judaism (1989) Vol. 2, *The Hellenistic Age*, eds. W. D. Davies and Louis Finkelstein, Cambridge: Cambridge University Press.
Campbell, John and Sherrard, Philip (1968): *Modern Greece*, London: Ernest Benn.
Canefe, Nergis (2005): "Turkish Nationalism and Ethno-Symbolic Analysis: The Rules of Exception," *Nations and Nationalism* 8, 2, 135–55.

Carr, Edward H. (1945): *Nationalism and After*, London: Macmillan.

Cartledge, Paul (1987): "The Greek Religious Festivals," in Easterling and Muir (1987, 98–127).

Cauthen, Bruce (1997): "The Myth of Divine Election and Afrikaner Ethno-Genesis," in Hosking and Schöpflin (1997, 107–31).

Cauthen, Bruce (2004): "Covenant and Continuity: Ethno-Symbolism and the Myth of Divine Election," in Guibernau and Hutchinson (2004, 19–33).

Cazelles, H. (1979): "The History of Israel in the Pre-Exilic Period," in G. W. Anderson (1979, 274–319).

Charlton, D. G. (1984): *New Images of the Natural in France*, Cambridge: Cambridge University Press.

Chatterjee, Partha (1986): *Nationalist Thought and the Colonial World: A Derivative Discourse*, London: Zed Books.

Cherniavsky, Michael (1975): "Russia," in Ranum (1975, 118–43).

Cinar, Alev (2005): *Modernity, Islam and Secularism in Turkey*, Minneapolis: University of Minnesota Press.

Citron, Suzanne (1989): *Le Mythe National*, Paris: Presses Ouvrières.

Clanchy, M. T. (1998): *England and Its Rulers, 1066–1272*, 2nd edition, Oxford: Blackwell.

Clark, J. C. D. (2000): "Protestantism, Nationalism and National Identity, 1660–1832," *Historical Journal* 43, 1, 249–76.

Cobban, Alfred (1963): *A History of Modern France*, Vol. 1: *1715–99*, 3rd edition, Harmondsworth: Penguin.

Cohen, Edward (2000): *The Athenian Nation*, Princeton: Princeton University Press.

Cohen, Shaye (1998): *The Beginnings of Jewishness: Boundaries, Varieties, Uncertainties*, Berkeley and Los Angeles: University of California Press.

Colley, Linda (1992): *Britons: Forging the Nation, 1707–1837*, New Haven: Yale University Press.

Connor, Walker (1990): "When is a Nation?," *Ethnic and Racial Studies* 13, 1, 92–103.

Connor, Walker (1994): *Ethno-Nationalism: The Quest for Understanding*, Princeton: Princeton University Press.

Connor, Walker (2004): "The Timelessness of Nations," in Guibernau and Hutchinson (2004, 35–47).

Conversi, Daniele (1997): *The Basques, the Catalans and Spain: Alternative Routes to Nationalist Mobilization*, London: C. Hurst.

Conversi, Daniele (ed.) (2002): *Ethno-Nationalism in the Contemporary World: Walker Connor and the Study of Nationalism*, London: Routledge.

Cook, J. M. (1983): *The Persian Empire*, London: Book Club Associates.

Cowan, Edward (2003): *"For Freedom Alone": The Declaration of Arbroath, 1320*, East Lothian: Tuckwell Press.

Crummey, Robert (1987): *The Formation of Muscovy, 1304–1613*, London and New York: Longman.
Dakin, Douglas (1972): *The Unification of Greece, 1770–1923*, London: Ernest Benn.
David, A. Rosalie (1982): *The Ancient Egyptians: Religious Beliefs and Practices*, London, Boston, and Henley: Routledge and Kegan Paul.
Davies, Norman (1979): *God's Playground: A History of Poland*, 2 vols., Oxford: Clarendon Press.
Davies, Philip (1992): *In Search of "Ancient Israel,"* Sheffield: Sheffield Academic Press.
Davies, Rees R. (2000): *The First English Empire: Power and Identities in the British Isles, 1093–1343*, Oxford: Oxford University Press.
Davies, W. D. (1982): *The Territorial Dimension of Judaism*, Berkeley and Los Angeles: University of California Press.
Day, John (ed.) (2004): *In Search of Pre-Exilic Israel*, London: T. and T. Clark International.
Detroit (1974): *French Painting, 1774–1830: The Age of Revolution*, Detroit, MI: Wayne State University Press.
Deutsch, Karl (1966): *Nationalism and Social Communication*, 2nd edition, New York: MIT Press.
Dever, William (2003): *Who Were the Early Israelites and Where Did They Come From?*, Grand Rapids, MI, and Cambridge: W. B. Eerdmans.
Dever, William (2004): "Histories and Non-Histories of Ancient Israel: The Question of the United Monarchy," in Day (2004, 65–94).
Dieckhoff, Alain and Jaffrelot, Christophe (eds.) (2005): *Revisiting Nationalism: Theories and Processes*, London: C. Hurst.
Doak, Ken (1997): "What is a Nation and Who Belongs? National Narratives and the Ethnic Imagination in Twentieth-Century Japan," *American Historical Review* 102, 4, 282–309.
Doumanis, Nicholas (2001): *Italy: Inventing the Nation*, London: Arnold.
Duncan, A. A. M. (1970): *The Nation of Scots and the Declaration of Arbroath*, London: Historical Association.
Dunlop, John B. (1985): *The New Russian Nationalism*, New York: Praeger.
Easterling, P. E. and Muir, J. V. (eds.) (1987): *Greek Religion and Society*, Cambridge: Cambridge University Press.
Edwards, John (1985): *Language, Society and Identity*, Oxford: Blackwell.
Eissfeldt, O. (1975): "The Hebrew Kingdom," in *Cambridge Ancient History* (1975, 537–605).
Elgenius, Gabriella (2005): "Expressions of Nationhood: National Symbols and Ceremonies of Contemporary Europe," unpublished PhD thesis, University of London.
Eller, Jack and Coughlan, Reed (1993): "The Poverty of Primordialism: The Demystification of Attachments," *Ethnic and Racial Studies* 16, 2, 183–202.

Ely, Christopher (2002): *This Meager Nature: Landscape and National Identity in Imperial Russia*, DeKalb, IL: Northern Illinois University Press.

Emerton, J. A. (2004): "The Date of the Yahwist," in Day (2004, 107–29).

Engelhardt, Juliane (2007): "Patriotism, Nationalism and Modernity," *Nations and Nationalism* 13, 2, 205–23.

Eriksen, Thomas H. (1993): *Ethnicity and Nationalism*, London: Pluto Press.

Finkelberg, Margalit (2005): *Greeks and Pre-Greeks: Aegean Prehistory and Greek Heroic Tradition*, Cambridge: Cambridge University Press.

Finkelstein, Israel and Silberman, Neil (2001): *The Bible Unearthed: Archaeology's New Vision of Ancient Israel and the Origin of its Sacred Texts*, New York: Free Press.

Finkelstein, Louis (1989): "The Men of the Great Synagogue (circa 400–170 BCE)" and "The Pharisaic Leadership after the Great Synagogue," in *Cambridge History of Judaism* (1989, 229–44, 245–77).

Finley, Moses (1986): *The Use and Abuse of History*, London: Hogarth Press.

Fishman, Joshua (1980): "Social Theory and Ethnography: Neglected Perspectives on Language and Ethnicity in Eastern Europe," in Sugar (1980, 69–99).

Flacke, Monica (ed.) (1998): *Mythen der Nationen: Ein Europaisches Panorama*, Berlin: German Historical Museum.

Fletcher, Anthony (1982): "The First Century of English Protestantism and the Growth of National Identity," in Mews (1982, 309–17).

Fondation Hardt (1962): *Grecs et Barbares, Entretiens sur l'Antiquité Classique* VIII, Geneva.

Foot, Sarah (2005): "The Historiography of the Anglo-Saxon Nation-State," in Scales and Zimmer (2005, 125–42).

Forde, Simon, Johnson, Lesley, and Murray, Alan (eds.) (1995): *Concepts of National Identity in the Middle Ages*, Leeds: School of English, Leeds Texts and Monographs, new series 14.

Frame, Robin (2005): "Exporting State and Nation: Being English in Medieval Ireland," in Scales and Zimmer (2005, 143–65).

Frankfort, Henri (1948): *Kingship and the Gods*, Chicago: Chicago University Press.

Franklin, Simon (2002): "The Invention of Rus(sia)(s): Some Remarks on Medieval and Modern Perceptions of Continuity and Discontinuity," in Smyth (2002a, 180–95).

Fraschetti, Augusto (2005): *The Foundation of Rome*, trans. Marian Hill and Kevin Windle, Edinburgh: Edinburgh University Press.

Frazee, C. A. (1969): *The Orthodox Church and Independent Greece, 1821–52*, Cambridge: Cambridge University Press.

Freeden, Michael (1998): "Is Nationalism a Distinct Ideology?," *Political Studies* 46: 748–65.

Frendo, Anthony (2004): "Back to Basics: A Holistic Approach to the Problem of the Emergence of Ancient Israel," in Day (2004, 41–64).

Friedman, Richard E. (1997): *Who Wrote the Bible?*, 2nd edition, San Francisco: HarperCollins.

Frye, Richard (1966): *The Heritage of Persia*, New York: Mentor.

Frye, Richard (1978): *The Golden Age of Persia: The Arabs in the East*, London: Weidenfeld and Nicolson.

Fulbrook, Mary (1997): "Myth-Making and National Identity: The Case of the GDR," in Hosking and Schöpflin (1997, 72–87).

Gallant, Thomas (2001): *Modern Greece*, London: Hodder Arnold.

Galloway, Andrew (2004): "Latin England," in Lavezzo (2004, 41–95).

Gans, Herbert (1979): "Symbolic Ethnicity," *Ethnic and Racial Studies* 2, 1, 1–20.

Garsoian, Nina (1999): *Church and Culture in Early Medieval Armenia*, Aldershot: Ashgate Variorum.

Geary, Patrick (2001): *The Myth of Nations: The Medieval Origins of Nations*, Princeton: Princeton University Press.

Geertz, Clifford (1973): "The Integrative Revolution," in Geertz, *The Interpretation of Cultures*, New York: Fontana.

Geiss, Immanuel (1974): *The PanAfrican Movement*, London: Methuen.

Gellner, Ernest (1964): *Thought and Change*, London: Weidenfeld and Nicolson.

Gellner, Ernest (1973): "Scale and Nation," *Philosophy of the Social Sciences* 3, 1–17.

Gellner, Ernest (1983): *Nations and Nationalism*, Oxford: Blackwell.

Geopolitics (2002): Special Issue on "When is the Nation?," 7, 2.

Gershoni, Israel and Jankowski, Mark (1987): *Egypt, Islam and the Arabs: The Search for Egyptian Nationhood, 1900–1930*, Oxford: Oxford University Press.

Giddens, Anthony (1984): *The Nation-State and Violence*, Cambridge: Cambridge University Press.

Gildea, Robert (1994): *The Past in French History*, New Haven and London: Yale University Press.

Gillingham, John (1992): "The Beginnings of English Imperialism," *Journal of Historical Sociology* 5, 392–409.

Gillingham, John (1995): "Henry Huntingdon and the Twelfth Century Revival of the English Nation," in Forde et al. (1995, 75–101).

Gillis, John R. (ed.) (1994): *Commemorations: The Politics of Identity*, Princeton: Princeton University Press.

Goldstein, Jonathan (1989): "The Hasmonean Revolt and the Hasmonean Dynasty," in *Cambridge History of Judaism* (1989, 292–351).

Goodblatt, David (2006): *Elements of Ancient Jewish Nationalism*, Cambridge: Cambridge University Press.

Gorski, Philip (2000): "The Mosaic Moment: An Early Modernist Critique of Modernist Theories of Nationalism," *American Journal of Sociology* 105, 5, 1428–68.

Grant, Susan-Mary (2005): "Raising the Dead: War, Memory and American National Identity," *Nations and Nationalism* 11, 4, 509–29.

Green, V. H. H. (1964): *Renaissance and Reformation: A Survey of European History between 1450 and 1660*, London: Edward Arnold.

Greenfeld, Liah (1992): *Nationalism: Five Roads to Modernity*, Cambridge, MA: Harvard University Press.

Grimal, Pierre (1968): *Hellenism and the Rise of Rome*, London: Weidenfeld and Nicolson.

Grosby, Steven (1991): "Religion and Nationality in Antiquity," *European Journal of Sociology* 33, 229–65.

Grosby, Steven (1994): "The Verdict of History: The Inexpungeable Tie of Primordiality – A Reply to Eller and Coughlan," *Ethnic and Racial Studies* 17, 1, 164–71.

Grosby, Steven (1995): "Territoriality: The Transcendental, Primordial Feature of Modern Societies," *Nations and Nationalism* 1, 2, 143–62.

Grosby, Steven (2002): *Biblical Ideas of Nationality, Ancient and Modern*, Winona Lake, IN: Eisenbrauns.

Grosby, Steven (2006): *A Very Short Introduction to Nationalism*, Oxford: Oxford University Press.

Gruen, Erich (1994): *Culture and National Identity in Republican Rome*, London: Duckworth.

Guibernau, Montserrat (1999): *Nations without States*, Cambridge: Polity.

Guibernau, Montserrat (2004): "Anthony D. Smith on Nations and National Identity: A Critical Assessment," in Guibernau and Hutchinson (2004, 125–41).

Guibernau, Montserrat and Hutchinson, John (eds.) (2004): *History and National Destiny: Ethno-symbolism and its Critics*, Oxford: Blackwell.

Hall, Edith (1992): *Inventing the Barbarian: Greek Self-Definition through Tragedy*, Oxford: Clarendon Press.

Hall, Jonathan (1997): *Ethnic Identity in Greek Antiquity*, Cambridge: Cambridge University Press.

Haller, William (1963): *Foxe's Book of Martyrs and the Elect Nation*, London: Jonathan Cape.

Handelman, Don (1977): "The Organization of Ethnicity," *Ethnic Groups* 1, 187–200.

Hankey, Teresa (2002): "Civic Pride versus Feelings for Italy in the Age of Dante," in Smyth (2002a, 196–216).

Harootunian, Harry (1999): "Memory, Mourning and National Morality: Yasukuni Shrine and the Reunion of State and Religion in Post-War Japan," in van der Veer and Lehmann (1999, 144–60).

Hastings, Adrian (1997): *The Construction of Nationhood: Ethnicity, Religion and Nationalism*, Cambridge: Cambridge University Press.

Hastings, Adrian (1999): "Special Peoples," *Nations and Nationalism* 5, 3, 381–96.

Hastings, Adrian (2003): "Holy Lands and their Political Consequences," *Nations and Nationalism* 9, 1, 29–54.

Hatzopoulos, Marios (2005): " 'Ancient Prophecies, Modern Predictions': Myths and Symbols of Greek Nationalism," unpublished PhD thesis, University of London.

Hayes, William (1973): "Egypt: Internal Affairs from Tuthmosis I to the Death of Amenophis III," in *Cambridge Ancient History* (1973, 313–416).

Hearn, Jonathan (2006): *Rethinking Nationalism: A Critical Introduction*, Basingstoke: Palgrave Macmillan.

Henze, Paul B. (2000): *Layers of Time: A History of Ethiopia*, London: C. Hurst.

Herbert, Robert (1972): *David, Voltaire, Brutus and the French Revolution*, London: Allen Lane.

Herzfeld, Michael (1982): *Ours Once More: Folklore, Ideology and the Making of Modern Greece*, Austin: University of Texas Press.

Highet, Gilbert (1959): *Poets in a Landscape*, Harmondsworth: Pelican.

Hill, Christopher (1994): *The English Bible and the Seventeenth-Century Revolution*, Harmondsworth: Penguin.

Hobsbawm, Eric (1983): "Mass-Producing Traditions: Europe, 1870–1914," in Hobsbawm and Ranger (1983, 263–307).

Hobsbawm, Eric (1990): *Nations and Nationalism since 1780*, Cambridge: Cambridge University Press.

Hobsbawm, Eric and Ranger, Terence (eds.) (1983): *The Invention of Tradition*, Cambridge: Cambridge University Press.

Hodgkin, Thomas (1964): "The Relevance of 'Western' Ideas in the Derivation of African Nationalism," in J. R. Pennock (ed.), *Self-Government in Modernising Societies*, Englewood Cliffs, NJ: Prentice-Hall.

Hofer, Tamas (1980): "The Ethnic Model of Peasant Culture: A Contribution to the Ethnic Symbol Building on Linguistic Foundations by East European Peoples," in Sugar (1980, 101–45).

Hooson, David (ed.) (1994): *Geography and National Identity*, Oxford: Blackwell.

Horowitz, Donald (1985): *Ethnic Groups in Conflict*, Berkeley and Los Angeles: University of California Press.

Horowitz, Donald (2002): "The Primordialists," in Conversi (2002, 72–82).

Hosking, Geoffrey (1985): *A History of the Soviet Union*, London: Fontana Press/Collins.

Hosking, Geoffrey (1993): *Empire and Nation in Russian History*, Baylor University, Waco, TX: Markham University Press.

Hosking, Geoffrey (1997): *Russia: People and Empire, 1552–1917*, London: HarperCollins.

Hosking, Geoffrey and Schöpflin, George (1997): *Myths and Nationhood*, London: Routledge.

Housley, Norman (2000): "Holy Land or Holy Lands? Palestine and the Catholic West in the Late Middle Ages and Renaissance," in Swanson (2000, 234–49).

Howard, Michael (1976): *War in European History*, London: Oxford University Press.

Howe, Nicholas (1989): *Migration and Myth-Making in Anglo-Saxon England*, New Haven: Yale University Press.

Hroch, Miroslav (1985): *Social Preconditions of National Revival in Europe*, Cambridge: Cambridge University Press.

Hubbs, Joanna (1993): *Mother Russia: The Feminine Myth in Russian Culture*, Bloomington, IN: Indiana University Press.

Huntington, Samuel (2004): *Who Are We? The Cultural Core of American National Identity*, New York: Simon and Schuster.

Hupchik, Dennis (2002): *The Balkans: From Constantinople to Communism*, Basingstoke: Palgrave Macmillan.

Hutchinson, John (1987): *The Dynamics of Nationalism: The Gaelic Revival and the Creation of the Modern Irish Nation State*, London: George Allen and Unwin.

Hutchinson, John (1994): *Modern Nationalism*, London: Fontana.

Hutchinson, John (2000): "Ethnicity and Modern Nations," *Ethnic and Racial Studies*, 23, 4, 651–69.

Hutchinson, John (2005): *Nations as Zones of Conflict*, London: Sage.

Hutchinson, William and Lehmann, Hartmut (eds.) (1994): *Many Are Chosen: Divine Election and Western Nationalism*, Minneapolis: Fortress Press.

Ichijo, Atsuko (2002): "The Scope of Theories of Nationalism: Comments on the Scottish and Japanese Experiences," *Geopolitics*, 7, 2, 53–74.

Ichijo, Atsuko (2004): *Scottish Nationalism and the Idea of Europe: Concepts of Europe and the Nation*, London and New York: Routledge.

Ichijo, Atsuko and Uzelac, Gordana (eds.) (2005): *When is the Nation? Towards an Understanding of Theories of Nationalism*, London and New York: Routledge.

Ignatieff, Michael (1993): *Blood and Belonging: Journeys into the New Nationalisms*, London: Chatto and Windus.

Ihalainen, Pasi (2005): *Protestant Nations Redefined: Changing Perceptions of National Identity in the Rhetoric of the English, Dutch and Swedish Public Churches, 1685–1772*, Leiden and Boston: Brill.

Im Hof, Ulrich (1991): *Mythos Schweiz: Identitat-Nation-Geschichte, 1291–1991*, Zürich: Neue Verlag Zürcher Zeitung.

Jacobsen, Thorkild (1976): *The Treasures of Darkness: A History of Mesopotamian Religion*, New Haven and London: Yale University Press.

Jaffrelot, Christophe (1996): *The Hindu Nationalist Movement and Indian Politics, 1925 to the 1990s*, London: C. Hurst.

James, Edward (1988): *The Origins of France: From Clovis to the Capetians, 500–1000*, Basingstoke: Macmillan Education.

James, Harold (2000): *A German Identity: 1770 to the Present Day*, London: Phoenix Press.

Jesperson, Knud (2004): *A History of Denmark*, trans. Ivan Hill, Basingstoke: Palgrave Macmillan.

Jones, A. H. M. (1978): *Athenian Democracy*, Oxford: Blackwell.

Jones, Howard M. (1974): *Revolution and Romanticism*, Cambridge, MA, and London: Harvard University Press and Oxford University Press.

Jones, Sian (1997): *The Archaeology of Ethnicity: Constructing Identities in the Past and the Present*, London and New York: Routledge.

July, Robert (1967): *The Origins of Modern African Thought*, London: Faber and Faber.

Just, Roger (1989): "The Triumph of the *Ethnos*," in Tonkin et al. (1989, 71–88).

Kaufmann, Eric (2002): "Modern Formation, Ethnic Reformation: The Social Sources of the American Nation," *Geopolitics*, 7, 2, 99–120.

Kaufmann, Eric (ed.) (2004a): *Rethinking Ethnicity: Majority Groups and Dominant Minorities*, London and New York: Routledge.

Kaufmann, Eric (2004b): "The Decline of the WASP in the United States and Canada," in Kaufmann (2004a, 63–83).

Kaufmann, Eric and Zimmer, Oliver (1998): "In Search of the Authentic Nation: Landscape and National Identity in Canada and Switzerland," *Nations and Nationalism* 4, 4, 483–510.

Keddie, Nikki (1981): *Roots of Revolution: An Interpretive History of Modern Iran*, New Haven: Yale University Press.

Kedourie, Elie (1960): *Nationalism*, London: Hutchinson.

Kedourie, Elie (ed.) (1971): *Nationalism in Asia and Africa*, London: Weidenfeld and Nicolson.

Keen, Maurice (1973): *The Pelican History of Medieval Europe*, Harmondsworth: Penguin.

Keeney, Barnaby (1972) [1947]: "Military Service and the Development of Nationalism, 1272–1327," *Speculum* 22, 534–49, partly reprinted in Tipton (1972, 87–97).

Kemilainen, Aira (1964): *Nationalism: Problems concerning the Word, the Concept and Classification*, Yvaskyla: Kustantajat Publishers.

Kemp, Barry (1983): "The Old Kingdom, the Middle Kingdom and Second Intermediate Period, 2686–1552 BC," in Trigger et al. (1983, 71–182).

Kennedy, Emmet (1989): *A Cultural History of the French Revolution*, New Haven and London: Yale University Press.

Kershaw, Ian (1989): *The Hitler Myth: Image and Reality in the Third Reich*, Oxford: Oxford University Press.

Kidd, Colin (1993): *Subverting Scotland's Past: Scottish Whig Historians and the Creation of an Anglo-British Identity, 1689–c. 1830*, Cambridge: Cambridge University Press.

Kitromilides, Paschalis (1979): "The Dialectic of Intolerance: Ideological Dimensions of Ethnic Conflict," *Journal of the Hellenic Diaspora* 6, 4, 5–30.

Kitromilides, Paschalis (1989): "'Imagined Communities' and the Origins of the National Question in the Balkans," *European History Quarterly* 19, 2, 149–92.

Kitromilides, Paschalis (1998): "On the Intellectual Content of Greek Nationalism: Paparrigopoulos, Byzantium and the Great Idea," in Ricks and Magdalino (1998, 25–33).

Kitromilides, Paschalis (2006): "From Republican Patriotism to National Sentiment: A Reading of *Hellenic Nomarchy*," *European Journal of Political Theory* 5, 1, 50–60.

Knapp, Peggy A. (2004): "Chaucer Imagines England (in English)," in Lavezzo (2004, 131–60).

Knoll, Paul (1993): "National Consciousness in Medieval Poland," *Ethnic Groups* 10, 1–3, 65–84.

Kohn, Hans (1940): "The Origins of English Nationalism," *Journal of the History of Ideas* 1, 69–94.

Kohn, Hans (1944): *The Idea of Nationalism*, New York: Macmillan.

Kohn, Hans (1967): *Prelude to Nation-States: The French and German Experience, 1789–1815*, New York: Van Nostrand.

Koliopoulos, John and Veremis, Thanos (2004): *Greece: The Modern Sequel, 1821 to the Present*, London: Hurst.

Kreis, Jacob (1991): *Der Mythos von 1291: Zur Enstehung des Schweizerisches Nationalfeiertags*, Basel: Friedrich Reinhardt Verlag.

Kreis, Jacob (1998): "Schweiz," in Flacke (1998, 446–60).

Kristof, Ladis (1994): "The Image and the Vision of the Fatherland: The Case of Poland in Comparative Perspective," in Hooson (1994, 221–32).

Kuhlemann, Ute (2002): "The Celebration of Dürer in Germany during the Nineteenth and Twentieth Centuries," in Giulia Bartrum (ed.), *Albrecht Dürer and His Legacy: The Graphic Work of a Renaissance Artist*, London: British Museum Press.

Kumar, Krishan (2003): *The Making of English National Identity*, Cambridge: Cambridge University Press.

Kumar, Krishan (2006): "English and French National Identity: Comparisons and Contrasts," *Nations and Nationalism* 12, 3, 413–32.

Larsen, Mogens Trolle (ed.) (1979a): *Power and Propaganda: A Symposium on Ancient Empires*, Copenhagen: Akademisk Forlag.

Larsen, Mogens Trolle (1979b): "The Traditions of Empire in Mesopotamia," in Larsen (1979a, 75–103).

Lartichaux, J. -Y. (1977): "Linguistic Politics in the French Revolution," *Diogenes* 97, 65–84.

Lavezzo, Kathy (ed.) (2004): *Imagining a Medieval English Nation*, Minneapolis and London: University of Minnesota Press.

Le Goff, Jacques (1998): "Reims, City of Coronation," in Nora (1997–8), Vol. 3, 193–251.

Lehmann, Jean-Pierre (1982): *The Roots of Modern Japan*, London: Macmillan.

Leith, James (1965): *The Idea of Art as Propaganda in France, 1750–99: A Study in the History of Ideas*, Toronto: Toronto University Press.

Levine, Donald (1974): *Greater Ethiopia: The Evolution of a Multiethnic Society*, Chicago: Chicago University Press.

Levine, Lee I. (1998): *Judaism and Hellenism in Antiquity: Conflict or Confluence?*, Seattle and London: University of Washington Press.

Lewis, Bernard (1968): *The Emergence of Modern Turkey*, Oxford: Oxford University Press.

Linehan, Peter (1982): "Religion, Nationalism and National Identity in Medieval Spain," in Mews (1982, 161–99).

Liverani, Mario (1973): "The Amorites," in Wiseman (1973, 100–33).

Liverani, Mario (1979): "The Ideology of the Assyrian Empire," in Larsen (1979a, 297–317).

Llobera, Josep (1994): *The God of Modernity: The Development of Nationalism in Western Europe*, Oxford and Providence: Berg.

Loades, David (1982): "The Origins of English Protestant Nationalism," in Mews (1982, 297–307).

Loades, David (1992): *Politics and the Nation, 1450–1660*, 4th edition, London: Fontana Press.

Loomis, Louise (1939): "Nationality at the Council of Constance: An Anglo-French Dispute," *American Historical Review* 44, 3, 508–27.

Luz, Efraim (1988): *Parallels Meet: Religion and Nationalism in the Early Zionist Movement*, trans. Lenn J. Schramm, Philadelphia: Jewish Publication Society of America.

Lydon, James (1995): "Nation and Race in Medieval Ireland," in Forde et al. (1995, 103–24).

Lyons, F. S. L. (1979): *Culture and Anarchy in Ireland, 1890–1939*, Oxford and New York: Oxford University Press.

MacCulloch, Diarmaid (2004): *Reformation: Europe's House Divided, 1490–1700*, London: Penguin.

MacDougall, Hugh (1982): *Racial Myth in English History: Trojans, Teutons and Anglo-Saxons*, Montreal and Hanover, NH: Harvest House and University Press of New England.

Machinist, Peter (1997): "The Fall of Assyria in Comparative Ancient Perspective," *Proceedings of the 10th Anniversary Symposium of the Assyrian Text Corpus Project*, eds. S. Parpola and R. M. Whiting, Helsinki: University of Helsinki, 179–95.

Mackie, John (1976): *A History of Scotland*, Harmondsworth: Penguin.

Malamat, A. (1973): "The Arameans," in Wiseman (1973, 134–55).

Mallowan, Max (1978): *The Nimrud Ivories*, London: British Museum Publications.

Mango, Cyril (1980): *Byzantium: The Empire of New Rome*, London: Weidenfeld and Nicolson.

Mann, Michael (1993): *The Sources of Social Power*, 2 vols., Cambridge: Cambridge University Press, Vol. 2.

Mann, Michael (1995): "A Political Theory of Nationalism and its Excesses," in Periwal (1995, 44–64).

Marcu, E. D. (1976): *Sixteenth-Century Nationalism*, New York: Abaris Books.

Martin, Ronald (1989): *Tacitus*, London: Batsford.

Martines, Lauro (2002): *Power and Imagination: City-States in Renaissance Italy*, London: Pimlico.

Marx, Anthony (2003): *Faith in Nation: Exclusionary Origins of Nationalism*, Oxford and New York: Oxford University Press.

Marx, Steven (2000): *Shakespeare and the Bible*, Oxford: Oxford University Press.

Mason, R. A. (1983): "Scotching the *Brut*: The Early History of Britain," *History Today* 35 (January), 26–31.

Mendels, Doron (1992): *The Rise and Fall of Jewish Nationalism*, New York: Doubleday.

Mendes-Flohr, Paul (1994): "In Pursuit of Normalcy: Zionism's Ambivalence towards Israel's Election," in Hutchinson and Lehmann (1994, 203–29).

Merridale, Catherine (2001): *Night of Stone: Death and Memory in Russia*, London: Granta.

Mews, Stuart (ed.) (1982): *Religion and National Identity*, Ecclesiastical History Society, Oxford: Blackwell.

Michalski, Sergiusz (1998): *Public Monuments: Art in Political Bondage, 1870–1997*, London: Reaktion Books.

Millard, A. R. (1973): "The Canaanites," in Wiseman (1973, 29–52).

Miller, David (1993): "In Defence of Nationality," *Journal of Applied Philosophy* 10, 1, 3–16.

Miller, David (1995): *On Nationality*, Oxford: Oxford University Press.

Milner-Gulland, Robin (1999): *The Russians*, Oxford: Blackwell.

Minogue, Kenneth (1976): "Nationalism and the Patriotism of City-States," in A. D. Smith (1976, 54–73).

Moore, R. I. (1987): *The Formation of a Persecuting Society: Power and Deviance in Western Europe, 950–1250*, Oxford: Blackwell.

Moscati, Sabatino (1973): *The World of the Phoenicians*, London: Cardinal, Sphere Books.

Mosse, George (1964): *The Crisis of German Ideology*, New York: Grosset and Dunlap.

Mosse, George (1975): *The Nationalization of the Masses: Political Symbolism and Mass Movements from the Napoleonic Wars through the Third Reich*, Ithaca, NY: Cornell University Press.

Mosse, George (1990): *Fallen Soldiers*, Oxford: Oxford University Press.

Mosse, George (1994): *Confronting the Nation: Jewish and Western Nationalism*, Hanover, NH: University Press of New England.

Mundy, John and Woody, Kennerly (eds.) (1961): *The Council of Constance: The Unification of the Church*, trans. L. Loomis, New York and London: Columbia University Press.

Nairn, Tom (1977): *The Break-up of Britain: Crisis and Neo-Nationalism*, London: Verso.

Nations and Nationalism (1999): Special Issue on "Chosen Peoples," 5, 3.

Nations and Nationalism (2003): "Religion and Nationalism: Symposium in Honour of Professor Adrian Hastings," with essays by Steven Grosby, Josep Llobera, Branka Magas, and Anthony D. Smith, 9, 1, 5–28.

Nations and Nationalism (2007): Debate on Krishan Kumar's *The Making of English National Identity*, 13, 2, 179–203.

Nersessian, Vrej (2001): *Treasures of the Ark: 1700 Years of Armenian Christian Art*, London: British Library.

Newman, Gerald (1987): *The Rise of English Nationalism: A Cultural History, 1740–1830*, London: Weidenfeld and Nicolson.

Nicholson, Ernest (1988): *God and His People: Covenant and Theology in the Old Testament*, Oxford: Clarendon Press.

Nora, Pierre (ed.) (1997–8): *Realms of Memory: The Construction of the French Past*, 3 vols., ed. Lawrence Kritzman, New York: Columbia

University Press (orig. *Les Lieux de Mémoire*, Paris: Gallimard, 7 vols., 1984–92).

Noth, Martin (1960): *The History of Israel*, London: Adam and Charles Black.

Novak, David (1995): *The Election of Israel: The Idea of the Chosen People*, Cambridge: Cambridge University Press.

Nylander, Carl (1979): "Achaemenid Imperial Art," in Larsen (1979a, 345–59).

Oakes, Lorna and Gahlin, Lucia (2005): *The Mysteries of Ancient Egypt*, London: Hermes House, Anness Publishing.

O'Brien, Conor Cruise (1988a): *God-Land: Reflections on Religion and Nationalism*, Cambridge, MA: Harvard University Press.

O'Brien, Conor Cruise (1988b): "Nationalism and the French Revolution," in G. Best (ed.), *The Permanent Revolution: The French Revolution and Its Legacy, 1789–1989*, London: Fontana, 17–48.

Odisho, Edward (2001): "The Ethnic, Linguistic and Cultural Identity of Modern Assyrians," in *Mythology and Mythologies* (Melammu Symposium II), ed. R. M. Whiting, Helsinki: University of Helsinki, 137–48.

Ogilvie, R. M. (1976): *Early Rome and the Etruscans*, London: Fontana.

Oguma, Eiji (2002): *A Genealogy of "Japanese" Self-Images*, trans. David Askew, Melbourne: Trans Pacific Press.

Okamura, J. (1981): "Situational Ethnicity," *Ethnic and Racial Studies* 4, 4, 452–65.

Oppenheim, A. Leo (1977): *Ancient Mesopotamia: Portrait of a Dead Civilization*, revised edition, Chicago and London: University of Chicago Press.

Ossowski, Stanislav (1962): *Class Structure in the Social Consciousness*, London: Routledge and Kegan Paul.

Ostergård, Uffe (1996): "Peasants and Danes: The Danish National Identity and Peasant Culture," in Geoff Eley and Ronald Suny (eds.), *Becoming National: A Reader*, Oxford and New York: Oxford University Press, 179–201.

Ozouf, Mona (1982): *L'Ecole, l'Eglise et la République, 1871–1914*, Paris: Editions Cana/Jean Offredo.

Ozouf, Mona (1998): "The Pantheon: The Ecole Normale of the Dead," in Nora (1997–8, Vol. 3, 325–46).

Panossian, Razmik (2002): "The Past as Nation: Three Dimensions of Armenian Identity," in *Geopolitics*, 121–46.

Parker, Geoffrey (1985): *The Dutch Revolt*, revised edition, Harmondsworth: Pelican.

Parpola, Simo (2004): "National and Ethnic Identity in the Neo-Assyrian Empire and Assyrian Identity in Post-Empire Times," *Journal of Assyrian Academic Studies* 18, 2, 5–40.

Pavlov, Andrei and Perrie, Maureen (2003): *Ivan the Terrible*, Harlow: Longman, Pearson Education.

Pearson, Raymond (1993): "Fact, Fantasy, Fraud: Perceptions and Projections of National Revival," *Ethnic Groups* 10, 1–3, 43–64.

Periwal, Sukumar (ed.) (1995): *Notions of Nationalism*, Budapest: Central European University Press.

Perkins, Mary Ann (1999): *Nation and Word: Religious and Metaphysical Language in European National Consciousness*, Aldershot: Ashgate.

Perkins, Mary Ann (2005): *Christendom and European Identity: The Legacy of a Grand Narrative since 1789*, Berlin and New York: Walter de Gruyter.

Perrie, Maureen (1998): "The Cult of Ivan the Terrible in Stalin's Russia," in Geoffrey Hosking and Robert Service (eds.), *Russian Nationalism, Past and Present*, Basingstoke: Macmillan.

Petrovich, Michael (1980): "Religion and Ethnicity in Eastern Europe," in Sugar (1980, 373–417).

Pilbeam, Pamela (1995): *Republicanism in Nineteenth-Century France, 1814–1871*, Basingstoke: Macmillan.

Pinard, Maurice and Hamilton, Richard (1984): "The Class Bases of the Quebec Independence Movement," *Ethnic and Racial Studies* 7, 1, 19–54.

Piscatori, James (1989): "Ideological Politics in Sa'udi Arabia," in James Piscatori (ed.), *Islam in the Political Process*, Cambridge: Cambridge University Press.

Plamenatz, John (1976): "Two Types of Nationalism," in Eugene Kamenka (ed.), *Nationalism: The Nature and Evolution of an Idea*, London: Edward Arnold, 22–36.

Poliakov, Leon (1975): *The Aryan Myth*, New York: Basic Books.

Pomian, Krzysztof (1997): "Franks and Gauls," in Nora (1997–8, Vol. 1, 27–75).

Pongratz-Leisten, Beate (1997): "The Other and the Enemy in the Mesopotamian Conception of the World," in *Mythology and Mythologies* (Melammu Symposium II), ed. R. M. Whiting, Helsinki: University of Helsinki, 195–231.

Poole, Ross (1999): *Nation and Identity*, London and New York: Routledge.

Potter, David (2003): *France in the Later Middle Ages*, Oxford: Oxford University Press.

Poulton, Hugh (1997): *Top Hat, Grey Wolf and Crescent: Turkish Nationalism and the Turkish Republic*, London: Hurst.

Pritchard, James (1975): *The Ancient Near East: A New Anthology of Texts and Pictures*, 2 vols., Princeton: Princeton University Press, Vol. 2.

Prost, Antoine (1998): "Monuments to the Dead," in Nora (1997–8, Vol. 2, 307–30).

Prost, Antoine (2002): *Republican Identities in War and Peace*, trans. Jay Winter with Helen McPhail, Oxford and New York: Berg.

Ranum, Orest (ed.) (1975): *National Consciousness, History and Political Culture in Early Modern Europe*, Baltimore, MD: Johns Hopkins University Press.

Reade, Julian (1979): "Ideology and Propaganda in Assyrian Art," in Larsen (1979a, 329–43).

Reade, Julian (1984): *Assyrian Sculpture*, London: British Museum Publications.

Redgate, Ann (2000): *The Armenians*, Oxford: Blackwell.

Renan, Ernest (1882): *Qu'est-ce qu'une nation?*, Paris: Calmann-Levy.

Reuter, Timothy (2002): "The Making of England and Germany, 850–1050: Points of Comparison and Difference," in Smyth (2002a, 53–70).

Reynolds, Susan (1983): "Medieval *origines gentium* and the Community of the Realm," *History* 68, 375–90.

Reynolds, Susan (1984): *Kingdoms and Communities of Medieval Europe, 900–1300*, Oxford: Clarendon Press.

Reynolds, Susan (2005): "The Idea of the Nation as a Political Community," in Scales and Zimmer (2005, 54–66).

Richter, Michael (2002): "National Identity in Medieval Wales," in Smyth (2002a, 71–84).

Rickard, Peter (1974): *A History of the French Language*, London: Hutchinson.

Ricks, David and Magdalino, Pauls (eds.) (1998): *Byzantium and Modern Greek Identity*, Centre for Hellenic Studies, Kings College, Aldershot: Ashgate Publishing.

Robertson, Martin (1987): "Greek Art and Religion," in Easterling and Muir (1987, 155–90).

Rose, Paul L. (1996): *Wagner: Race and Revolution*, London and Boston: Faber and Faber.

Rosenberg, Jakob (1968): *Rembrandt, Life and Work*, London and New York: Phaidon.

Rosenblum, Robert (1961): "Gavin Hamilton's *Brutus* and its Aftermath," *Burlington Magazine* 103, 8–16.

Rosenblum, Robert (1967): *Transformations in Late Eighteenth Century Art*, Princeton: Princeton University Press.

Rosenblum, Robert (1985): *Jean-Dominique-Auguste Ingres*, London: Thames and Hudson.

Roshwald, Aviel (2006): *The Endurance of Nationalism: Ancient Roots and Modern Dilemmas*, Cambridge: Cambridge University Press.

Roudometof, Victor (1998): "From *Rum* Millet to Greek Nation: Enlightenment, Secularization and National Identity in Greek Society, 1453–1821," *Journal of Modern Greek Studies* 16, 1, 11–48.

Roudometof, Victor (2001): *Nationalism, Globalization and Orthodoxy: The Social Origins of Ethnic Conflict in the Balkans*, Westport, CT: Greenwood Press.

Routledge, Bruce (2003): "The Antiquity of Nations? Critical Reflections from the Ancient Near East," *Nations and Nationalism* 9, 2, 213–33.

Roux, Georges (1964): *Ancient Iraq*, Harmondsworth: Penguin.

Rublack, Ulinka (2005): *Reformation Europe*, Cambridge: Cambridge University Press.

Sacks, Jonathan (2002): *The Dignity of Difference: How to Avoid the Clash of Civilizations*, London: Continuum.

Sarkisyanz, Emanuel (1964): *Buddhist Backgrounds of the Burmese Revolution*, The Hague: Nijhoff.

Scales, Len (2000): "Identifying 'France' and 'Germany': Medieval Nation-Making in Some Recent Publications," *Bulletin of International Medieval Research* 6, 23–46.

Scales, Len (2005): "Late Medieval Germany: An Under-Stated Nation?," in Scales and Zimmer (2005, 166–91).

Scales, Len and Zimmer, Oliver (eds.) (2005): *Power and the Nation in European History*, Cambridge: Cambridge University Press.

Schama, Simon (1987): *The Embarrassment of Riches: An Interpretation of Dutch Culture in the Golden Age*, London: William Collins.

Schama, Simon (1989): *Citizens: A Chronicle of the French Revolution*, New York and London: Knopf and Penguin.

Schama, Simon (1995): *Landscape and Memory*, London: HarperCollins (Fontana).

Scheuch, Erwin (1966): "Cross-National Comparisons with Aggregate Data," in Richard Merritt and Stein Rokkan (eds.), *Comparing Nations: The Use of Quantitative Data in Cross-National Research*, New Haven: Yale University Press.

Schniedewind, William (2005): *How the Bible Became a Book*, Cambridge: Cambridge University Press.

Schwartz, Seth (2004): *Imperialism and Jewish Society, 200 BCE to 640 CE*, Princeton: Princeton University Press.

Scott, Franklin D. (1977): *Sweden: The Nation's History*, Minneapolis: University of Minnesota Press.

Scurr, Ruth (2006): *Fatal Purity: Robespierre and the French Revolution*, London: Chatto and Windus.

Seton-Watson, Hugh (1977): *Nations and States*, London: Methuen.

Shafir, Gershon (1989): *Land, Labour and the Origins of the Israeli–Palestinian Conflict, 1882–1914*, Cambridge: Cambridge University Press.

Shiiyama, Chiho (2005): "Nationalism and Supranational Regional Solidarity: The Case of Modern Japanese Nationalism and Its Perception of Asia, 1868–2001," unpublished PhD thesis, University of London.

Shils, Edward (1957): "Primordial, Personal, Sacred and Civil Ties," *British Journal of Sociology* 7, 13–45.

Shimoni, Gideon (1995): *The Zionist Ideology*, Hanover, NH: Brandeis University Press.

Smith, Anthony D. (ed.) (1976): *Nationalist Movements*, London and Basingstoke: Macmillan.

Smith, Anthony D. (1979): *Nationalism in the Twentieth Century*, London: Martin Robertson.

Smith, Anthony D. (1981): "War and Ethnicity: The Role of Warfare in the Formation, Self-Images and Cohesion of Ethnic Communities," *Ethnic and Racial Studies* 4, 4, 375–97.

Smith, Anthony D. (1983) [1971]: *Theories of Nationalism*, 2nd edition, London and New York: Duckworth and Holmes and Meier.

Smith, Anthony D. (1986): *The Ethnic Origins of Nations*, Oxford: Blackwell.

Smith, Anthony D. (1991a): *National Identity*, Harmondsworth: Penguin.

Smith, Anthony D. (1991b): "The Nation: Invented, Imagined, Reconstructed?," *Millennium, Journal of International Studies* 20, 3, 353–68 (also in A. D. Smith 2004).

Smith, Anthony D. (1997): "The Golden Age and National Renewal," in Hosking and Schöpflin (1997, 36–59) (also in A. D. Smith 2004).

Smith, Anthony D. (1998): *Nationalism and Modernism: A Critical Survey of Recent Theories of Nations and Nationalism*, London and New York: Routledge.

Smith, Anthony D. (1999a): *Myths and Memories of the Nation*, Oxford: Oxford University Press.

Smith, Anthony D. (1999b): "Sacred Territories and National Conflict," *Israel Affairs* 5, 4, 13–31.

Smith, Anthony D. (2000a): *The Nation in History: Historiographical Debates about Ethnicity and Nationalism*, Jerusalem: Historical Society of Israel; Hanover, NH: University Press of New England; and Cambridge: Polity Press.

Smith, Anthony D. (2000b): "The 'Sacred' Dimension of Nationalism," *Millennium, Journal of International Studies* 29, 3, 791–814.

Smith, Anthony D. (2001): *Nationalism: Theory, Ideology, History*, Cambridge: Polity Press.

Smith, Anthony D. (2003): *Chosen Peoples: Sacred Sources of National Identity*, Oxford: Oxford University Press.

Smith, Anthony D. (2004): *The Antiquity of Nations*, Cambridge: Polity Press.

Smith, Anthony D. (2005): "Nationalism in Early Modern Europe," *History and Theory* 44, 3, 404–15.

Smith, Anthony D. (2006): "'Set in the Silver Sea': English National Identity and European Integration," *Nations and Nationalism* 12, 3, 433–52.

Smith, S. Tyson (2003): *Wretched Kush: Ethnic Identities and Boundaries in Egypt's Nubian Empire*, London and New York: Routledge.

Smyth, Alfred P. (ed.) (2002a): *Medieval Europeans: Studies in Ethnic Identity and National Perspectives in Medieval Europe*, Basingstoke: Palgrave.

Smyth, Alfred P. (2002b): "The Emergence of English Identity, 700–1000," in Smyth (2002a, 24–52).

Staab, Andreas (1998): *National Identity in Eastern Germany: Inner Unification or Continued Separation?*, Westport, CT and London: Praeger.

Steinberg, Jonathan (1976): *Why Switzerland?*, Cambridge: Cambridge University Press.

Stergios, James (2006): "Language and Nationalism in Italy," *Nations and Nationalism* 12, 1, 15–33.

Sternhell, Zeev (1999): *The Founding Myths of Israel: Nationalism, Socialism and the Making of the Jewish State*, trans. David Maisel, Princeton: Princeton University Press.

Strath, Bo (1994): "The Swedish Path to National Identity in the Nineteenth Century," in Oystein Sorenson (ed.), *Nordic Paths to National Identity in the Nineteenth Century*, Oslo: Research Council of Norway, 55–63.

Strayer, Joseph (1971): *Medieval Statecraft and the Perspectives of History*, Princeton: Princeton University Press.

Sugar, Peter (ed.) (1980): *Ethnic Diversity and Conflict in Eastern Europe*, Santa Barbara, CA: ABC-Clio.

Sugar, Peter and Lederer, Ivo (eds.) (1969): *Nationalism in Eastern Europe*, Seattle: University of Washington Press.

Suleiman, Yasir (2003): *The Arabic Language and National Identity*, Edinburgh: Edinburgh University Press.

Swanson, Robert (ed.) (2000): *The Holy Land, Holy Lands and Christian History*, Ecclesiastical History Society, Woodbridge: Boydell Press.

Tadmor, Hayim (1991): "On the Role of Aramaic in the Assyrian Empire," *Near Eastern Studies, Bulletin of the Middle Eastern Cultural Centre in Japan*, Vol. 5, 419–26, Wiesbaden: Otto Harrassowitz.

Tadmor, Hayim (1997): "Propaganda, Literature, Historiography: Cracking the Code of the Assyrian Royal Inscriptions," in Simo Parpola and R. M. Whiting (eds.), *Assyria 1995*, Helsinki: University of Helsinki, 325–7.

Talmon, Shmaryahu (1986): *King, Cult and Calendar in Ancient Israel*, Jerusalem, Hebrew University: Magnes Press.

Templin, J. Alton (1999): "The Ideology of a Chosen People: Afrikaner Nationalism and the Ossewa Trek," *Nations and Nationalism* 5, 3, 397–417.

Thaden, Edward (1964): *Conservative Nationalism in Nineteenth-Century Russia*, Seattle: University of Washington Press.

Thompson, Leonard (1985): *The Political Mythology of Apartheid*, New Haven: Yale University Press.

Thomson, Robert (1982): *Elishe: History of Vardan and the Armenian War*, trans. R. Thomson, Cambridge, MA: Harvard University Press.

Tipton, C. Leon (ed.) (1972): *Nationalism in the Middle Ages*, New York: Holt, Rinehart, and Winston.

Tilly, Charles (ed.) (1975): *The Formation of National States in Western Europe*, Princeton: Princeton University Press.

Toftgaard, Anders (2005): "Letters and Arms: Literary Language, Power and Nation in Renaissance Italy and France, 1300–1600," unpublished PhD thesis, University of Copenhagen.

Tonkin, Elisabeth, McDonald, Maryon, and Chapman, Malcolm (eds.) (1989): *History and Ethnicity*, London and New York: Routledge.

Tønnesson, Stein and Antlöv, Hans (eds.) (1996): *Asian Forms of the Nation*, Richmond: Curzon Press.

Triandafyllidou, Anna (2001): *Immigrants and National Identity in Europe*, London and New York: Routledge.

Trigger, B. G., Kemp, B. J., O'Connor, D., and Lloyd, A. B. (1983): *Ancient Egypt: A Social History*, Cambridge: Cambridge University Press.

Tudor, Anthony (1972): *Political Myth*, London: Pall Mall Press.

Tuveson, E. L. (1968): *Redeemer Nation: The Idea of America's Millennial Role*, Chicago: Chicago University Press.

Ulker, Erol (2005): "Contextualising 'Turkification': Nation-Building in the Late Ottoman Empire, 1908–1918," *Nations and Nationalism* 11, 4, 613–36.

Ullendorff, Edward (1988): *Ethiopia and the Bible*, Oxford: Oxford University Press.

Uzelac, Gordana (2002): "When is the Nation? Constituent Elements and Processes," *Geopolitics*, 7, 2, 33–52.

Van den Berghe, Pierre (1995): "Does Race Matter?," *Nations and Nationalism* 1, 3, 357–68.

Van den Berghe, Pierre (2005): "Ethnies and Nations: Genealogies Indeed," in Ichijo and Uzelac (2005, 113–18).

Van der Veer, Peter and Lehmann, Hartmut (eds.) (1999): *Nation and Religion: Perspectives on Europe and Asia*, Princeton: Princeton University Press.

Vasiliev, A. A. (1958): *History of the Byzantine Empire, 324–1453*, 2 vols., Madison: University of Wisconsin Press, Vol. 2.

Viroli, Maurizio (1995): *For Love of Country: An Essay on Patriotism and Nationalism*, Oxford: Clarendon Press.

Vital, David (1990): *The Future of the Jews: A People at the Cross-roads?*, Cambridge, MA, and London: Harvard University Press.

Waley, Daniel (1969): *The Italian City-Republics*, London: Weidenfeld and Nicolson.

Walzer, Michael (1984): *Exodus and Revolution*, New York: HarperCollins, Basic Books.
Warner, Marina (1983): *Joan of Arc: The Image of Female Heroism*, Harmondsworth: Penguin.
Watkins, Frederick M. (ed.) (1953): *Rousseau, Political Writings*, Edinburgh and London: Nelson.
Weber, Eugene (1991): *My France: Politics, Culture, Myth*, Cambridge, MA: Harvard University Press.
Weber, Max (1948): *From Max Weber: Essays in Sociology*, eds. Hans Gerth and C. Wright Mills, London: Routledge and Kegan Paul.
Weber, Max (1968): *Economy and Society*, 3 vols., eds. G. Roth and C. Wittich, New York: Bedminster Press.
Webster, Bruce (1997): *Medieval Scotland: The Making of an Identity*, Basingstoke: Macmillan.
Welsby, Derek and Anderson, Julie (eds.) (2004): *Sudan: Ancient Treasures*, London: British Museum Press.
Westermann, Mariet (2004): *The Art of the Dutch Republic, 1585–1717*, London: Laurence King.
Widengren, Geo (1973): "The Persians," in Wiseman (1973, 312–57).
Wiesehofer, Josef (2004): *Ancient Persia from 550 BC to 650 AD*, London and New York: I. B. Tauris.
Wilkinson, L. P. (1976): *The Roman Experience*, London: Paul Elek.
Williamson, Arthur (1979): *Scottish National Consciousness in the Age of James VI*, Edinburgh: John Donald.
Wilmsen, Edwin and McAllister, Patrick (eds.) (1995): *The Politics of Difference: Ethnic Premises in a World of Power*, Chicago: University of Chicago Press.
Wilton, Andrew and Barringer, Timothy (eds.) (2002): *American Sublime: Painting in the United States, 1820–1880*, London: Tate.
Winichakul, Thongchai (1996): "Maps and the Formation of the Geobody of Siam," in Tønnesson and Antlöv (1996, 67–91).
Winter, Irene (1997): "Art in Empire: The Royal Image and the Visual Dimensions of Assyrian Ideology," in Simo Parpola and R. M. Whiting (eds.), *Assyria 1995*, Helsinki: University of Helsinki, 359–81.
Winter, Jay (1995): *Sites of Memory, Sites of Mourning: The Great War in European Cultural History*, Cambridge: Cambridge University Press.
Wiseman, D. J. (ed.) (1973): *Peoples of Old Testament Times*, Oxford: Clarendon Press.
Wormald, Patrick (1984): "The Emergence of Anglo-Saxon Kingdoms," in Lesley Smith (ed.), *The Making of Britain: The Dark Ages*, Basingstoke: Macmillan.

Wormald, Patrick (2005): "Germanic Power Structures: The Early English Experience," in Scales and Zimmer (2005, 105–24).

Yack, Bernard (1999): "The Myth of the Civic Nation," in Ronald Beiner (ed.), *Theorising Nationalism*, Albany, NY: State University of New York, 103–18.

Young, Crawford (1985): "Ethnicity and the Colonial and Post-Colonial State," in Brass (1985, 57–93).

Zacek, Joseph F. (1969): "Czechoslovakia," in Sugar and Lederer (1969, 166–206).

Zadok, Ran (1991): "Elements of Aramean Prehistory," in *Ah, Assyria, Scripta Hierosolymitana* 33, 104–17.

Zeitlin, Irving (1984): *Ancient Judaism*, Cambridge: Polity Press.

Zeitlin, Irving (1988): *Jesus and the Judaism of His Time*, Cambridge: Polity Press.

Zernatto, Guido (1944): "Nation: The History of a Word," *Review of Politics* 6, 351–66.

Zernov, Nicolas (1978): *Eastern Christendom: A Study of the Origin and Development of the Eastern Orthodox Church*, London: Weidenfeld and Nicolson.

Zimmer, Oliver (1998): "In Search of Natural Identity: Alpine Landscape and the Reconstruction of the Swiss Nation, 1870–1900," *Comparative Studies in Society and History* 40, 4, 637–65.

Zimmer, Oliver (2000): "Competing Memories of the Nation: Liberal Historians and the Reconstruction of the Swiss Past, 1870–1900," *Past and Present* 168, 194–226.

Zimmer, Oliver (2003): *A Contested Nation: History, Memory and Nationalism in Switzerland, 1761–1891*, Cambridge: Cambridge University Press.

Zubaida, Sami (1978): "Theories of Nationalism," in G. Littlejohn, B. Smart, J. Wakeford, and N. Yuval-Davis (eds.), *Power and the State*, London: Croom Helm.

Index